# A Short Guide to Writing about Chemistry

## HOLLY B. DAVIS
*Jacobson Center for Writing, Teaching, and Learning*
*Department of English*
*Smith College*
*Department of Chemistry*
*University of Massachusetts Amherst*

## JULIAN F. TYSON
*Department of Chemistry*
*University of Massachusetts Amherst*

## JAN A. PECHENIK
*Biology Department*
*Tufts University*

D0226104

**Longman**

Boston   Columbus   Indianapolis   New York   San Francisco   Upper Saddle River
Amsterdam   Cape Town   Dubai   London   Madrid   Milan   Munich
Paris   Montreal   Toronto   Delhi   Mexico City   Sao Paulo   Sydney
Hong Kong   Seoul   Singapore   Taipei   Tokyo

Senior Sponsoring Editor: Virginia L. Blanford
Marketing Manager: Bonnie Gill
Production Manager: Jacqueline A. Martin
Electronic Page Makeup: GGS Higher Education Resources, A division
    of PreMedia Global, Inc.
Cover Designer/Manager: John Callahan
Cover Image: iStockphoto
Senior Manufacturing Buyer: Dennis J. Para

**Library of Congress Cataloging-in-Publication Data**
Holly Davis
  A short guide to writing about chemistry / Holly Davis, Julian Tyson. Jan A.
Pechenik,—1st ed.
    p. cm.
Includes bibliographical references and index.
ISBN-13: 978-0-205-55060-9 (alk. paper)
ISBN-10: 0-205-55060-6 (alk. paper)
  1. Chemistry—Authorship. 2. Communication in chemistry. 3. Technical writing. I.
Davis, Holly, 1951– II. Tyson, Julian, 1949– III. Title.
  QD8.5.P43 2009
  808'.06654—dc22

                                                                    2009040894

**Longman**
**is an imprint of**

www.pearsonhighered.com

ISBN 13: 978-0-205-55060-9
ISBN 10: 0-205-55060-6

# Contents

iii

# PART II
*Guidelines for Specific Tasks 97*

# Preface

Writing clearly, correctly, and concisely is essential to success in chemistry, and in this electronic age chemists are writing more than ever before. Recently, after surveying many companies, including major employers of trained chemists, the National Commission on Writing suggested that employers perceive college graduates as ill-prepared to do the kind of writing necessary in the modern workplace, where writing clearly and cogently is not only a threshold skill but also vital to career advancement. The simple truth that writing well matters is hard to sell to students inclined to believe that experience with chemical instrumentation and techniques or the possession of excellent laboratory skills will compensate for an inability to communicate well. We know that addressing student writing while covering the essential chemistry content in the course of a semester challenges even the most gifted and energetic instructor; nevertheless, our students really must learn to communicate well. Our goal in creating this book is to provide a resource to help students learn how to communicate effectively in writing, as well as in other forms of communication that are extremely important in chemistry, such as oral and poster presentations.

The material in this book comes primarily from two sources: the highly successful *Short Guide to Writing about Biology*, now in its seventh edition, a vital component of the Pearson Short Guide Series, written by Jan, and the material that Holly and Julian developed over the course of many years for the junior-year "Writing in Chemistry" course at the University of Massachusetts Amherst. We have also drawn from *The ACS Style Guide: Effective Communication of Scientific Information* 3rd Edition edited by Anne Coghill and Lorrin Garson (Oxford University Press, New York, 2006).

Certain fundamental convictions about writing and the teaching of writing inform all aspects of this book. For one thing, we believe that revision is essential to writing well, for novices and experts alike. Writing is both a process and a product, and writing well is a skill acquired and honed through practice; the more constructive and timely the feedback the students get, the more rapidly their skills will improve. We regard writing as a tool for learning: students benefit from being required to write about chemistry not only because it improves their skills as communicators, but also because it enhances their understanding of content. Writing is a means of discovering what one actually knows and, at times, what one does not know. Clear writing and clear thinking are inseparable, and bad writing often reveals fuzzy thinking. Students who embrace writing about chemistry with seriousness and purpose benefit immeasurably, and instructors who incorporate writing into their teaching of chemistry perform an invaluable service to their students.

Just as Jan's book is grounded in the premise that "Biology is a way of thinking about the world," this book is informed by the belief that chemistry represents a distinct way of understanding the world. Being a chemist is not just about memorizing facts and terminology or about learning to use laboratory apparatus, instruments, and computer software. It is about understanding how the world works by making careful observations, asking specific questions, designing ways to address those questions, manipulating data thoughtfully and thoroughly, and interpreting those data and related observations in terms of the behavior of matter at the atomic and molecular levels. In common with all professionals in academic communities, chemists reevaluate past work, ask new questions, and redefine older questions. Of course, chemistry also requires writing. The hard work of thinking and writing about chemistry is at least as important as the work of doing it. Writing provides a way to examine, to evaluate, and to refine the ideas and insights that come from thinking about chemistry and, ultimately, to share them.

Aware that "we only get one chance to make a first impression" and that often this impression is made through our writing, we remind readers that making a good first impression means paying attention to detail. For chemists, many, many details of style and format are important. We have tried not to swamp readers with the minutiae of chemistry conventions, but rather to deal with only the more commonly encountered situations. We strongly recommend that readers who are on track to be professional chemists obtain a copy of *The ACS Style Guide*.

## ORGANIZATION

In addition to convincing our readers that writing plays an extremely important role in doing chemistry, we expect that students will find this textbook worth consulting repeatedly for reference and guidance throughout their academic careers. To meet the needs of chemistry students when they are initially introduced to the discipline, we provide guidance on lab notebooks, lab reports, and disciplinary conventions about format and citations. We also anticipate the needs of student writers as they advance in their study by providing material on specific tasks such as writing summaries, critiques, and research proposals, as well as communicating through oral and poster presentations. Finally we provide advice about writing applications and personal statements most likely to be useful to students as they transition from undergraduate life to the workplace or graduate study.

The book is divided into two parts: Part I covers general issues that apply to all types of writing (and reading) in chemistry; Part II provides guidelines for specific tasks. In Chapter 1, we emphasize the benefits of learning to write well in chemistry, describe the sorts of writing that professional chemists do, and review some key principles that characterize all sound scientific writing. Chapter 2 emphasizes the struggle for understanding that must precede any concern with how something is articulated. In it, we discuss how to read the formal scientific literature, how to take useful notes, and how to take them in ways that prevent unintentional plagiarism. Chapter 3 explains how to cite references and prepare a References section. Chapter 4 focuses on the process of revision—for content, clarity, and completeness. Chapter 5 focuses on editing for concision and issues of correctness, including observing the conventions of American Chemical Society (ACS) style. Chapters 4 and 5 also address certain usage issues that loom large when writing about chemistry such as passive and active voice, modifier placement, and concision. We have also included a brief tutorial on using punctuation in Appendix A, which we think will aid anyone unable to use punctuation with confidence.

The rest of the book covers most of the specific writing tasks encountered in chemistry coursework and in professional life: keeping laboratory notebooks (Chapter 6), writing laboratory and other research reports (Chapter 7), writing summaries and critiques (Chapter 8), writing essays and review papers (Chapter 9), writing research reports (Chapter 10), writing research proposals (Chapter 11), answering timed essay questions (Chapter 12), preparing oral and poster presentations (Chapter 13), and writing letters of application for jobs and graduate school (Chapter 14). We recognize that there are significant differences between the conventions of the different branches of chemistry and that, for example, advice about writing a lab report for an organic chemistry class may not be completely applicable to a report for a physical chemistry lab. However, we have not provided detailed commentary on such differences; rather, we have tried to keep the material at a more generic level, with the suggestion (made many times) that students should, when there are likely to be such differences, consult their instructors for further details.

Checklists at the ends of the chapters allow students to evaluate their own work and that of their peers. Some of these checklists include page numbers to help students locate the text on which each item is based. Instructors can easily turn these checklists into grading rubrics, which should be shared with students well before the assignments are due. In addition, we have provided a more general "Rubric for Science Writing" in Appendix B, which lays out in descriptive terms the attributes of science writing along a continuum from excellence to serious deficiency, and we encourage instructors to modify it to suit particular assignments. We find that students benefit immensely from knowing what exemplary completion of an assignment looks like, and we recommend sharing positive examples as well.

We recognize that there are ethical issues related to scientific writing. Plagiarism and other acts of academic dishonesty related to the production of written material need to be addressed and have been at the appropriate places. Readers are invited to take the two quizzes on the more common aspects of academic dishonesty at the end of Chapter 9, for which we provide answers and commentary at the end of the book.

We do not anticipate that students will read the chapters in the sequence in which we have presented them or that all readers will find all chapters equally compelling and useful. Thus, we repeat certain key ideas as they become relevant to various aspects of writing about chemistry to make individual chapters capable of standing alone and being useful even if a student has not read or recently reread the other chapters. We sincerely hope that not only will students find the text useful as they progress through their undergraduate careers, but instructors will also regard it as a valuable resource on which to rely as they educate the next generation of chemists to be not only conscientious, disciplined, and innovative scientists, but excellent communicators as well.

## ACKNOWLEDGMENTS

We gratefully acknowledge many useful discussions, thoughtful reading of drafts, and helpful comments from Madeleine Blais, University of Massachusetts Amherst; Paulina Borrego, Integrated Sciences & Engineering Library, University of Massachusetts Amherst; Debra Carney, Smith College; Ray D'Alonzo, University of Massachusetts Amherst; Elizabeth Ilnicki-Stone, Brock University; Kevin Shea, Smith College; Sharon Palmer, Amherst Regional High School; Peter Samal, University of Massachusetts Amherst; Jeff Seelye, Procter and Gamble;

Cristina Suarez, Smith College; Lynmarie Thompson, University of Massachusetts Amherst; William Vining, SUNY Oneonta; Peter Khalifah, SUNY Stony Brook. For his excellent artwork, we gratefully acknowledge Abraham Reyes Pardo of Boston, MA.

We thank the following reviewers of this edition for their many useful comments, many of which have been incorporated into the text: Gary D. Christian, University of Washington; Cindy DeForest Hauser, Davidson College; Neil Fitzgerald, Marist College; Katherine Kantardjieff, California State University Fullerton; Jeffrey Kovac, University of Tennessee; Carl Salter, Moravian College; Jack Steehler, Roanoke College; Sharon Williams, Hamilton College. It is also a pleasure to thank Rebecca Gilpin and our editor, Ginny Blanford, for their invaluable assistance and support during the revision and production of the book. We would also like to thank our many, many students in the "Writing in Chemistry" course from whom, as all attentive teachers do, we have learned much over the years. Many of our students offered insightful feedback that we have gratefully incorporated. We welcome comments from readers of this first edition of the new *A Short Guide to Writing about Chemistry*, instructors and students alike.

HOLLY DAVIS
JULIAN TYSON
JAN PECHENIK

# I

# GENERAL ADVICE ABOUT WRITING AND READING ABOUT CHEMISTRY

# 1

# WRITING: A THRESHOLD SKILL

*In science credit goes to the [scientist] who convinces the world, not to the [scientist] to whom the idea first occurs.*

SIR WILLIAM OSLER

## WHAT DO CHEMISTS WRITE ABOUT AND WHY?

An ability to write well is one of the most valuable but difficult skills that can be mastered in college, and the chemistry classroom is an excellent place to practice this skill. Writing is not an elusive, magical skill granted only to some. Ample evidence shows that everyone has the capacity to write and that people learn to write by writing, that is, writing is a skill best acquired through practice.

The ability to write clearly, correctly, and concisely is essential to success in virtually every professional field, including chemistry. In this electronic age, more employees—including chemists—have to write more than ever before. Neither experience with chemical instrumentation and techniques nor the possession of excellent laboratory skills will compensate for an inability to communicate well. In fact, a recent report from the National Commission on Writing, based on a survey of companies that included major employers of trained chemists, such as DuPont, Procter and Gamble, Bristol-Meyers Squibb, Eli-Lilly, Dow, and Pfizer, suggests that employers are unhappy with the preparation of college graduates to do the kind of writing necessary in the modern workplace. Such companies view an ability to write clearly and cogently as a "threshold skill"—that is, one that is necessary even to enter into the workplace.

The sort of writing that professional chemists do (grant proposals, research reports, literature reviews, oral and poster presentations for meetings, letters of recommendation for hiring and promotion) is similar in many respects to the sort of writing you are asked to do in typical college chemistry courses (essays, literature reviews, term papers, and laboratory and research reports). Just like your writing in college, every piece of professional writing must be written clearly, developed logically, and proofread carefully. All statements of opinion must be supported with facts or examples, and all uses of other people's work must be appropriately referenced.

Basically, most of what chemists write is an argument: an attempt to persuade or convince an audience of something. The success of a research proposal, for example, depends on your ability to convince a panel of other chemists that what you want to do is worth doing, that you are capable of doing it, that you are capable of interpreting the results, that the work cannot be done without the funds requested, and that the amount of funding requested is appropriate for the research planned. Research money is not plentiful. Even well-written proposals have a difficult time; poorly written proposals don't stand a chance.

Chemists also spend time preparing the results of their research for publication or for presentation at meetings in order to communicate with other chemists who are doing similar or related research. Academic journals and professional conferences are the means by which scholars in all fields communicate with one another to share their ideas and, in the case of chemistry, their most recent findings, and to consider the implications. Research articles are really just laboratory reports based on data collected over a period much longer than the typical laboratory session; the goals of a research article, as for a laboratory report, are to present data clearly and to interpret the results thoroughly in the context of previous work and basic chemical principles—to convince your audience, in other words, through the clarity of your writing that your results are new, true, and important.

While in all these cases—lab reports, grant proposals, journal articles, literature reviews—chemists are writing for an audience of other chemists, scientists are also frequently called upon to write for readers who are not part of their own professional community, to explain technical information to the general public, and to address scientific issues for broad audiences. Writing such explanations is a much more difficult task than it may at first seem. The additional challenge is to explain what is often highly complex or technical information in such a way that a reader who does not have your scientific expertise can grasp the seriousness of a situation or problem and its broader implications well enough to form a thoughtful opinion about it.

Clearly, being able to write effectively will help advance your career, yet when students in a chemistry course get critical feedback on their writing, they sometimes complain that "this is not an English course." However, clear, concise, logical writing is an important tool of the chemist's trade, and learning how to write well is at least as important as learning how to use a spectrophotometer or a pH meter. And unlike the specialized laboratory techniques that you might learn as a student, mastering the art of effective writing will reward you regardless of the field in which you eventually find yourself. If your chemistry instructor is willing to help you by providing feedback on your writing and allowing you to revise it before the grade is assigned, take full advantage of this wonderful opportunity to develop your writing skills.

## THE KEYS TO SUCCESS

**All good writing involves two struggles: the struggle to gain understanding and the struggle to communicate that understanding to readers.** Anyone who has done much writing is acutely aware that it is difficult and that there is no easy way to learn to write well in chemistry or in any other field. Reading a lot of good writing (see Chapter 2), and not just in chemistry, will help, as will keeping in mind that someone is going to be reading what you write. Whether your audience is your college instructor, your classmates, fellow professional chemists, or your supervisor at work, you need to create a document that your readers will understand and accept.

When you write, there is an implied contract between you and your reader. Your reader's obligation is to be alert and make a good-faith effort to pay attention to the argument you are making. Your obligation as a writer is to create a clear, concise, forward-moving, and accurate text. **The less you make your readers work, the more they will appreciate your writing.** If your reader has to stop, back up, or reread to make sense of what you're saying, you are in danger of losing that reader. Vague phrasing, inaccurate word choice, poor organization, even a lack of attention to the conventions of Standard Written English, such as punctuation and spelling, may all breach the contract between you and your reader.

There are no shortcuts to good writing, but there are some basic strategies that will help considerably. We offer here a list of practices that will help you write clearly and effectively about chemistry. Each is discussed more fully in later chapters (note the relevant page numbers). This list is worth reviewing at the start of each semester or whenever you begin a new assignment.

A useful general principle to keep in mind whenever you write is that **good writing is writing that achieves its own particular objectives.**

## TEN STRATEGIES FOR PREPARING YOUR FIRST DRAFT

**Strategy 1. Work to understand your sources (pp. 18–32).**  Before you begin to write—or even plan what you will write—you need to understand the data you are writing about. Examine laboratory data until you are confident that you see its significance; read books or research articles carefully, reread sentences you don't understand, and look up unfamiliar words. Confirm your understanding by making notes in your own words, rather than cutting and pasting or copying from sources; if you can't put what you have read into your own words, you probably don't completely understand it. All good scientific writing begins here: with understanding your sources.

**Strategy 2. Think about why you are writing before you begin and as you write (pp. 144–156).**  As we said above and will remind you frequently in this book, **good writing is writing that achieves a particular objective.** For example, the words, the voice, and the tone you would choose were you setting out to write a really passionate love letter are not the same words, voice, and tone that you would choose in writing the experimental section of a chemistry lab report because, as we hope you recognize, the two have very different goals. Having a clear sense of your objectives when you write allows you to make better choices about *what* to include (opinions or facts? how much detail?) and *how* to say it (use *I* and active voice or impersonal passive voice?) The *why* is key to *what* and *how* you write; therefore, it is important to have a clear sense of what your objectives are when you set out to write, even if you do not yet have a clear sense of how you will achieve them.

**Strategy 3. Write in anticipation of discovery (pp. 143–144).**  Your ideas about what you want to say and how best to say it may well change as you write and revise, since the act of writing invariably clarifies your thinking and often brings entirely new ideas into focus. Instructors know that asking students to respond in writing to a well-constructed assignment is a very effective way of developing students' awareness of what they know and don't know and of developing critical thinking skills, as well as developing their writing skills. This is called "writing to learn," and it is intimately linked with "learning to write."

**Strategy 4. Write to illuminate, not to impress (pp. 58, 127, 146).** Once you do begin to write, use the simplest words and the clearest phrasing available. Make sure your writing is consistent with the needs of your readership. Even if your intended reader is your instructor, try keeping your classmates in mind as you write: what words and concepts will they understand? What needs to be explained? Avoid overusing acronyms and abbreviations, and remember to define specialized terminology. Your goal is to communicate: focus on making your argument or getting your point across, not on trying to impress your readers with big words or highly technical vocabulary or jargon.

**Strategy 5. Use sources responsibly (pp. 156–158).** Passing off someone else's ideas as your own, or presenting someone else's words as though they were your original creation, is plagiarism. **Plagiarism is an academic crime.** The result will almost always be a failing grade on your paper and perhaps a failing grade in the course. Plagiarism can get you expelled from college and may cost you a career later. Whenever you restate another writer's ideas or concepts, you must do so in your own words, and you must credit your source explicitly. Simply changing a few words here and there or changing the order of words in a sentence or paragraph without acknowledging your source is still plagiarism. Incorporating source material into your own writing is always acceptable, but such material must always be incorporated appropriately and acknowledged specifically.

**Strategy 6. Use your own words; do not quote from sources (pp. 27–32).** Direct quotations rarely appear in the formal chemical literature. This practice distinguishes writing in the sciences from writing in disciplines like English or history, where invoking the actual words of an original text serves a useful purpose. In writing about chemistry, your goal is to describe what others have done and the ideas they have presented, but in your own words.

**Strategy 7. Show rather than tell. Support all statements of fact or opinion with evidence (pp. 54, 234, 154).** In any argument, a statement of fact or opinion becomes convincing to the critical reader only when that statement is supported by evidence, research, or explanation; provide it. Cite relevant authoritative sources according to the conventions of chemistry.

**Strategy 8. Always distinguish fact from possibility (pp. 55–56).**
In the course of examining your data or reading your notes, you may
form an opinion. This is splendid, and it represents the way science
advances: by offering opinions based on data, to which other scientists
may respond by adding supporting—or contradictory—evidence. But
you must be careful not to state your opinion as though it were fact,
based on your data alone. For example, "The concentration of
trimethylselenonium ion was always less than those of the selenosugars"
is a statement of fact and must be supported with references. "Our data
suggest that when selenized yeast supplements have been taken, the
species of greatest concentration in the urine are selenosugars"
expresses your opinion and should be supported by drawing the reader's
attention to relevant results.

**Strategy 9. Write to show that you can "think like a chemist"
(pp. 196–197).**    Much of the writing you are called on to produce for
your instructors in college is a request to show that you can interpret the
properties of materials, and their behavior under certain circumstances,
in terms of the behavior of the atoms and molecules of the materials and
of the nature of the electronic structure of atoms and molecules. Be sure
that you take full advantage of the opportunity to do so, especially in
"high-stakes" writing, such as answers to exam questions or reports of laboratory work, whether it is a short-term activity (an instructional lab class)
or long-term project (a senior thesis).

**Strategy 10. Allow time for revision (pp. 51–69).**    Once your
first draft is done, you are only partway to the finish line. Accurate, concise, persuasive communication is not easily achieved. Although the act of
writing can itself help clarify your thinking, you need to allow time to step
away from the first draft and reread it with fresh eyes before making revisions. A "revision" is, after all, a re-vision: another look at what you have
written. This second (or third or fourth) look allows you to see whether
you have really said what you intended to say and whether you have
guided the reader from point to point as masterfully as you had hoped.
Remember you are constructing an argument: making an argument fully
convincing requires thoughtful revision. Start a writing assignment as
soon as possible after receiving it, and always allow a few days between
the penultimate and final drafts. If you follow this advice, the quality of
what you submit will improve dramatically. You will also, almost certainly,
learn more from the assignment.

# TEN STRATEGIES FOR REVISING AND EDITING: GETTING TO YOUR FINAL DRAFT

**Strategy 1. Make sure you say what you mean to say (pp. 60–63).**   Words are tricky. If they end up in the wrong place—especially as misplaced modifiers—they can add considerable ambiguity to your sentences. Consider the following sentence.

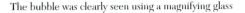 The bubble was clearly seen using a magnifying glass

In this case, the dangling modifier probably leads only to laughter, not to real misunderstanding; clearly a gas bubble is not capable of using a magnifying glass. The writer meant the bubble was clearly seen when a magnifying glass was used. Sometimes, however, this kind of sloppy language introduces significant misunderstandings. Good science writing is precise. Be sure you say what you mean. It sometimes helps to read aloud what you have written and to listen carefully to what you say as you read.

**Strategy 2. Use transitional words and phrases to keep the reader moving forward (p. 58).**   Part of your obligation as a writer is to offer your reader the simplest possible path forward through what you have written. You should try to take the reader by the nose in your first paragraph and lead him or her through to the end, line by line, paragraph by paragraph. Link your sentences carefully, using such transitional words as "therefore" or "in contrast," or by repeating key words so that a clear argument is developed logically. Link your paragraphs using transitions to continue the thought and to remind readers periodically of what they have already read.

**Strategy 3. Avoid using pronouns like *it, this,* and *they* without clear antecedents, that is, without clarifying what such pronouns refer to (pp. 63–65).**   Here is an example to show what we mean:

Our results were based upon observations of short-term changes in temperature. **They** showed that reaction rates did not depend on the amount of formaldehyde.

The pronoun *they* could refer to *results, observations,* or *changes in temperature.* Granted, the reader can back up and figure out what *they* are, but this ambiguity can be clarified by changing *they* to *these results*. Don't be afraid to repeat a word or phrase from the preceding sentence. If it is the right word and avoids ambiguity, use it. Repetition can at times be an effective way to keep readers moving forward.

**Strategy 4. Don't make readers work harder than they have to; do the work for the readers (pp. 66–68).**    If there is interpreting to be done, you, the writer, should be the one to do it. For example, never direct your readers to a table of data without setting them up to see what you consider significant.

    The difference in reaction rates is clearly shown in Table 1.

Such a statement puts the burden of effort on the readers and leaves them wondering, "So what?" Instead, provide the readers with guidance that facilitates their ability to grasp more quickly what is being presented.

As can be seen from the results in Table 1, peptides were more rapidly hydrolyzed in the presence of the protease enzyme than in acid solution, even when the temperature was raised.

Readers now know clearly what you have in mind and can examine Table 1 to see whether they agree with your interpretation.

**Be concise.** Give all the information necessary, but avoid using more words than you need. The next three rules are particular strategies we recommend for achieving concision in your writing when you revise.

**Strategy 5. Eliminate throat clearing (pp. 73–76).**    When we write, we often employ mindless little phrases to buy ourselves a little time to think of what to say next. We call this **written throat clearing** as it is the written equivalent of the "ahem, ahem" sound that serves the same purpose in speech. Written throat clearing is a natural part of the process of thinking and writing, of how people wrestle meaning into words, but when you revise, it pays to be alert for instances of unnecessary words, modifiers, or phrases that can be eliminated. Here are two sentences that provide ample illustration of what we mean by written throat clearing.

There is a considerable body of evidence in the literature to show that the quality of instrumental measurements of trace metallic elements in the environment has improved significantly over the most recent two decades. In view of the fact that the concentrations of trace elements in open and coastal ocean water have been decreasing, according to the results presented in published papers, it may be deduced that some of the earlier measurements were made under circumstances in which the many and varied interference effects that can be encountered with this type of sample material were not accounted for fully. (99 words)

Here is the same passage edited for throat clearing.

 The reported concentrations of metals in seawater have decreased over the past 20 years because improvements in instrument quality mean that measurements no longer suffer from the interferences that produced the earlier inaccurate high results. (35 words)

By revising for throat clearing, we achieve a reduction of 64%.

**Strategy 6. Avoid a too heavy reliance on weak verbs, such *as to be and to use* (pp. 77–78).**    The verb *to be* often serves a useful purpose early in the writing process helping the writer make connections or articulate relationships; consequently, it often gets overused at the draft stage. Utilitarian and serviceable, the verb *to be* is also colorless and bland. By working while you edit to avoid a too heavy reliance on it, you can pare down and breathe some life into the flat, unnecessarily wordy prose it produces.

The verb *to use* is a similar sort of work-horse verb that produces lifeless and flat prose when repeatedly employed in place of more specific verbs, as often occurs in the experimental section of research reports. For example:

A model ZX-100 chronospectrometer **was used** for all endochronic measurements. For the time dilation experiments a modified 3-electropode cell **was used.** To remove dissolved gases from the solutions, high purity helium **was used**, and an infrared radiation lamp **was used** to heat the solutions. A saturated calomel reference electrode with a triple junction **was used** as this prevented contamination of the solutions with mercury ions. To record the data, a home-built analog-to-digital converter **was used** to connect the spectrometer to a personal computer. (83 words)

We replace all of the *was used* constructions with more specific action verbs, and get this revision.

 Endochronicity was measured with a model ZX-100 chronospectrometer, equipped with a modified 3-electropode cell for the time dilation experiments. Solutions were degassed with high purity helium and heated with an infrared lamp. Mercury contamination from the saturated calomel reference electrode was avoided with a triple junction. Data were recorded by a personal computer interfaced via an analog-to-digital converter built in-house. (60 words)

The revision contains 27% fewer words and much less monotony than the original.

**Strategy 7. Excise unnecessary prepositions (pp. 76–77).** These little connecting words (*of, in, to*) tend to proliferate when we are still thinking our way through a sentence, making connections, and piecing together bits of information. Much like throat clearing and using forms of *to be* to link together concepts, prepositions may serve a useful purpose when we are struggling to understand, but they, too, can contribute to unnecessary wordiness. When you are editing your final draft, you should be vigilant to remove as many unnecessary prepositions as possible. Consider, for example, the following passage in which we have highlighted the prepositions.

The immobilization **of** biomolecules is a key feature **of** the basis **of** the development **of** biosensing devices. **In** order to understand the nature **of** the processes responsible **for** the change **in** oscillation frequency **of** a piezoelectric quartz crystal when subjected **to** the increased mass load **of** an adsorbed protein, many different forms **of** the spectroscopy **of** surfaces have been used. Several researchers **in** this area have found that useful information may be obtained **from** examination **with** ellipsometry, a form **of** spectroscopy that depends **on** the changes **in** polarization **of** light reflected off **of** a surface. (95 words)

Removing the unnecessary prepositions and some instances of throat clearing produces the following considerably shorter, less plodding passage.

Biomolecule immobilization is a key feature of biosensing device development. Processes responsible for the changes in a piezoelectric quartz crystal oscillation frequency due to protein adsorption have been studied by surface spectroscopy. Ellipsometry, in which the polarization changes on reflection are measured, is particularly useful. (45 words)

**Strategy 8. Use passive and active voice effectively (pp. 80–83).** In English it is possible to describe the same action using two different voices: the active voice or the passive voice. The active voice is preferable in most situations for a number of reasons. Passive voice obscures who or what is responsible for the central action in a sentence.

> Passive: Errors were made in the lab, and as a result the findings were deemed invalid.

Active voice makes it very clear who or what is the agent of the central action, who is doing what, and is usually more direct, concise, and economical than passive voice.

> Active: He made errors in the lab that invalidated the findings.

Passive voice does have its uses, especially in scientific writing, but it is often a great enemy of concise writing, which is also highly valued in scientific writing. So which should you use when writing about chemistry? **Use the voice that best suits your purpose in a particular situation.** We discuss passive and active voice in greater detail in Chapter 5.

**Strategy 9. Ensure that your writing is gender neutral (pp. 70–73).** Work to eliminate sexist language habits from your writing by avoiding using masculine nouns such as *man* to refer to both males and females or modifiers derived from masculine nouns such as *manmade*. Instead, substitute neutral alternatives such as nouns like *people* or *chemists* or modifiers like *synthetic* or *artificial*. Also avoid using the masculine pronouns (*he, his,* and *him*) to refer to both males and females. This can be accomplished by eliminating pronouns, occasionally using masculine and feminine pronouns in tandem (he or she), or recasting the sentence in the plural. We do not recommend the use of singular *they*, that is, the substitution of the plural pronoun *they* for the singular pronouns *he* and *she* as a means of achieving gender-neutral prose. Although this usage is a common feature of informal English and may eventually become accepted as Standard Written English, we recommend—that when writing formal prose, you adopt other strategies to avoid sexism in your writing.

**Strategy 10. Handle electronic files carefully and responsibly (p. 151).** Back up your file in a safe location, and leave yourself enough time for printing out a hard copy to account for such possible accidents as printer malfunctions or running out of ink. Never miss a deadline because of a computer-related problem. Instructors do not believe that printer cartridges run out at deadlines any more than they believe that dogs eat homework or flash drives.

# RULES AND CONVENTIONS: THE EASY STUFF

Like all academic disciplines, the field of chemistry has developed its own set of conventions for communicating information among its members. These conventions constitute a kind of shorthand or code that allows chemists to communicate more effectively and efficiently with one another. In order to write successfully about chemistry, you must understand and be able to employ these various conventions correctly.

**1. Follow rules from the American Chemical Society about abbreviation (pp. 84–86).**    Abbreviate units of measurement that are preceded by numbers, and always use the same symbol for all values regardless of quantity: 1 mm (millimeter), 50 mm; 1 h (hour), 2 h; 1 g (gram), 454 g. Note that there is no period after the symbol unless it terminates a sentence (pp. 89–90). Many commonly used instrumental techniques can be referred to by an abbreviation. For example, high-performance liquid chromatography can be abbreviated to HPLC. Such abbreviations are in capital letters, and there are no periods. You should define an abbreviation when the term is first encountered in the text, and then just use the abbreviation.

Be careful not to use an abbreviation inappropriately. You can determine the number of compounds in the reaction mixture by HPLC, but you cannot run the sample on the HPLC. In other words, do not use the abbreviation for the technique to stand for the instrument, even though, in informal conversation, we often do just that.

The following abbreviations are well-known and do not need to be defined: DNA (deoxyribonucleic acid), GC (gas chromatography), IR (infrared), M (molar), NMR (nuclear magnetic resonance), RNA (ribonucleic acid), and UV (ultraviolet) (pp. 84–86).

**2. Observe the conventions of the American Chemical Society about capitalization (pp. 86–87).**    Do not capitalize the names of chemical elements, the names of chemical compounds, the periodic table, the names of species, the common names of equipment or techniques, or surnames used as units of measure. Be careful with capitalization in chemical formulae: CO is carbon monoxide; Co is cobalt (p. 92). Capitalize adjectives formed from proper names (such as Boolean), genus names used as formal names (*Bacillus subtillis*), trade names (Teflon), and surnames when used as modifiers (Erlenmeyer flask). Capitalize the words *figure*, *table*, *chart*, and *scheme* only when they refer to specified numbered items (p. 87).

**3. Pay attention to the discipline-specific conventions of chemistry regarding hyphens and suffixes (pp. 87–89).** Most prefixes are not hyphenated. Use a hyphen to join two or three words that together function as a single modifier (ion-exchange resin), a modifier that contains *well, still, ever, ill,* or *little* (well-deserved award), spelled out fractions (one-tenth), spelled out numbers from 21 to 99 (forty-three), a word that is formed from a word and an initial capital letter (H-bomb), and double surnames (Elizabeth Davis-Calhoun). Use a hyphen to attach prefixes such as *anti, non,* and *pre* only under these special circumstances: when the second word in the combination begins with a capital letter (anti-Markovnikov) or a number (pre-2000), when the second word in the combination begins with the same letter that occurs at the end of the prefix (pre-equilibrium), or when the second word in the combination is a chemical term (non-phenyl).

Do not use a hyphen in modifiers that are chemical names (amino acid concentration), to attach multiplying prefixes (triatomic), to join an *ly* adverb and an adjective (accurately measured), or to attach prefixes such as *anti, non,* and *pre* to common adjectives (nonspecific).

**4. Pay attention to form and format (pp. 16, 120).** Everything you write should demonstrate that you took the time to read any style and formatting guidelines given to you by your instructor, supervisor, or potential publisher; that you took the assignment seriously and are proud of the result; and that you welcome constructive criticism of your work. Carefully follow guidelines about margins, spacing, length, and typeface, where to put your name and a date, and other formatting issues. Number pages so that a reader can tell immediately if a page is missing or out of order and so that readers can easily reference a particular part of the text ("In the middle of page 7, you imply...").

## THE ESSENTIAL LAST PASS: PROOFREADING

After you have read your final draft carefully and revised it for clarity, concision, and appropriate use of transitional word and phrases as well as capitals, abbreviations, and formatting, you still have one important task left. Although it is a crucial part of the writing process, few of us like to proofread. By the time we have arrived at this point in the project, we have put in a considerable amount of work and are certain we have done the job correctly. Who wants to read the paper yet another time? Moreover, finding an error means having to make a correction. But put yourself in the position of your reader. Your reader typically starts off on your side, wanting to give you a good grade or find your paper suitable for publication. A sloppy paper—for example, one with too many typing errors—can lose you a considerable amount of good will as a student and, later, as a practicing scientist. Sloppy writing may suggest to the reader that you are equally sloppy in your work and in your thinking, or that you take little pride in your own efforts. Furthermore, failure to proofread your paper and to make the required corrections implies that you don't value the reader's time, which is neither a flattering nor particularly wise message to send. Never forget that you get only one chance to make a first impression. Shoddily prepared material can easily lower a grade, damage a writer's credibility, reduce the likelihood that a manuscript will be accepted for publication or that a grant proposal will be funded, or cost an applicant a job or admission to professional or graduate school. Why put yourself in such jeopardy for a mere half-hour saved? **Turn in a piece of work that you are proud to have produced.**

## DO NOT DEPEND ON YOUR COMPUTER TO DO YOUR WORK FOR YOU

Although a computer makes revision and editing much easier than if a draft is handwritten, a computer can do little to help you in that all-important first struggle—the struggle for understanding. Nor can it read and synthesize the material from your sources or organize your paper conceptually; it cannot, in short, think. And keep in mind that it cannot even proofread for you—at least not very effectively.

Computerized spell and grammar checkers can catch some typographical and spelling and syntax errors, but chemistry is a field with considerable specialized terminology, much of which is of no use to non-chemists. Many chemical terms are not included in the dictionaries that accompany computerized spelling programs. If you are fortunate enough to be working on your own personal computer, you can easily add words to the computer's dictionary, but the terminology in your papers will be changing with every new assignment. Many of the words you add for today's assignment will probably not be used in next week's assignment. Moreover, spell-check programs cannot distinguish between homophones like *to* and *too*, *there* and *their*, or *it's* and *its*, and the program will miss typographical errors that are real words. Your computer will not know that you have typed *an* when you meant to type *and*. A grammar checker might spot this error—but it might not. By all means use spell-

and grammar-check programs if they are readily available, but don't depend on them as infallible. Use your own sharp eyes and keen intellect—moving word by word and sentence by sentence—to complete the necessary process of proofreading your work.

**Pay attention to formatting issues.**   Check, for example, that sections are numbered correctly and that Greek letters or other signs or symbols you may have included have not been transformed by changes you may have made to font or style. Be especially careful with the global "find and replace" feature in the edit toolbox. If you are not absolutely sure how your proposed edit will work, try it on the first few examples you encounter before letting it loose on the entire document. Some changes cannot be reversed easily.

Chemistry writing can contain many superscripts and subscripts: check that these are correctly formatted. Sometimes material that has been created by another program does not print as you expect it to, even though it looks fine on the screen. Pay close attention to any pictures or diagrams that you have inserted from elsewhere, since these may not "translate" well into another software program. Look especially for tables or charts that break inconveniently between pages or for headings that sit by themselves at the bottom of pages. Insert additional page breaks or move elements around to avoid this kind of problem.

Finally, use one part of your word-processing program that really is efficient: the word count feature. Make sure that your paper is within the targeted length of your assignment or publication guidelines.

## CHECKLIST FOR WRITING ABOUT CHEMISTRY

- ❑   Work to understand your sources (p. 5).
- ❑   Think about why you are writing before you begin to write and as you write (pp. 5–6).
- ❑   Write in anticipation of discovery (p. 5).
- ❑   Write to illuminate, not to impress (p. 5).
- ❑   Use sources responsibly (p. 6).
- ❑   Use your own words; do not quote from sources (p. 6).
- ❑   Show rather than tell. Support all statements of fact or opinion with evidence (p. 6).
- ❑   Always distinguish fact from possibility (p. 7).

❑   Write to show that you can "think like a chemist" (p. 7).

❑   Allow time for revision (p. 7).

❑   Make sure you say what you mean to say (p. 8).

❑   Use transitional words and phrases to keep the reader moving forward (p. 8).

❑   Avoid using pronouns like *it, they, this,* and *their* without clear antecedents, that is, without clarifying what such pronouns refer to (pp. 8–9).

❑   Do not make readers work harder than they have to; do the work for the reader (p. 9).

❑   Be concise: Eliminate throat clearing (pp. 9–10).

❑   Avoid a too heavy reliance on weak verbs (pp. 10–11).

❑   Excise unnecessary prepositions (p. 11).

❑   Use passive and active voice effectively (pp. 11–12).

❑   Ensure that your writing is gender neutral (p. 12).

❑   Handle electronic files carefully and responsibly (p. 12).

❑   Follow rules from the American Chemical Society about abbreviation (p. 13).

❑   Observe the conventions of the American Chemical Society about capitalization (p. 13).

❑   Pay attention to the discipline-specific conventions of chemistry regarding hyphens and suffixes (p. 14).

❑   Pay attention to form and format (p. 14).

❑   Proofread, proofread, proofread (pp. 14–15).

❑   Do not rely too heavily on your spelling- and grammar-checking software (pp. 15–16).

❑   Pay attention to formatting issues (p. 16).

❑   Use the word count tool. (p. 16).

# 2

---

# GENERAL ADVICE ON READING AND TAKING NOTES

*That is one of the worst feelings I can think of, to have had a wonderful moment or insight or vision or phrase, to know you had it, and then lose it. So now I use note cards.*

ANNE LAMOTT

## WHY READ AND WHAT TO READ

By now you will have realized that a college education consists mostly of guided self-teaching, a pedagogy in which reading features prominently. That is, much of what you learn in college, particularly with regard to the content of your various courses, you learn by interacting with "written" material whether it be on the screen of your computer, in the pages of a book, or in an original research article in a scientific journal. Chemists refer to articles in scientific journals as the primary literature.

The **primary literature** is based on original observations and experiments; it includes information about how those observations or experiments were made or conducted. Review articles, which summarize the primary literature, that appear in scientific journals are known as the **secondary literature**. Chemists call textbooks and encyclopedia entries the **tertiary literature**.

Reading secondary and tertiary sources is an excellent way to get up to speed in a new area, but you will generally be learning more about what is known than about how we have come to know it or what remains to be found. For many assignments in upper-level undergraduate chemistry courses, and certainly in a graduate program, you will be asked to go beyond the factual foundation of the field to interpret, evaluate, synthesize, ask new questions, and maybe even design experiments to address those questions.

To see the basis for—and often the limits of—our current knowledge, you will need to explore the primary literature. Reading that literature is very different from reading the secondary or tertiary literature. It is a skill that requires some practice and guidance.

## EFFECTIVE READING

Too many students think of reading as the mechanical act of moving the eyes left to right, line by line, to the end of the page, and repeating the process page after page to the end of the chapter or assignment. We call this "brain-off" reading. When the last page has been "read," the task is over and it's on to something else. In the same way, some students typically "listen" to a lecture by furiously copying whatever the instructor writes or says, without really thinking about the information while it is being presented.

Whether you are reading a textbook, a review article, or a paper from the primary research literature, you must interact intellectually with the material if you hope to understand it in a useful way and to have something worthwhile to write about later. As you read, you must become a "brain-on" reader, wrestling thoughtfully with every sentence, every graph, every figure, and every table. If you do not fully understand any part of what you are reading, you must work through the problem until it is resolved rather than skipping over the difficult material and moving along to something more accessible. This is especially true when reading the primary research literature; it must be read slowly, thoughtfully, and patiently, and a single paper must usually be reread several times before it can be thoroughly understood. Don't become discouraged after only one or two readings. As with playing tennis or sight reading music, reading the primary literature gets easier with practice.

This kind of reading is inevitably a time-consuming process, but you can do a number of things to smooth the way. Always begin by carefully reading the appropriate sections of your textbook and any relevant class notes to get a solid overview of your general subject. You should also look for review articles or other books on the subject, and at this point, you might find it helpful to talk to a reference librarian about finding such suitable secondary and tertiary sources. In addition to books specifically written for students, there are books specifically written for professional chemists. These books fall into two categories: **monographs**, which are in-depth treatments of one particular topic, and **handbooks**, which are in-depth treatments of a particular field. Your library will probably have a number of these books available.

Almost all articles published in chemistry journals appear in a standard format containing the following sections: Title, Abstract, Introduction, Experimental, Results, Discussion, Acknowledgments, and References. Often, the Results and Discussion are combined into one section, and some journal articles also have a Conclusion section. A more recent trend is to decrease the number of experimental results that appear in the print version of the article and make these available as supplemental material that can be downloaded from a Web site. First, read the Title and Abstract to get an overview of the paper. Next, read the last paragraph of the Introduction. If the paper is written well, this is where the researchers will describe what is new about the material in the article and will state the specific issues or questions that were addressed. Then read the titles of the tables and the captions for the figures, so that you can see exactly what sorts of data are being presented. At this point you may find that the article is not really relevant to your topic after all or that it is of little help in developing your theme. If so, this preliminary reading will have saved you from wasted note taking. On the other hand, if the paper is of interest, you can now start at the beginning and read the material in the sequence that the researchers present it.

As you read, pay special attention to the following:

- What was the goal of the work reported?
- Did the researchers achieve this goal?
- What evidence is presented to convince you that the goal was achieved?
- Do you believe the evidence?
- Are numerical results accompanied by appropriate statistical evaluations of errors?
- Are any results presented that are not discussed?
- What questions remain unanswered?

If you are planning to write a research proposal, you should ask one additional question:

- What are the next steps to be taken?

# EFFECTIVE NOTE-TAKING AND NOTE-ORGANIZING

We all know that if you want to learn something from an oral presentation or seminar, taking notes is a good idea. Taking notes keeps you active: you have to engage with the material to decide whether to write or not. Note-taking is a basic skill that college instructors assume you have mastered and one you will need in many professional settings. The purpose of taking notes is to create a fuller written document containing all of the important material at a later time. The sooner you revisit those notes, the more you will be able to recall. Too many students do not revisit their notes until it is (almost) too late—often just before a test or exam. One of your goals in attending college is to acquire skills that will transfer over into life after college, when you are responsible for your own learning. It is a good idea to get into the habit of rewriting your lecture notes within 24 hours rather than 24 days.

Taking notes about what you are reading is much like taking notes during a lecture: you are keeping active, you are identifying the material that is unfamiliar, you are collecting material that is potentially useful, and you are creating a record of your thoughts and activity. If you are in the early stages of gathering material from multiple sources to create an essay or term paper, you will want to record accurately the details of what information came from what source. You will probably need to provide citations to your sources (for more details see Chapter 3), and since you may well want to find a particular source again, keep careful records of what you read.

It is worth giving a little thought to how you are going to organize your notes. Almost certainly you will not want to record material in a bound notebook because it can be difficult to rearrange the order of the material or to insert new material other than at the end. You may want to use a loose-leaf, three-ring binder, or perhaps you should invest in some file index cards, and a suitable box with dividers. It is, of course, perfectly possible to create notes as electronic text on your computer, although there are certain logistical issues to be considered such as portability, battery life, and, if your reading is to be done in the library, work-surface availability. Viewing and organizing notes about even modest numbers of topics can be difficult on the virtual desktop.

If you are reading the original literature in the form of text you have printed for your own use from a pdf version of the article, then do not hesitate to write all over it. In this way, you can readily identify those parts of the article you do not understand or find convincing, and you can write appropriate comments and questions in the margins. You should still make separate notes about each article that you read and add those to your collection for the project.

## READING DATA: PLUMBING THE DEPTHS OF FIGURES AND TABLES

In addition to text, most research articles will contain tables and figures in which the researchers present the results of experiments. The claims the authors make will be based on the data or information presented in the tables and figures, and so you should pay particular attention to those results. If the tables and figures were carefully executed, there will be enough information in the figure caption and in the axis labels for you to understand the essential details of the experiment. As you scrutinize the figures and tables, ask yourself *what* experiment was done, *why* it was done, *how* it was done, and *what* the key results seem to be. Try to form your own opinions about what the data mean before you read the text of the Results section.

An example of a table from a journal article is shown in Figure 1. The title of the article is "Arsenic Speciation in Rice and Soil Containing Related Compounds of Chemical Warfare Agents"; the authors are Koji Baba, Tomohito Arao, Yuji Maejima, Eiki Watanabe, Heesoo Eun, and Masumi Ishizaka; and the journal, year, volume, and page numbers are *Anal. Chem.* **2008,** *80,* 5768–5775. We see that the title of the table does not tell us what the numbers are, and we have to read the heading above the numbers to find that these are concentrations expressed in mg kg$^{-1}$ (or ppm) of arsenic. We also note that there are three materials (grain, straw, and soil) even though there are only two "straddle" headings (as the horizontal lines with text above are called). Each number is accompanied by a ± term, but this is not defined (we would look to see if there was a footnote to explain this) and so we make a mental note that maybe this information is in the text. We note that each number is based on the results for three samples (this is how we interpret "$n = 3$"). We see that for each extraction solvent the concentration of each species is given, and that several of the arsenic-containing compounds are referred to by 3-, 4-, and 5-letter abbreviations, as is one of the solvents. We will have to look in the text to find the identity of these. We note that the solvents used for extracting arsenic compounds from soil are not the same as those for extracting arsenic compounds from the rice, grain, and straw.

**Table 1. Extraction of Arsenic Species with Various Media ($n = 3$)**

| grain | extraction media (mg of As kg$^{-1}$) | | | | digest (mg of As kg$^{-1}$) |
|---|---|---|---|---|---|
| | H$_2$O | 50% CH$_3$OH | TFA | HNO$_3$ | |
| inorganic As | 0.167 ± 0.005 | 0.164 ± 0.019 | 0.226 ± 0.034 | 0.255 ± 0.039 | |
| DPAA | 0.048 ± 0.006 | 0.072 ± 0.005 | 0.076 ± 0.007 | 0.071 ± 0.005 | |
| MPAA | 0.262 ± 0.013 | 0.323 ± 0.008 | 0.426 ± 0.024 | 0.408 ± 0.010 | |
| total | 0.475 ± 0.011 | 0.555 ± 0.021 | 0.732 ± 0.009 | 0.729 ± 0.027 | 0.752 ± 0.032 |
| overall recovery (%)[a] | 63.2 ± 1.5 | 73.8 ± 2.8 | 97.3 ± 1.2 | 96.9 ± 3.6 | |
| straw | | | | | |
| inorganic As | 1.094 ± 0.100 | 1.068 ± 0.012 | 1.062 ± 0.105 | 1.661 ± 0.038 | |
| MAA+DMAA | 0.064 ± 0.004 | 0.067 ± 0.004 | 0.091 ± 0.003 | 0.272 ± 0.028 | |
| MPAA | 0.107 ± 0.007 | 0.125 ± 0.007 | 0.209 ± 0.003 | 0.216 ± 0.010 | |
| DMPAO | 0.834 ± 0.064 | 1.162 ± 0.089 | 1.112 ± 0.022 | 1.742 ± 0.032 | |
| MDPAO | 0.072 ± 0.005 | 0.115 ± 0.011 | 0.125 ± 0.005 | 0.124 ± 0.004 | |
| total | 2.189 ± 0.138 | 2.537 ± 0.100 | 2.599 ± 0.094 | 4.020 ± 0.096 | 5.018 ± 0.134 |
| overall recovery (%)[a] | 43.6 ± 2.8 | 50.6 ± 2.0 | 51.8 ± 1.9 | 80.1 ± 1.9 | |

| | extraction media (mg of As kg$^{-1}$) | | | | digest (mg of As kg$^{-1}$) |
|---|---|---|---|---|---|
| | H$_2$O | H$_3$PO$_4$ | NaOH | HNO$_3$ | |
| soil | | | | | |
| inorganic As | nd[b] | 0.863 ± 0.069 | 1.041 ± 0.048 | 5.856 ± 0.191 | |
| MAA+DMAA | nd[b] | 0.173 ± 0.018 | 0.208 ± 0.012 | 0.524 ± 0.015 | |
| PAA | 0.051 ± 0.005 | 1.130 ± 0.027 | 1.247 ± 0.066 | 1.355 ± 0.070 | |
| DPAA | 0.107 ± 0.007 | 0.217 ± 0.008 | 0.267 ± 0.025 | 0.338 ± 0.022 | |
| MPAA | 0.152 ± 0.007 | 0.626 ± 0.032 | 0.750 ± 0.031 | 0.762 ± 0.058 | |
| DMPAO | 0.071 ± 0.002 | 0.142 ± 0.014 | 0.188 ± 0.007 | 0.347 ± 0.019 | |
| MDPAO | 0.117 ± 0.007 | 0.232 ± 0.003 | 0.373 ± 0.027 | 0.449 ± 0.025 | |
| total | 0.498 ± 0.004 | 3.383 ± 0.137 | 4.074 ± 0.193 | 9.632 ± 0.364 | 9.803 ± 0.396 |
| overall recovery (%)[a] | 5.1 ± 0.0 | 34.5 ± 1.4 | 41.6 ± 2.0 | 98.3 ± 3.7 | |

[a] $100 \times$ [chromatographic total As]/[digested total As]. [b] Below instrumental detection limit.

Figure 1. Table 1 from the article "Arsenic Speciation in Rice and Soil Containing Related Compounds of Chemical Warfare Agents."

We note that the concentrations of the phosphoric acid, sodium hydroxide, and nitric acid are not given, and therefore we will have to find this information in the text. We also see that the researchers have analyzed the materials for total arsenic, and the values are given in the column headed "digest." We see that the units are the same (and note that there is a word-processing error in one of these where a ")" and "−1" appear in the wrong order).

The way the overall original figure has been calculated is explained in the footnote for which we have to interpret the use of "[]" to mean concentration. There is enough information to check the researchers' calculations. So for the extraction of arsenic compounds from rice grain by water, we can add $0.167 + 0.048 + 0.262$ to get $0.477$, which is close to the value of $0.475$ given in the table. We note that there are similar issues with the other columns of numbers, but as 475 divided by 752 is 0.632, the 63.2% given as the overall recovery is correct. We note that not all compounds are listed for each of the three materials, and so we assume that compounds not listed were not detected in any of the extracts. We see that in terms of accounting for all the arsenic, nitric acid is the best solvent, though TFA took out nearly all of the arsenic from the rice grains. We can see that compared with the relative proportions of inorganic arsenic and organic arsenic compounds in the soil, the rice grain and straw contain higher amounts of organic arsenic. We probably think it would be easier to express some of these numbers in a bar chart format, and so we are gratified to find on the next page of the article some figures that do just that. One of these figures is shown in Figure 2.

Because the caption of the figure does not explain how these numbers were obtained, we speculate that this was based on the analysis of a nitric acid extract, as we already know that for grain and soil, this solvent can extract about 97% of the arsenic present. We can look to see whether the numbers in the figure agree with the numbers in the table. Now we encounter a problem, as we see, for example, that the total arsenic in the straw was about 13 mg kg$^{-1}$ according to the figure but only 5 mg kg$^{-1}$ according to the table. We can, however, clearly see that there is not much arsenic in the rice grain, but there is much more in the straw. We can also see that the compound DMPAO is taken up by the straw to a much greater extent than any other compound, even though the concentration in soil was one of the lowest.

An important part of the way in which science advances is that other scientists scrutinize the results presented and ask whether the data really support the conclusions drawn. It is unlikely that your instructor will assign you an article to read that contains seriously flawed interpretations

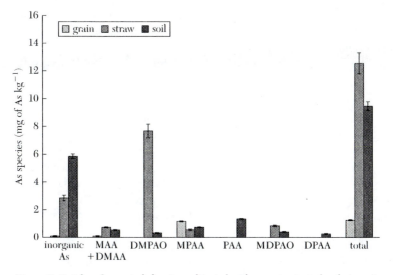

Figure 9. Uptake of arsenicals by rice cultivated with a contaminated soil. Arsenic concentrations in rice grain, straw, and soil were expressed by the white, gray, and black bars, respectively ($n = 3$).

Figure 2. Figure from the article "Arsenic Speciation in Rice and Soil Containing Related Compounds of Chemical Warfare Agents."

of the data, but if you have selected the article yourself, then you should be aware that publication in a primary journal is no guarantee that the science is flawless, and no guarantee that the presentation is error free (as we saw above from examining the figures and tables in a published article). The scientists who reviewed the material before publication may have had some questions that were not fully answered in the resubmission, but in the judgment of the journal's editor, the positive features of the work outweighed the negative features, and the article was accepted for publication. Always reading with a skeptical eye can give you interesting things to write about, and sometimes it even leads to interesting new research questions. We discuss the process by which chemists publish their research results to the rest of the community in Chapter 10.

## READING TEXT: SUMMARIZE AS YOU GO

Resist the temptation to copy your source's words verbatim. Instead, try to summarize sections of the material as you read. In this way, you will be processing information as you read it, and you will be one major step closer to having something interesting to write about later. To summarize effectively, you must first determine what is important. Consider the following paragraph from a 2004 review article, published in the journal *Clinical Chemistry*, by Kevin Francesconi and Florence Pannier.

> In addition to the scientific interest in selenium, there is also considerable public awareness because of its purported efficacy as a treatment against certain types of cancer. Encouraging results, reported in 1996 from a study carried out in the United States [5]*, provided the impetus for an ongoing 12-year study involving 32,000 individuals to test the efficacy of selenium intake against prostate cancer [6]. Furthermore, although there are no demonstrated health benefits from having selenium intake above physiologic requirements, there is a general perception that increased selenium ingestion is beneficial, which has led to a flourishing market in selenium supplements. These supplements are thought to be more effective when the selenium is ingested in an "organic" form, and many suppliers provide the selenium as selenized yeast, which contains largely selenomethionine bound in proteins in addition to many other unknown selenium species [7]. Consumers of such products intent on improved health should be aware, however, of the toxicity of selenium and the possible toxic consequences of overindulgence.

What are the key points in this paragraph? What information would the authors be unhappy to see left out?

- Selenium compounds may prevent some cancers.
- People should be aware that selenium compounds are toxic, so overdosing with supplements may be dangerous.

Here is a possible one-sentence summary that incorporates both points:

> People who take selenium supplements should be aware that, although there is evidence that selenium prevents some types of cancer, overdosing is dangerous because selenium compounds are toxic.

---

*A number that appears in the text like this (sometimes as a superscript) refers to the source from which the writers are taking their information. This is known as "citing" a source. At the end of the article, there will be a collection of sources cited under the heading "References." In Chapter 3, we discuss references and how to cite them.

The original paragraph illustrates one or two conventions of chemistry writing, which have been incorporated into the summary sentence. The first is that **writers use the name of the element as shorthand for "a variety of compounds of the element."** When we are told that selenium may prevent prostate cancer, the writers do not mean that participants in the trial will be eating ground-up elemental selenium. They mean that participants will be given a compound of selenium, an example of which—selenomethionine—is given later in the original paragraph. The other convention is that **it is understood that all chemicals are toxic, but that not all chemicals are equally toxic**, and that in addition to dose and the time over which the interaction occurs, toxicity depends on how the chemical and organism interact. It is not necessary to write that selenium compounds are toxic at high doses because, by definition, anything is toxic at a "high" dose. What we are really being told is that compared with the amounts of chemicals commonly eaten such as various compounds of, for example, calcium, carbon, hydrogen, nitrogen, oxygen, sodium, sulfur, and phosphorus, the amount of a selenium compound that it is safe to eat is much lower.

The important features of the summary sentence are that it is (1) accurate, (2) complete, (3) self-sufficient (it makes sense even if the reader has never read the original text), and (4) in your own words. Although taking these kinds of notes may be a real challenge at first, if you get into the habit of writing such summaries as you read, you will find that the eventual payoff is tremendous. Moreover, summarizing in your own words is an excellent way to avoid plagiarism, an act of academic dishonesty that is not tolerated in academic and professional communities. Submitting anyone else's work under your own name is plagiarism, even if you alter some words or reorder some sentences. Presenting someone else's ideas as your own is also plagiarism. We discuss plagiarism in more detail in Chapter 7, which deals with writing essays and reviews.

## Take Notes in Your Own Words

Photocopying an article or book chapter does not constitute note taking; neither does highlighting or even copying a passage by hand, occasionally substituting a synonym for a word in the original text. Take notes using your own words. Do not be awed and overwhelmed by other people's words; rather, build confidence in your own thoughts and phrasings.

Taking notes involves critical evaluation; as you read you must decide either that particular facts or ideas are relevant to your topic or that they are not. **If an idea is relevant, you should jot down a summary in your own words,** as discussed earlier. Try not to write complete sentences as you take notes as this will help you avoid unintentional plagiarism later and will encourage you to see through to the essence of a statement. For the same reasons, do not write while looking at the source.

Sometimes the author's words seem so perfect that you cannot see how they might be revised to best advantage for your paper. In this case, you may wish to copy a phrase or sentence or two verbatim in your notes, but be sure to enclose the material in quotation marks as you write, and clearly indicate the source from which the quotation derives. If you modify the original wording slightly as you take notes, you should indicate this as well, perhaps by using modified quotation marks: ⁄. . . ⁄. If you feel that there is any danger that you will not be able to distinguish between your words and those of the original text, we suggest preceding your notes with the word *Me* and a colon. If you take notes this way, you will avoid the unintentional plagiarism that might occur if you later forget who is responsible for the wording of your notes or for the origin of an idea.

If you find yourself copying verbatim or paraphrasing your source, be sure it is not simply because you do not understand what you are reading. Be honest with yourself. **It is always best to summarize in your own words**; at the very least, you should think your way to some good questions about what you are reading and write those questions down. Sooner or later serious intellectual engagement is required; there are no shortcuts available here.

Here is an example of some notes taken using the suggested system of notation based on the introduction to a review paper by Dan Melamed (*Anal. Chim. Acta*, **532**, 2005, 1–13). The notes were being taken for the introduction to a research proposal concerning the determination of arsenic in drinking water. Note that **the student has avoided using complete sentences**, focusing instead on the basic points and pinning down a few words and phrases that might be useful later. Notice also that **the student has taken notes selectively** and has **clearly distinguished his or her own thoughts from those of Melamed** by preceding such thoughts with *Me* and a colon. The original text is shown in Figure 3, and the student's notes are shown in Figure 4.

Having been selective and taken care to label his or her own thoughts while recording these notes, this student will not have to worry

Arsenic is a relatively common, toxic element that is also a known carcino-
gen [1]. Arsenic is found in a wide variety of chemical forms throughout the
environment and can be readily transformed by microbes, changes in geo-
chemical conditions, and other environmental processes [2]. While arsenic
occurs naturally, it also may be found as a result of a variety of industrial     ←①
applications [3], including leather and wood treatments [4], and pesticides [5].
Anthropogenic arsenic contamination results from a variety of activities: manufacturing metals and alloys, refining petroleum, and burning fossil fuels and
wastes. These activities have created a strong legacy of arsenic pollution
throughout the world. The combination of high toxicity and widespread occur-
rence has created a pressing need for effective monitoring and measurement
of arsenic in soils and groundwater. Toxic concentrations of arsenic have been
detected in water supply wells in the United States [6] and abroad [7], creating   ←②
a health risk for a large fraction of the world's population [8]. Arsenic is second
only to lead as the main inorganic contaminant in the original National Priority
List (NPL) of Superfund sites [9]. It also is one of the toxic materials regulated
under the Resource Conservation and Recovery Act (RCRA). Therefore, the        ←③
need exists for arsenic monitoring at Superfund sites, RCRA landfills, facilities
handling arsenic-containing wastes, and sites where arsenic is found at toxic
concentrations in groundwater. The current maximum contaminant level
(MCL) for all forms of arsenic in groundwater is 50 $\mu$g/l (50 ppb), set by EPA
in 1975 based on a Public Health Service standard originally established in
1942. On 22 January 2001, EPA adopted a new standard for arsenic in drinking
water at 10 ppb, to be enforced by January 2006 [10]. Arsenic-contaminated    ←④
waste is restricted under RCRA as a hazardous waste and must be treated to
meet limits determined by a prescribed aqueous extraction protocol, the toxicity characteristic leaching procedure (TCLP), usually performed in a laboratory. However, recent studies have shown that the TCLP may *not* accurately      ←⑤
measure the ability for arsenic to migrate from a landfill [11]. Arsenic-contaminated soil is often treated as a hazardous waste with the same limitations on
treatment or disposal, and often, additional regulations [12,13]. Specific limits
requirements vary but soil arsenic requires measurements down to mg/kg (ppm)
concentrations. The new groundwater limits may affect disposal procedures for
waste-containing arsenic, increasing the pressure to directly monitor RCRA
waste sites, as well as arsenic containing soils for their potential to leach arsenic
into groundwater. Unlike organic pollutants, arsenic cannot be transformed into
a non-toxic material; it can only be transformed into a form that is less toxic to    ←⑥
organisms in the environment. Because arsenic is a permanent part of the environment, there is a long-term need for regular monitoring at sites where arsenic-
containing waste is collected and at sites where it occurs naturally at elevated
concentrations. A range of analytical field assays for pollutants such as arsenic
provide valuable tools to support improved site characterization [14].

Figure 3. Taken from Melamed, D. *Anal. Chim. Acta*, **2005,** 532, 1–13. The
numbers and arrows indicate the text that informs the notes shown in Figure 4.

Arsenic widely distributed in environment, especially soils and waters, at concentrations likely to be harmful.

1. Sources of arsenic both natural and human, including some deliberate applications in the environment such as pesticides and wood preservation. Inadvertent release from metal prodn, leather treat, fossil fuel burn, petrol refine and wastes. **Me:** does this mean landfills? Possible quote: "strong legacy of arsenic pollution throughout the world." What about chicken manure? Known to contain residues of arsenic-containing feed additives, but maybe not a major source of contamination?

2. Concs in some drinking waters too high in both US and rest of world. **Me:** where has arsenic come from and what chemical forms?

3. US has regulations about pollutants: National Priority list (Pb first then As), Superfund sites, Resource Conservation and Recovery Act. **Me:** Superfund? better check ref 9.

4. USEPA limit for drinking water now (Jan 2006) 10 ppb.

5. Waste treatment not relevant except that if As leaches from waste sites it may contaminate ground water. **Me:** surely landfills are made so that they don't leak? Could be important topic, but off-task.

6. Arsenic compounds cannot be made non-toxic. **Me:** what about arsenobetaine and arsenocholine? Need to check if these turn up in environment. So need to measure at As-containing waste sites and places where background concs are high. Check ref 14 for more info about on-site measurements.

Figure 4. Handwritten notes based on the passage shown in Figure 3. Numbers in the margin correspond to the indicated portions of Figure 3.

about accidental plagiarism when writing a proposal based on these notes. Moreover, all of the active thinking the student has done while reading has generated the foundation for a good introduction to a research proposal.

## Split-Page Note-Taking: A Can't-Fail System

*Perfectly organized notes that cover everything are beautiful, but they live on paper, not in your mind.*

PETER ELBOW

If you have trouble taking notes in your own words and thinking while you read, try the split-page note-taking system. With this system, you divide a page into left and right halves. On the left side, you write factual information as you read—preferably in your own words, but it is also okay to quote directly. On the right side, write your response to the entry you just made on the left side. Try to respond to everything that you write on the left as you read. Your response could be a simple question ("Is arsenic *common*?"), a more thoughtful question ("What other environmental processes could be involved?"), a reminiscence ("That reminds me of what Professor Shea said in last week's seminar about..."), or a comparison ("Interesting: the issue of chicken manure contaminated with residues of arsenic-containing drugs is not mentioned and so may not be as important as these other sources"). Write whatever you happen to think of when you look at what you wrote on the left side. Figure 5 is an example based on the material from the Melamed article.

## Final Thoughts on Note-Taking: Document Your Sources

As you take notes, be sure to make a complete record of each source used: author(s), title of article, title of journal, year of publication, volume number, and page numbers. It is not always easy to relocate a source once it has been returned to the library stacks; in fact, the source you forgot to record completely is always the one that vanishes as soon as you realize that you need it again. Furthermore, before you finish with a source, it is good practice to read the material one last time to be sure that your notes accurately reflect the content.

| Facts | Responses |
|---|---|
| Arsenic is a relatively common, toxic, carcinogen, occurs in a wide variety of chemical forms throughout the environment. Can be readily transformed by microbes, changes in geochemical conditions, and other environmental processes. | "Arsenic" means arsenic compounds.<br><br>Example of biogeochemistry in action. |
| Occurs naturally, but also from industrial applications: leather and wood treatment and pesticides, manufacturing metals and alloys, refining petroleum, and burning fossil fuels and wastes. | Some contamination from As into environment deliberately; some contamination is accidental. What about residues from chicken drugs? |
| These activities have created a strong legacy of arsenic pollution throughout the world. | Good quote to use. |
| The combination of high toxicity and widespread occurrence has created a pressing need for effective monitoring and measurement of arsenic in soils and groundwater. | Could be another useful quote or maybe just paraphrase? |
| Toxic concentrations of arsenic found in wells in the United States and elsewhere. Large fraction of the world's population at risk. | Hmm—just how large a fraction? |
| As second only to Pb as inorganic contaminant on the original National Priority List (NPL) of Superfund sites [9]. Also regulated under the Resource Conservation and Recovery Act (RCRA). | What are Superfund sites? How do inorganic contaminants compare with organics on the list? Do Gov't regulations just address total elemental As, or is speciation involved? Prob. not. Approach would be to measure total arsenic and then assume all present as most toxic compound. But this ignores bioavailability. Not a problem for drinking water (assume all bioavailable) but what about soil? |

Figure 5. An example of split-page note taking based on part of the material shown in Figure 3.

## CHECKLIST FOR READING AND TAKING NOTES

❑    Become a brain-on reader: work to understand your sources fully, sentence by sentence, figure by figure, table by table.

❑    Take notes thoughtfully. In particular, practice summarizing information as you go along. Your summary must be accurate, complete, self-sufficient, and written in your own words.

❑    When taking notes, be careful to distinguish your words and thoughts from those of the author(s) to avoid unintentional plagiarism.

❑    Be sure to record the complete citation information for everything on which you take notes.

# 3

## CITING SOURCES AND LISTING REFERENCES

### CITING SOURCES

As described briefly in Chapter 1, **all statements of fact and opinion require support in order to be convincing to the thoughtful, critical reader**. The firmer the statement, the more important it is to your argument, the greater the need for support. As the writer, you should expect your readers to ask, "How do you know?" or "Who says?" In research reports (including lab reports), review papers ("term papers"), theses, and dissertations, factual statements are usually supported by reference to the source (or sources) of the facts presented. In a separate section at the end of your manuscript, you must list all the books, research articles, Web sites, and any other sources referred to so that they can be located by interested (or skeptical) readers.

While you should try to cite only sources that are reliable (i.e., have been subject to the peer review process) and verifiable (i.e., can be independently consulted by your readers), you may sometimes need to cite sources that are more difficult to check in order to avoid being dishonest (see page 40). There are also instances when, as a student, you may need to cite the manual for your laboratory class or even something that was said by an instructor in a lecture. We will explain how to deal with such sources of information later.

When backing up assertions, some judgment is called for, because there are many facts that the chemistry community will accept without question. The challenge is to determine which facts are considered "common knowledge." As a general rule, when making statements that need to be supported by reference to authoritative sources, consider that you are writing for an audience of your peers—other students at the same stage of their careers as you are—even though what you are writing will be read (and graded) by one of your professors. For example, you would not need to cite any sources to support the statement that elemental mercury is a liquid at room temperature and atmospheric pressure, nor to support the statement that the vapor pressure of the monatomic vapor is such that mercury can be detected by atomic absorption spectroscopy at room temperature. These are phenomena that are so reproducible that they are considered to be facts. However, if you were to state that mercury may be determined in fish tissue at concentrations below 1 ng kg$^{-1}$ using cold vapor atomic absorption spectrometry (AAS), you would need to support that statement, even if you were writing for an audience that is knowledgeable about the capabilities of AAS. Why? Because the capabilities of AAS are such that the detection claimed seems beyond the scope of current measurement technology.

Clearly, for the student writer, there are issues here. Until you become very familiar with the topic about which you are writing, you will have some difficulty judging what needs to be supported and what does not. In general, if you think that you might need the support of some well-known authority of the scholarly chemistry community to convince your classmates that your statements are valid, provide references to appropriate sources.

What does the chemistry community regard as an authoritative source? As we explain in Chapter 10, research findings are disseminated to other members of the relevant community by a process of peer review; through this process, other knowledgeable scientists scrutinize the quality of the material before it is added to the record in the form of a journal article. Peer review is not a foolproof procedure. There are plenty of examples of pathological science (the researchers were deluding themselves), of inaccurate science (the measurement tools were not up to the job), and, unfortunately, of deliberate fraud that have fooled the reviewers and appeared in print. On the other hand, there are also examples of major breakthroughs that have been rejected by the review process when first presented for consideration. So, although the system is slightly flawed, it is what the community works with, and articles in peer-reviewed journals are considered to be accurate accounts of extensive experiments by reputable researchers. If the material has not been subjected to the peer-review process, it must be regarded as suspect.

Although it is quite acceptable to use Internet sources, such as Wikipedia, as a first stage in finding information, you cannot use such sources to substantiate your claims, because such material has not been subjected to peer review. Here is a quotation from the Wikipedia "About" page:

> Because Wikipedia is an on-going work to which in principle anybody can contribute, it differs from a paper-based reference source in some very important ways. In particular, older articles tend to be more comprehensive and balanced, while newer articles may still contain significant misinformation, unencyclopedic content, or vandalism. Users need to be aware of this in order to obtain valid information and avoid misinformation that has been recently added and not yet removed.

Just to clarify what we said earlier about writing for an audience of your peers: you must cite a source if you think that your classmates might not accept your statement, but the source that you cite must be acceptable to your instructor. Most chemistry professors will not accept Wikipedia as an authoritative source. On the other hand, most will accept the *Encyclopædia Britannica* (On-line). Ask your instructor for guidance.

## SOME GUIDELINES FOR CITING SOURCES IN CHEMISTRY

Here are a few general rules to follow when citing sources to back up your statements or to acknowledge prior experimental work or the origin of an idea. These rules apply to review papers, essays, and research reports (theses, dissertations, manuscripts submitted for publication, and perhaps reports of laboratory exercises, depending on the format that is required by your instructor). We will deal first with how to cite a source in your text and then explain how to assemble the sources (chemists refer to them as "references") at the end of your piece. At first you may think that all this attention to "superscripts after the punctuation" and how to refer to more than one author and other rules is just so much busywork; however, all these details are really important. Chemists, like other scientists, are fanatical about paying attention to detail, and if you show in your writing that you are not paying attention, you may give the impression that you don't pay attention to other things, such as your experimental design or the care with which you analyze and present your data.

**1. Cite by inserting a number in the text.** In most published chemistry research papers, references are cited by inserting a superscript number at the most appropriate place, as in the following example:

> Arsenobetaine, which occurs in seafood, is not toxic.[1]

Note that the number comes after the punctuation. This rule also applies when the number is more appropriately inserted before the end of the sentence:

> As a result of the widespread application of lead-containing pesticides to fruit trees,[2] the soils of old orchards may be severely contaminated.

**2. Cite references in numerical order, starting with number one.** The sequence is disrupted only if you need to cite a source again, when you will use the same number again. Multiple references are indicated by the appropriate numbers separated by commas with no spaces. If you revise your text and change the order of the citations, you will need to renumber. This can be taken care of automatically with suitable software, such as EndNote. The superscript number convention is not the only one in current use: some journals use a parenthetical style such as (1) or *(1)* or [1]. In this case, the convention is that the number comes before the punctuation. Note that chemistry publications rarely use the "author-date" convention often found in biology publications. In this convention, the citation is given in the form of the surname of the first-named author together with the year of publication, e.g., (Bunsen, 1855). None of the 35 journals published by the American Chemical Society use this convention.

You can, however, create more interesting text if you incorporate the names of the researchers into your writing. For example,

> The copper concentration in the sediment was determined by Jones using atomic absorption spectrometry.[3]

The sentence can be considerably improved by adopting the active voice (see Chapter 5), thereby replacing the feeble word *using* with some real action (the determination of copper):

> Jones determined the copper concentration in the sediment by atomic absorption spectrometry.[3]

## 3. Observe the established practices in chemistry when referring to authors.

- The usual convention is to give **only the surname and not the researcher's first name, initials, or title**.
- When **two researchers' names** appear on a publication, the standard practice is to give both names separated by *and*. For example,

  Agrawal and Wood devised a cost-effective procedure for decreasing NOX emissions.[4]

- When **more than two names are associated with the publication**, the convention is that the first-named author is given together with the abbreviation *et al.*, which is short for *et alii* meaning, in Latin, *and the others*.

  Driscoll et al. have examined many aspects of acid rain in the Northeastern United States.[5]

  As *al.* is an abbreviation created by removing some letters from the end of the word, the convention is that it terminates in a period.

- When you want to cite multiple sources that have the same principal author but a variety of coauthors (probably transient members of the research group, such as students, academic visitors, and postdoctoral researchers), the convention is to **identify the principal researcher by name and add *and coworkers*.** For example,

  Steehler and coworkers have characterized the surfaces of acrylate polymers by X-ray photoelectron spectroscopy.[1-4,5,8]

The person directing the research enterprise usually can be identified by a footnote showing which of the researchers is the "corresponding author"–meaning the person to whom comments and questions (correspondence) about the article's contents should be addressed. Note the hyphen-like character between the *1* and the *4*. This is the convention for dealing with three or more consecutive reference numbers. Also there should be no spaces after the commas.

We think it is a good idea to use the researchers' names in your writing, even though you will see many pages in published chemistry journals and books in which the writing is in the disembodied passive voice. Rather than identifying the researcher by name and using the active voice as above,

"Steehler and coworkers devised . . .," sometimes you will see sentences or even entire articles written in the passive voice in which the human beings actually doing the original creative work are never identified, as in this rewrite of the previous example:

> A number of strategies for characterizing the surfaces of acrylate polymers have been devised.[1–4,5,8]

You should bear in mind that much of what is published in the original chemical literature is not necessarily written very well, and one of the goals of this book is to improve the quality of what is written by the next generation of chemists. Real people do research, and if you have ambitions to be a researcher yourself, you need to know who the key players are. Also, if you use the names of the researchers, it is much less likely that you will overlook mistakes in your references. If your text indicates that the number refers to an article by Driscoll et al., you are unlikely to mistakenly assign a paper written by Agrawal and Wood to this number in your reference list.

**4. Make the relevance of the cited reference clear to the reader.** It is quite permissible to put the reference number at a location other than the end of the sentence. Indeed, this is desirable if you are going to mention more than one set of researchers in the same sentence. For example, if you were to write,

> D'Ulivo and coworkers investigated the mechanism by which arsine is formed from the reaction between arsenite and tetrahydroborate in acid solution by adopting the deuterated reagent approach of Pergantis et al.[12,15,16]

your readers must turn to your list of references to be reassured that you are not citing three papers by Pergantis et al. and have neglected to cite the D'Ulivo work. If you place the numbers as in the following sentence, then you do not interrupt the flow of communication:

> D'Ulivo and coworkers[12,15] investigated the mechanism by which arsine is formed from the reaction between arsenite and tetrahydroborate in acid solution by adopting the deuterated reagent approach of Pergantis et al.[16]

**Notice the different tenses in the sentence:** D'Ulivo's group *investigated,* but arsine *is* formed. The convention is that any chemical phenomenon that can be considered reproducible (i.e., there is no argument that the phenomenon is a fact) is referred to in the present tense.

What the researchers did in the behavioral sense is referred to in the past tense, since the work was completed in the past. This whole business of what tense to adopt when writing about published work can be a bit tricky. (See also pp. 63, 115, 127, 136, 139, and 187).

**5. Is it necessary to have read everything that I am citing?** For most students the answer is "yes." In most cases, you are citing sources to support statements in your own writing and you need to be confident that you are in fact getting the support you require from your source. You may also be citing the source to demonstrate that you are knowledgeable about relevant work that has already been done, and you may be called upon to demonstrate such knowledge in a high-stakes situation, such as answering questions after an oral presentation on your lab report, senior thesis, original research proposal, or even doctoral dissertation defense.

You may, however, occasionally have to cite a source that you have not actually read. For example, significant chemistry research has been—and, to a lesser extent, still is—published in foreign-language journals, and you may not be able to read the original paper even if you could obtain a copy. In this case, you would have to rely on your reading of the English-language abstract.

**6. When citing a review of a paper, also cite the original article.** When citing a review of a paper that does not include the original data supporting a particular statement that you wish to make, **reference both the original article and the review article and indicate in your text that you are relying on the reviewer's interpretation**. For example,

> Evans et al. reviewed sample introduction for atomic spectrometry[9] and concluded that the only significant advance in hydride generation procedures was the procedure for the determination of lead devised by Chuachuad and Tyson.[10]

As a general strategy in your writing, taking someone else's word for the content of a paper is to be discouraged, although it is probably acceptable when you are writing about your first research activities (junior-year independent study report, for example). The purpose of a review article, after all, is to draw the reader's attention to the worthwhile information, and if you are interested you should read the original article. As you will discover as you advance in your scientific career, the literature contains some errors; you should not propagate them. It is possible, for example, that in the process of sifting through the 2000-odd publications that Evans et al. considered before writing their review, they made a mistake in describing the work of Chuachuad and Tyson in such glowing terms, or maybe the Chuachuad and Tyson paper was about the determination of cadmium and not lead.

**7. Avoid citation overkill.** How many references should you cite? This is another good question; the answer depends on the purpose of the piece of writing and the audience. Most undergraduate writing assignments will come with some guidelines from the instructor; if not, ask your instructor. In writing an introduction to a research report, you need to exercise some judgment about the number of references you cite. Many such reports are going to be evaluated on the basis of your ability to "read and make critical use of the literature" (to quote from the UMass Graduate School bulletin's instructions for the preparation of master's theses and doctoral dissertations). This criterion also applies to undergraduate-project reports, independent-study reports (maybe even lab reports), introductions to manuscripts being submitted for publication, and proposals submitted to external-funding agencies, such as the National Science Foundation. At one end of the spectrum, citing every paper on a topic does not demonstrate a critical evaluation of the material; continuing advances in research eventually make it unnecessary to cite much of the early literature. We will offer a word of warning about that later. On the other hand, if you cite only one or two papers (assuming that there are, in fact, many on the topic), your readers will think that you have been lazy about your literature search and that your writing is not very authoritative because you do not know what has been done previously.

Deciding how many references to cite is tricky. Context is everything. For students writing about the literature as an exercise assigned by an instructor, or creating a "full" laboratory report, or writing a report on a semester-long independent study, our advice is ask for guidance. If the guidance is vague or if you think your readers may not be knowledgeable about the extent of activity in the field, then it can be helpful to survey the field. It is very easy, with the aid of databases such as the Web of Science and SciFinder Scholar, to analyze any subset of articles you have identified according to the year of publication or the identity of the principal author or the country where the work was done. For example, you might start your term paper on the cancer chemoprevention properties of selenium as follows:

> Over the past 25 years there has been a steady increase in the number of journal articles dealing with the impact of selenium compounds on cancer, such that the current rate is 35–40

publications per year. Nearly 60% of the total literature of about 500 publications describes work conducted in the U.S. with significant contributions from as many as 20 research groups. The single largest contribution is from The Roswell Park Cancer Institute. The cancer chemoprevention literature contains the results of 8 trials with humans and 100 trials with small animals.

Now you could make a good case for concentrating on a small subset of the publications, say those that dealt with the eight human trials.

Deciding how many references to cite can also be a matter of experience. The more you read the professional literature, the more familiar you will become with the normal practice.

Now for that caveat about citing the early work: chemists, like other scientists, can be touchy about the issue of getting credit for something new; consequently, if there is any possibility that your piece will be read by one of the senior figures in the relevant field, it is a good idea to acknowledge his or her early work.

## PREPARING THE REFERENCES SECTION

### Listing the References—General Rules

**Include only those references that you specifically mention in your report or paper, and include all of the references that you cite.** As discussed earlier (p. 40), do not cite references that you have not read. Unless you are told otherwise by your instructor, list references in the numerical order in which they appear in your text.

Many possible sources exist, including journal articles, books, electronic media (including Web sites), magazines, patents, conference proceedings, theses, dissertations, technical reports, material safety data sheets, and personal communications. We will show you how to deal with journal articles, books, and Web sites, as well as instructions in laboratory handouts, manuals, and the information that instructors give you in the lab. Guidelines on how to deal with other sources can be found in *The ACS Style Guide*.

The number one rule is to **be consistent—use the same format for all references.** The number two rule is to **adopt the format of a major publisher** (such as the American Chemical Society or the Royal Society of Chemistry). Note that the formats of these two publishers are very different. Note also that some agencies are very strict about the format for references. For example, the National Science Foundation (NSF) will not review proposals unless the references are in the NSF's particular format. All journals and granting agencies provide very specific guidelines on citation formatting, so read them carefully. You can also look at copies of journals, but beware: journals change the format every now and then, so look at only very recent issues. Also, some journals have a different format for references at the end of review articles than at the end of regular research articles. A uniform model for formatting acceptable to all publishers would be in the best interest of scholarship and science, but no such consensus exists at present.

## Format for Journal Articles

**When citing journal articles, the minimum information** you must include is as follows: the **initials and surnames of all the authors** (in the order they appear on the first page of the article), **the name of the journal suitably abbreviated** (more about this later), **the year of publication, the volume number of the journal**, and **the first page number of the article**. In some cases, you will also need to provide the title of the article and the **last page number of the article**. This latter requirement is called **"inclusive pagination."** You may also need to give the issue of the journal, which often corresponds to the month in which the issue was published. Here is an example of a reference to a journal article in the ACS format.

Offley, S. G.; Tyson, J. F.; Seare, N. J.; Kibble, H. A. B. *J. Anal. At. Spectrom.* **1991**, *6*, 133–138.

Notice the order of surname and initials and the convoluted punctuation with semicolons, commas, and periods. Notice that the year of publication is in bold type and the volume is in italics. Notice that the journal title (*The Journal of Analytical Atomic Spectrometry*) has been abbreviated according to the *Chemical Abstracts Service Source Index* (*CASSI*) abbreviations and is in italics. *The ACS Style Guide* includes a list of more than 1,000 commonly cited journals.

Just a word or two about **the convention for numbers**: the basic goal is to avoid confusion between year, volume, and page number. In the previous example, there is no ambiguity (inclusive pagination means the page numbers are obvious), but consider for a moment a style that does not rely on inclusive pagination. Many journals publish several thousand pages each year, so if the numbers "1991, 6, 1996" appeared after the journal title, you would not be able to distinguish between the year of publication and the page number. The volume number, if it can be identified (possible confusion with page number), may not help because many journals publish more than one volume each year, in which case there may not be a simple relationship between these two numbers.

Here is the same reference in the Royal Society of Chemistry (RSC) format.

> S. G. Offley, N. J. Seare, J. F. Tyson and H. A. B. Kibble, *J. Anal. At. Spectrom.*, 1991, **6**, 133–138.

Notice the order of surname and initials, and the slightly less convoluted punctuation with commas and periods. Notice that there is no comma before *and*, but there are commas after the last-named author and after the journal title. Notice that the year of publication and page numbers are in regular type and the volume is in bold type.

## Format for Books

By now, you should have gotten the general idea: **provide sufficient information to describe the source completely and unambiguously in a consistent format**. Basically there are two types of scientific books: either the book was written by one or more authors, or each chapter was written by a different author (or authors) and one person collected the material and turned it into a coherent account. The following are examples, using the ACS conventions, of references to these two types of books.

### A book written by one author (or several authors)

> Marcus, R. K.; Broekaert, J. A. C. *Glow Discharge Plasmas in Analytical Spectroscopy*; John Wiley and Sons Ltd: Chichester, 2003; pp 125–130.

Note the punctuation and that the information given is as follows: authors (and here there are two), title (in italics), publisher, place of publication (may be difficult to discern, pick a major city listed in the publisher's address), year of publication, and page numbers (pp is an abbreviation for *pages*). It is a good idea to try to give relevant page numbers, since citing a whole book may not be all that helpful to a reader who wants to check out one of your sources.

### A book in which one author has collected the materials of many different authors

> Montaser, A.; Minnich, M. G.; McLean, J. A.; Liu, H.; Caruso, J. A.; McLeod, C. W. Sample Introduction in ICP-MS, In *Inductively Coupled Plasma Mass Spectrometry;* Montaser, A., Ed.; Wiley-VCH: New York, 1998; pp 87–102.

## Format for Internet Sources

The same rules apply. Identify the author (indicate if this is a home page) or the organization responsible and give the title of the article and the uniform resource locator (URL), together with the month, day, and year accessed. For example, once again according to the ACS convention:

> Julian Tyson's Arsenic Project at UMass. http://courses.umass.edu/chemh01/(accessed Aug 30, 2006).

Because Internet sources can be ephemeral, here today and gone tomorrow, it is important that you tell your readers the date on which you obtained the information. Just to keep you on your toes, the ACS format does not put a period at the end of the abbreviation for the month of the year, though as you will have noticed, a period does appear at the end of the abbreviations for journal titles.

Despite the temptation to do so, since the relevant material can be easily copied and pasted, do not give references to journal articles by simply pasting in the URL that corresponds to the final stages of your Internet search, as in the following example:

> Katz, S. A.; Salem, H. Chemistry and toxicology of building timbers pressure-treated with chromated copper arsenate: a review. http://www.ncbi.nlm.nih.gov/entrez/query.fcgi?db=pubmed&cmd= Retrieve&dopt=AbstractPlus&list_uids=15669035&query_hl= 1&itool=pubmed_docsum (accessed Aug 30, 2006).

Or

> Katz, S. A.; Salem, H. Chemistry and toxicology of building timbers pressure-treated with chromated copper arsenate: a review. http://www3.interscience.wiley.com/cgi-bin/abstract/109875414/ ABSTRACT (accessed Aug 30, 2006).

These formats ask your reader (needlessly) to retrace your search steps and do not disclose the nature of the source (such as the title of the journal, for example). The format that is acceptable is the one that allows the reader to find the article by knowing the details of the journal in which the article was published.

 Katz, S. A.; Salem, H. Chemistry and toxicology of building timbers pressure-treated with chromated copper arsenate: a review. *J. Appl. Toxicol.* **2005**, *25*, 1–7.

Notice that giving the journal title conveys much more information than does the format without the journal title (e.g., Katz, S. A.; Salem, H. *J. Appl. Toxicol.* **2005**, *25*, 1–7.). Unfortunately, many journals do not adopt the "with title" format.

As noted above (see page 35) information posted on Web sites is ephemeral and has usually not been peer reviewed. Avoid using Web pages as sources of information unless you are fully confident of the accuracy of the material presented. In general, this means relying only on peer-reviewed electronic journals or Web sites maintained by recognized scientific authorities, such as those associated with major museums, research institutions, or government organizations, such as the National Academies of Science or National Institutes of Standards and Technology. Some reputable journals are only published electronically and therefore only accessible via the Web. Many other journals have both a print version and an electronic version that, again, is accessible via the Web. In addition, many journals publish material electronically on the Web before the print version is available. These "prepublication" articles are legitimate sources and will be identified by a unique digital object identifier (DOI) code that should be cited together with the indication that the material is "on-line early access." An example of this is given in the sample reference list on page 48.

## Format for a Laboratory Manual or Handout

Refer to the laboratory manual or handout as though it were a book: if the instructor's name appears on the document, then start with this. For example,

Sommerfeld, D., Determination of Calcium in Orange Juice; *Chem. 312 Laboratory Manual*, UMass, Amherst, 2006; pp 25–28.

If the instructor is not identified, start with the "chapter" title.

Determination of Roxarsone in Chicken Manure; *Chem. 312 Laboratory Manual*, UMass, Amherst, 2006; pp 46–50.

If your source is just a handout for one particular experiment, the page numbers are not informative.

> Determination of Gold Nanoparticles in Rat Brain Tissue, *Chem. 513 Laboratory Instructions*, UMass, Amherst, 2006.

## Format for Information Received from Your Instructor

This material comes under the general classification of a "personal communication," a category which includes electronic communication such as e-mail or "instant messenger," or material created by an instructor that might be posted on the course Web site (such as lecture notes transcripts). Unlike the lab manual situation described above, **this is a serious professional category of citation**. If someone comes by your poster presentation at an ACS national or regional conference and makes a substantive suggestion that you subsequently try out back at the lab and the work is published, you need to acknowledge the input of the person you met at the conference as a personal communication. You need to get the full names of people you talk to at professional meetings (ask for their business cards).

This is how you cite such a source:

> Mendeleev, D. University of St. Petersburg, Russia, Personal communication, 2006.

## A SAMPLE REFERENCES SECTION

The examples above should help you prepare your own reference sections, but since citation formats differ so much among journals, check to see if your instructor wants you to follow a particular format or the format used by a particular journal.

The most important rule in preparing the references section is **to provide all the information required and to be consistent in the manner in which you present it**. If you are using bibliographic management software, this can be specified with a few clicks of the mouse. When preparing a paper for publication, follow the format used by the specific journal to which you are submitting the paper, and follow it to the last detail. The same advice applies to grant applications, theses, and dissertations: locate and download the guidelines, read them, and follow them. Remember, you only get one chance to make a first impression. Don't blow it by not paying attention to the formatting of your references.

The following list contains examples of the format for a multiauthor journal article (1), a journal that is only published electronically (2), an article that has been published on the Web in advance of the print publication (3), a textbook without an editor or editors (4), a textbook with an editor (5), a chapter in a textbook with an editor (6), and, finally, a Web site (7). All of the references appear in the American Chemical Society (ACS) format.

## References

1. Block, E; Glass, R. S.; Jacobsen, N. E.; Johnson, S.; Kahakachchi, C.; Kaminski, R.; Skowronska, A.; Boakye, H. T.; Tyson, J. F.; Uden, P. C. Identification and Synthesis of a Novel Selenium-Sulfur Amino Acid Found in Selenized Yeast: Rapid Indirect Detection NMR Methods for Characterizing Low-Level Organoselenium Compounds in Complex Matrices. *J. Agric. Food Chem.* **2004,** *52,* 3761–3771.
2. Fahey, A. M.; Tyson, J. F. Education and Training of BS Analytical Chemists for Entry-Level Positions in Industry: A Survey. *Chem. Educator* [Online], **2006,** *11,* 445–450. http://chemeducator.org/index.htm (accessed Dec 13, 2006).
3. Hernandez, P. C.; Tyson, J. F.; Uden, P. C.; Yates, D. Determination of Selenium by Flow Injection Hydride Generation Inductively Coupled Plasma Optical Emission Spectrometry, *J. Anal. At. Spectrom.* [Online early access]. DOI: 10.1039/b612658h. Published Online: Dec 12, 2006. http://www.rsc.org/Publishing/Journals/JA/Article.asp?Tyzpe=AdvArticle (accessed Dec 13, 2006).
4. Skoog, D. A.; West, D. M.; Holler, F. J.; Crouch, S. R. *Analytical Chemistry An Introduction;* 7th ed.; Thompson Learning: USA, 2000.
5. *Trace Elements in Clinical Medicine;* Tomita, H., Ed.; Springer-Verlag: Tokyo, 1990.
6. Tyson, J. F.; Yourd, E. Flame Atomic Absorption Spectroscopy, Including Hydride Generation and Cold Vapour Techniques. In *Atomic Spectroscopy in Elemental Analysis,* Cullen, M., Ed., Blackwell Publishing: Oxford, 2004; pp. 239–281.
7. The Grainger Challenge, National Academy of Engineering of the National Academies. http://www.nae.edu/nae/grainger.nsf (accessed Dec 16 2006).

## A Word or Two about *Italics* and Bold Type

It is common practice in scholarly writing to italicize foreign words, especially Latin words. However, in the particular cases of *et al.* and one or two other abbreviations of Latin words (see page 85 in Chapter 5) that are in common use in the U.S. chemistry community, the practice is generally not to italicize, though it is still done in the U.K. chemistry community. Note that in almost all reference formats, however, the journal title is given in italics, as are the titles of books. In the chemical literature, underlining is almost never used, and certainly never in the references section, but bold-faced type may be used for headings and one or two items in the reference section, such as the year of publication or volume number (depending on which journal format is adopted).

## Reference-Management Software

Bibliographic-management or citation-management software typically consists of a database in which details of the article or book can be stored together with a way of creating selective lists of subsets of your stored material. Depending on the services offered by your library, it may be possible to populate your personal database directly from a larger database to which your institution has access (such as the Web of Science). Bibliographic software can interact with your word-processing software to create reference lists in any one of several user-defined formats while you are creating your text. Using such software means that you will avoid inserting a reference that is not cited in the text and that it is unlikely that you will cite the same reference twice with different numbers. Of greater importance, it ensures that all of your references are in the same format, assuming that the various fields in the database have been populated correctly. Some institutions may offer access to bibliographic-management software as part of the library services. Ask your reference librarian for information and a training session.

## CHECKLIST FOR CITING SOURCES

- ❏ Cite references by inserting numbers in the text, in numerical order, starting with number one.
- ❏ Observe the established practices in chemistry when referring to authors.

    Use only the surnames of researchers.

    When there are two researchers, use both surnames separated by *and*.

    When there are more than two researchers, use the first-named author followed by *et al.*

❑ Try to make the relevance of the cited reference clear to the reader.

❑ Cite only sources you have actually read.

❑ When citing a review of a paper, cite the original article as well.

❑ Exercise good judgment regarding how many sources you cite; when in doubt, seek guidance from your instructor.

## CHECKLIST FOR PREPARING THE REFERENCES SECTION

❑ Include only those references specifically mentioned in your report or paper.

❑ Include a reference for every source cited in your paper.

❑ Adopt the format of a major publisher, such as the American Chemical Society.

❑ Use the same format consistently for every reference.

❑ Provide all the information required for each type of entry.

# 4

# REVISING

*The biggest problem with communication is the illusion that it has been accomplished.*

## WHY REVISE?

Much of this book concerns the reading, note-taking, thinking, synthesizing, and organizing that permit you to capture your thoughts in a first draft. This chapter concerns the revising that must follow. As do most experienced writers, we, the authors of this book, revise our own writing four or five times before letting anyone else see it, and several more times after others have reviewed it. Only those who have had little experience actually writing harbor delusions that it is possible to do a really excellent job with a writing task without spending time revising. Don't feel inadequate for not producing flawless prose on your first or second draft: **the key to good writing is revision**—a lot of it.

Writing a first draft gives you the opportunity to get facts, ideas, and phrases on paper, where they won't escape. Writing involves a process of discovery. Sometimes you discover that you need to do more research or more reading or more in-depth thinking in order to write something that makes sense. If you wait until the night before the paper is due to begin to write and make this discovery (shocking thought, but *some* students *do* procrastinate), you won't have time to do a thorough job.

Once you have a working draft and have captured your thoughts, you can concentrate on reorganizing, expanding, and rephrasing them in the clearest, most logical way. **All writing benefits from revision**. Writing and then rereading what you have written typically clarify your thinking. Then, even when you know precisely what it is you want to say, there is the universal difficulty of getting any point across intact to a reader. Revising your work improves communication and often leads you to a firmer understanding of your subject.

It is difficult to revise your own work effectively unless you can examine it with fresh eyes. You know what you wanted to say, but without some distance from the work, you can't really tell whether you have actually said it. For this reason, **plan to complete your first draft at least three days before (and even more when possible) the final product is due, to allow time for careful revision**. Reading your paper aloud—and listening to yourself as you read—often reveals weaknesses that you would otherwise miss. It also helps to have one or more fellow students read and comment on your draft; it is always easier to identify writing problems—wordiness, ambiguity, faulty logic, factual errors, faulty organization, spelling and grammatical errors—in the work of others. Most colleges and universities have writing centers staffed by tutors trained to help you recognize patterns in your own writing, such as problems with clarity or wordiness or a too heavy reliance on passive voice. Choose whatever system works best for you, but **always revise your papers before submitting them**.

No matter how sound, or even brilliant, your thoughts and arguments are, how you express them will determine whether they are understood and appreciated. With pencil or pen at the ready, the time has come to revise your first draft: for content, for clarity, for completeness, for conciseness, and for correctness. If you are writing with a computer, make at least your first set of revisions on printed copy rather than on the screen. To edit effectively you must see more than one screen of text at a time. Continue editing and revising—printout by printout—until your work is ready for the eyes of the instructor, admission committee, journal editor, or potential employer. This chapter, as well as Chapter 5, should help you recognize when you have arrived at that point.

## REVISING FOR CONTENT

### Make Sure Every Sentence Says Something Worth Saying

Consider the following sentence for a paper on the dangers posed worldwide by arsenic contamination of groundwater.

> Arsenic is a naturally occurring and potentially harmful element.

What does this sentence say? Does the writer really think the readers need to be told that arsenic occurs naturally in the environment or that it can harm humans? Even though it is true that not all elements occur naturally, this is one of those sentences that provokes the reader to ask, "So what?" It amounts to little more than what we call written throat clearing, a bid for time while the writer thinks of something more substantive and specific to say. (For a more detailed discussion of throat clearing, see Chapter 5, pp. 73–76). A careful editor will delete the sentence and begin anew with a sentence that says something worth reading. For example,

 Arsenic compounds are widespread in nature and are drawing increasing attention due to the contamination of ground water used for drinking and irrigation in several parts of the world.

Similarly, a sentence like

 Arsenic can be harmful to humans if ingested.

could profitably be revised to read,

Chronic arsenic exposure may increase the risk of skin, lung, and bladder cancer or damage the immune and cardio vascular systems.

The authors of the revised opening sentences know where their essays are headed, and so does the reader. The original versions got the writers started; the revision process focused the writers' attention on a destination.

Take a careful look at the first sentence of each paragraph that you write for a first draft. You will often find instances of throat clearing, with the substance of the paragraph delayed until the second or even third sentence. Consider the following example from a student's paper on the biological role of selenium in which the opening sentence suggests that the topic here is the chemical form and concentration of selenium:

The multiple roles of selenium depend on the chemical form and concentration. The active site of the enzyme glutathione peroxidase contains selenium in the form of the aminoacid selenocysteine. This enzyme catalyses the reduction of reactive oxygen species, such as hydrogen peroxide and lipid hydroperoxides. It also has cancer prevention properties. Selenium deficiency has been linked to some diseases in China. DNA damage by reactive oxygen species could arise from antioxidant deficiency. Much research suggests that selenium plays an important role in human health.

The first sentence is a classic example of throat clearing, but it provides an excellent illustration of why even effective writers resort to throat clearing when they are still thinking on paper or, in the case of most writers these days, thinking at the keyboard as the words appear on the screen. The first sentence serves a useful purpose in writing the early draft: it buys the writer a few seconds to come up with the next, more substantive observation and then the next. Then, like a horse out of the gate, the writer is off and moving, accumulating a series of considerably more specific observations that, when it comes time to revise, make the first sentence seem inane because it is so general and, in this case, misleading. *That* is the beauty of revision. From the vantage point of increased insight, you can go back, eliminate the throat clearing and the rat-a-tat-tat cadence that thinking on screen often produces, and you can rethink the sequence in which you offer the observations to the reader, as illustrated by the following revision:

> Selenium plays an important role in human health.[1-5] For example, selenium, in the form of the aminoacid selenocysteine, is found in the active site of the enzyme glutathione peroxidase that catalyses the reduction of reactive oxygen species, such as hydrogen peroxide and lipid hydroperoxides. Some diseases arising from DNA damage by reactive oxygen species have been associated with selenium deficiency, particularly in parts of China. Selenium also has cancer prevention properties that are related to the chemical form and concentration.

In the original draft, it is not until the end of the paragraph that the writer finally articulates the central point of the paragraph: that selenium plays an important role in human health. Now able to *re-vision* his paragraph, the writer crafts a much more effective topic sentence, dispenses with unnecessary verbiage ("Much research suggests"), and directs the reader's attention to the relevant research that supports his assertion by referencing articles in superscript. As soon as the writer has figured out where the paragraph is going, reorganizing the rest of the sentences is relatively easy, and the result is a paragraph that does the work for the reader, instead of requiring the reader to make sense of a jumble of seemingly random observations.

## Show Rather Than Tell

A very useful principle to bear in mind when writing, not only about chemistry but writing in general, is to show rather than simply tell. As readers, we prefer to draw conclusions for ourselves as opposed to being told what to think. Writing that provides sufficient evidence to allow readers to draw their own evaluative conclusions is more effective than writing that offers glib opinions or unsupported conclusions.

**For example, never tell a reader that something is *interesting*.** Provide sufficient information to allow the reader to be the judge. Consider this rather uninformative sentence:

 Surfactants are a particularly interesting class of molecules.

Are surfactants interesting? If so, don't waste time simply telling the reader. Ask yourself why you find them interesting, and then share that information with your readers; *show* how this is true, so that they are right there with you, nodding, concluding as you have that there is indeed something interesting about surfactants. This example could, for instance, be rewritten as follows:

As the concentration of a surfactant in aqueous solution increases, the molecules spontaneously assemble into clusters in which the less polar parts of the molecule form the interior and the more polar parts are on the outside.

Given this information, readers can conclude for themselves that surfactants deserve their attention.

As a second example, consider the use of the word *relatively* in the following sentence in which the writer **tells** rather than shows:

 Dendrimer molecules are relatively large.

The thoughtful reader wonders, "Relative to what?" because the writer has some evidence in mind that has lead her to this conclusion but has not shared it with the reader. Consider the different effect when the writer **shows** what she means by "relatively large" by including the detail that informs her conclusion that will lead the reader to the very same conclusion:

Dendrimer molecules can contain many hundreds of atoms.

 Dendrimers are made up of several smaller molecules connected in successive layers of branches.

Each of these sentences provides sufficient information to allow the readers to conclude for themselves that, on the scale of molecular sizes, dendrimers are toward the large end.

## Be Cautious in Drawing Conclusions but Not Overly So

When interpreting chemical data, it is always wise to be careful, particularly with access to only a few experiments or small data sets. For instance, write, "These data suggest" rather than "These data demonstrate," or "prove that." Do not get carried away, as in the following example:

 The data suggest the possibility that copper (II) ions may catalyze the formation of the fibrils.

Here the author hedges three times in one sentence, using the words *suggests, possibility,* and *may.* Limit yourself to one hedge per sentence, as in the following rewrite:

 The data suggest that copper (II) ions catalyze the formation of the fibrils.

If you are too unsure of your opinion to write such a sentence, re-examine your opinion.

## Ensure That Your Writing Is Self-Sufficient

Good writing is always self-sufficient: the reader should not have to leave the text itself to consult textbooks or other sources in order to understand what you are saying. To make your writing self-sufficient, **you must anticipate the needs of your audience**. In particular, be sure to define all scientific terms and abbreviations; it is not enough simply to use them properly. Brief definitions will help keep the attention of readers who may not know or may not remember the meaning of some terms. It will also demonstrate to your instructor that you know the meaning of the specialized terminology you are using.

For example, the author of this sentence assumes the reader's familiarity with laser ablation sample introduction in a way that may confuse some readers:

 Laser ablation sample introduction overcomes the problems associated with the dissolution of samples to form aqueous solutions.

The addition of a simple definition of what is involved in laser ablation makes the sentence much more reader friendly and effective.

 The problems associated with the dissolution of samples to form aqueous solutions can be overcome by laser ablation, in which an aerosol of the solid is generated by the interaction of a pulse of laser light with the sample surface.

By incorporating a brief explanation, the writer ensures that the reader moves steadily forward, head nodding, able to follow what was written.

# REVISING FOR CLARITY

When revising for clarity, it is essential to keep in mind the writer's obligation to do the work for the reader. Your goal is a reader whose head is nodding in a way that signals comprehension and engagement.

## Tip #1 Anticipate the Needs of Your Reader

To do the work for your readers, you need to anticipate their needs, but to do so, you need to know *who* your readers are. When you write papers or lab reports in chemistry classes, for whom are you writing? Writing with your professor in mind as your audience can create problems. Your professor, of course, knows much more than you do about the subject you are studying, and you may be tempted to think that he or she knows what you mean and not explain everything as clearly as you might otherwise. Or you may be so concerned with impressing the professor that you inadvertently sacrifice being clear and concise. We advise that you **think of your reader as being someone who is at the same level in his or her academic career as you**. Anticipating the needs of your reader can help you with many of the judgment calls you make such as *what* you write (what to include and how much detail) as well as *how* you write (what words to use and how formal to be).

For example, if you were writing the experimental section of a lab report for organic chemistry on synthesizing bromobutane, and part of the procedure is to add two boiling stones, if you think of your reader as someone less knowledgeable, you might feel a need to explain why this step was necessary.

Two boiling stones were added to the mixture in order to prevent bumping, namely the slight super heating followed by a large release of vapor, which produces smooth boiling on the edge of the stones where gas bubbles are nucleated. The mixture was boiled for 30 min.

If you envision your reader as a peer, you will probably conclude that your fellow student already knows why the boiling stones are added, so this is unnecessary wordiness. So, you can write a much more clear, more concise sentence:

Two boiling stones were added and the mixture was boiled for 30 min.

Anticipating and meeting the needs of your reader are key to writing effectively.

# Tip #2 Avoid Overusing Acronyms and Abbreviations

Overuse of acronyms and abbreviations can drive away potentially interested readers. Keep in mind though that *acronym* and *abbreviation* are not synonyms. *DNA* and *IR* are examples of abbreviations; *FACSS*, which stands for the Federation of Analytical Chemistry and Spectroscopy Societies, is an example of an acronym because the initial letters form a pronounceable word. Some abbreviations, like DNA, are so widely known they never need to be defined. (See pp. 84–86 for more on abbreviations and acronyms.) When you are in doubt, err on the side of caution. You may be steeped in reading and thinking about a particular research topic, but you risk confusing your reader if you do not clarify the meaning of acronyms and abbreviations that are not widely used.

**Write to inform and enlighten, not to impress.** Often the names of techniques and chemicals are very long and are repeated frequently throughout a paper; in which case, it makes sense to use acronyms and abbreviations. What is a thoughtful writer to do? The American Chemical Society (ACS) advises that the first time you use a term, spell it out in full and place the abbreviation or acronym immediately after in parentheses. Once you have defined it, you can use the abbreviation or acronym throughout the rest of the paper.

First use:

> The yield was significantly increased when the surfactant cetyltrimethylammonium bromide (CTAB) was added.

Thereafter:

> All subsequent reactions were carried out in 0.1 M CTAB solutions.

# Tip #3 Keep the Reader Moving Forward

When you write a sentence that the reader finds confusing, you force the reader to back up and reread that sentence and puzzle out the intended meaning. As the author of the sentence, you, of course, know the intended meaning. It therefore requires some additional effort on your part to anticipate any source of potential confusion lurking in your sentence that might elicit head scratching on the part of the reader. For example, writers often find it difficult to write clearly about comparisons.

Consider the following sentence, in which the reader's progress is impeded because of ambiguity about what is being compared.

> The column packed with silica particles accumulated 67% more phosphomolybdate than Teflon beads.

The initial assumption is that the ability of silica to accumulate two different materials is being compared, but when the reader encounters the words *Teflon beads*, it becomes clear that the writer is comparing two different packing materials and that silica accumulated more of the target compound than did Teflon. The alert reader can back up and figure out what the writer means, but if you are doing your job as a writer, you will avoid writing sentences that make it necessary for the reader to work so hard to grasp your meaning. The following revision makes clear in one straight-forward sentence exactly what is being compared to what:

> The columns packed with silica particles accumulated 67% more phosphomolybdate than did the columns containing Teflon beads.

Here is another example, in which the points of comparison are not quite clear and the reader is forced to pause and ask, "In good agreement with what?"

> When compared with the reference materials, the mercury concentrations were in good agreement.

Backing up a couple sentences and rereading and giving it a moment's thought will lead the astute reader to conclude that the writer means "in good agreement with the mercury concentrations in the reference materials." The reader, however, should not need to puzzle over the intended meaning and should not have to backup and reread. With the simple goal of **keeping the reader moving forward in mind**, we would write a much better sentence:

> The mercury concentrations measured were in good agreement with those of the reference materials.

Readers should never have to guess what the proper comparisons are; the less your readers have to work, the more they will appreciate your writing.

In your efforts to keep the reader moving forward, you should make effective use of punctuation whenever possible. Punctuation marks such as commas, semicolons, and dashes are, after all, simply graphic symbols used by writers to assist their readers in grasping the intended meaning of the words in a sentence on a first reading. For example, read the following sentences silently to yourself and notice what happens while you read:

1. For pharmaceuticals development and approval can take over seven years.
2. For some time after these results were regarded as definitive.
3. Finally the two liquid phases turned blue and green crystals formed.
4. While the crystals were forming a white solid appeared at the surface.
5. When a wet gas cools a mist may form.

More than likely you began reading the sentence with one expectation of the direction in which the sentence was headed, and then in each instance reached a point where you realized you had been misled by the absence of punctuation and were forced to go back and reread. When a writer anticipates the needs of the reader and uses punctuation effectively, rereading is not necessary. A comma signals the reader to pause ever so slightly in order to grasp the intended meaning in each of the sentences above. When in doubt, read your sentence aloud. If you find yourself pausing in order to convey the meaning you intend, a comma will assist the reader in reading it that way as well. Placing a comma to denote a pause is not a failsafe rule for comma use, but it can help in many situations. For a more thorough discussion of comma rules as well some other forms of punctuation that you will find helpful in making your writing more clear and correct, see Appendix A.

## Tip #4 Beware of Modifiers and Their Perils

**Misplaced Modifiers.**   In English, word order matters; that is, where words are placed relative to other words in a sentence affects meaning, especially words or phrases that modify other words in a sentence. Writing a sentence with either a misplaced modifier (one placed in such a way it modifies the wrong word) or a dangling modifier (one that is left dangling because no word appears in the sentence that it can sensibly modify) can lead to ambiguity. Modifiers can take the form of a single word, a phrase, or even a clause, and in terms of meaning, they attach to the nearest noun or verb possible. Consider, for example, the following sentence from a campus newspaper describing a potentially disastrous incident in the chemistry building (we have bolded the errant modifier).

The fire in the lab was put out before any damage was done **by the local fire department**.

In all likelihood, the student reporting on this incident did not intend to malign the local fire department whose prompt arrival and efficient handling of the fire were essential in averting what could have been a much more serious event. Written in this way, however, the modifying phrase *by the local fire department* attaches to the closest verb *done* so that the meaning of this sentence is that the fire was extinguished before the local fire department was able to do any damage. The author of this report probably meant to say,

The fire in the lab was put out **by the local fire department** before any damage was done.

Repositioning the modifier here makes it clear that the worthy, dependable local firefighters arrived in time to put out the fire before the blaze did any damage.

Clearly, placement of modifiers matters because it affects meaning and clarity. Writing in chemistry often calls for the passive voice, and whenever a writer abandons the active voice, the perils of modifiers loom larger and additional vigilance is required to avoid misusing them. For example, consider the following sentence written in the passive voice:

Much research has been published in recent years **on single-walled carbon nanotubes**.

Single-walled carbon nanotubes seem an odd medium for publishing groundbreaking research. The modifying phrase *on single-walled carbon nanotubes* is misplaced and attaches to the verb *published*. Revision that places the modifying phrase so as to modify the noun *research* conveys a more sensible meaning:

Much research **on single-walled carbon nanotubes** has been published in recent years.

**Dangling Modifiers**.   While the revisions above required merely moving the misplaced modifiers to a different position, modifiers are sometimes left "dangling" because the word they should modify does not appear in the sentence. Dangling modifiers require more active intervention. Writing the experimental section of lab reports is a veritable minefield when it comes to dangling modifiers because of the need to use passive voice and avoid the personal pronouns *I* or *we*. For example, consider the following sentence written in the passive voice:

 Before running the reaction, the apparatus was flame dried from bottom to top.

The phrase *before running the reaction* should attach to and modify a human being, presumably the author of the sentence who did the experimental procedure, but disciplinary convention prohibits mention of the author. Thus the modifying phrase dangles and instead attaches to the word *apparatus* creating the ridiculous meaning that the apparatus ran the reaction. If active voice were an option, we could insert a human agent into the sentence and remedy the problem this way:

 Before I ran the reaction, I flame dried the apparatus from bottom to top.

However, if required to use the passive voice, we need to bring the modifying phrase in line with the rest of the sentence:

 Before the reaction was run, the apparatus was flame dried from top to bottom.

Problems with modifiers also frequently occur when students write about what appears in the published literature, especially when they introduce the research findings reported in a scientific paper with prepositional phrases such as *in this article* or *in this paper*. Even when using the active voice, as in the sentence below, it is easy to slip and place the phrase so that it attaches to the wrong verb and inadvertently misrepresent what occurs in the article. For example,

 In this article, Kemery, Steehler, and Bohn studied electric field mediated transport in nanometer diameter channels.

 In this paper, Caruso et al. interface chromatography with element-specific detection.

Each of these sentences makes it sound as if the studying and interfacing actually occurred *in* the article, which is of course impossible. The modifying phrases *In this article* and *In this paper* are left dangling because a more suitable verb, such as *report* or *discuss*, simply does not appear in the sentence. Remember to make clear that the work was not done *in the article*, but rather that that the article *reports* on the work that was done prior to the writing of the paper, most likely in a laboratory setting.

👍 In this article, Kemery, Steehler, and Bohn discuss . . .

👍 In this paper, Caruso et al. report the results obtained by . . .

*Note: Observe the convention of the eternal present*    When you write, the convention with regard to verb tense, in chemistry and all academic writing, is to **refer to what appears in print**, electronically or in hard copy, whether it is a textbook, a scholarly article, or a magazine article, **in the present tense.** For example, it may have taken Joe Caruso and his grad students a year to complete the research, but in the article they publish, they "describe" in the present tense what they "found when they interfaced" in the past tense. When you, in turn, write about their research, you should **refer to what they *claim* or *report* in their paper in the present tense and what they *did* in the past tense.**

## Tip #5 Avoid Ambiguity: The Dangers of *It*, *This*, and Other Pronouns

Frequent use of the pronouns *it, they, this, them, these, those,* **and** *that* in your writing should sound an alarm: probable ambiguity ahead. It is the writer's job to make sure that the antecedent (the word the pronoun refers back to) is absolutely clear to the reader.

The following example demonstrates the ambiguity that can be caused by the pronoun *it*:

👎 As long as the number of protons in the nucleus of an atom does not change, **it** preserves its chemical individuality.

To what does *it* refer? What preserves its chemical individuality, the nucleus or the atom?

Similarly, the pronoun *it* makes the second part of the following sentence equally ambiguous.

👎 The chemical signal compound must then be transported to the specific target tissue, but **it** is effective only if **it** possesses appropriate receptors.

Are these receptors needed by the chemical signal compound or the target tissue? It is not clear.

In the next example, *these* causes similar problems for the reader.

Broadening processes occur in the injection valve, column, and connecting tubings. **These** combine to give the overall chromatographic peak shape.

Presumably the "Broadening processes," not the "connecting tubings," are combining, although the author has certainly not made this clear.

The ambiguity created by the use of *these* in this sentence could be eliminated in several ways. We could begin the second sentence with *The broadening processes....*, but this results in a somewhat irritating singsong repetition. Another possibility is to use the relative pronoun *that* as follows:

Broadening processes that occur in the injection valve, column, and connecting tubings combine to give the overall chromatographic peak shape.

In the following sentence, the ambiguity about what the pronoun *them* refers to creates two distinct solutions to the problem of safe handling of volatile chemicals in the laboratory setting.

To ensure that students do not have access to volatile chemicals, lock them in a storage facility.

Does *them* refer to the students or the volatile chemicals? While locking students in the closet would prevent them from having access to dangerous chemical substances, this hardly seems the most practical solution, and incarcerating students is not likely to be popular with students, parents, or the administration. Placing the chemicals under lock and key seems a much more sensible solution, so we suggest a revision that makes clear that intended meaning:

Volatile chemicals should be locked in a storage facility to ensure that students do not have access to them.

A patient reader will puzzle out the more sensible meaning, but its author has certainly violated one of our key principles: **never make the reader back up**.

In short, when revising your work, read it carefully and with skepticism, checking that you have said exactly what you mean. Never make the reader guess what you have in mind. Everything you write must make sense—to you and to your reader. As you read each sentence you have written ask yourself: what does this sentence really say? What did I mean to say? Make each sentence work on your behalf, leading the reader easily from fact to fact, from thought to thought.

You need not be a grammarian to write clearly and correctly. With a little practice, especially if you read your work aloud, you can quickly learn to recognize a sentence in difficulty and sense how to fix it without even knowing the name of the grammatical rule that was violated.

## Tip #6 Revise for Parallelism

Parallelism—the use of similar grammatical structures to express similar elements of meaning—is a time-honored principle of style. Parallel structures not only create an ear-pleasing cadence, rhythm, and balance, but also allow a writer to create emphasis to help the reader grasp the intended meaning. When you are listing or pairing ideas or joining them together, use similar or parallel grammatical forms whenever possible to clarify and support content.

For example, consider this informative, but plodding, statement about the characteristics of aluminum.

 Aluminum is more abundant than any other metal in the earth's crust, is easy to reshape, silvery white in color, and after refinement from bauxite it costs less than fifteen cents per pound.

The sentence is not only leaden, but wordy and cumbersome. By listing each of the characteristics ascribed to aluminum in a parallel way, we get a much more clear, more concise sentence.

Aluminum is abundant, malleable, silvery white, and inexpensive.

If concision is not the main goal, and we really want to retain some of the detail of the original sentence because it suits our purposes, revising for parallelism makes it possible to work in a lot of information, but still write a balanced, more ear-pleasing sentence.

Aluminum, the most abundant metal in the earth's crust, is malleable, silvery white, and inexpensive, at fifteen cents per pound when refined from bauxite.

Let's consider some special attributes of another element and revise for parallelism.

Calcium does play a role that is very significant in the biological functioning of the body because for one thing blood clotting is helped by it, and it plays a role in heartbeat regulation and also in enabling muscle contractions.

Calcium, which plays a vital role in biological functions, serves to facilitate blood clotting, to regulate heartbeat, and to enable muscle contractions.

At the thinking and drafting stage, ideas don't necessarily pour forth in perfect parallel structure, but once you have a draft, parallelism is a very useful tool to provide clarity to help your reader grasp your intended meaning, and to streamline and balance your sentence.

## REVISING FOR COMPLETENESS

### Do Not Assume the Reader Knows What You Mean

Revising for completeness brings us back once again to anticipating the needs of the reader. Sometimes writing is unclear because we are still mired in the struggle to understand what we are writing about. Even when we do understand, writing clearly is difficult because, in deciding how best to communicate what we know, it requires us to anticipate the needs of the reader who does not necessarily share our own knowledge or point of view. When we write, we must always think about how much information the reader needs in order to grasp what we are trying to say. Because it seems clear to us, we sometimes stop short of providing enough information for the reader to grasp our meaning, thereby invoking the "you-know-what-I-mean" defense.

When writing, you may know what you mean, but that does not guarantee that your reader will know what you mean. Remember that it is the writer's job **to do the work for the reader, and part of that is to make sure that each thought is complete**. Be specific in making assertions. For example, the following statement is much too vague because the writer has not provided sufficient context for the reader to grasp the meaning of *many*.

Many selenium compounds have been detected in urine.

How many is *many*? You may have a clear sense of what this means in the context that you are referring to, but will your reader? After editing, the sentence might read,

About a dozen selenium compounds have been detected in urine.

Similarly, the following sentence gives us only a general sense of what the rate of arsine formation was when borohydride was the generating reagent in contrast to when powdered zinc and acid were the generating reagents.

 The rate of arsine formation was higher when the generating reagent was borohydride compared with the rate for the reaction with powdered zinc and acid.

Why stop with the vague *higher*, if you know it was 10 times higher?

 The rate of arsine formation was 10 times higher when the generating reagent was borohydride compared with the rate for the reaction with powdered zinc and acid.

## Do the Work for the Reader: Avoid Using *Etc.*

Be especially careful to revise for completeness whenever you find that you have written *etc.*, an abbreviation for the Latin term *et cetera*, meaning *and other things* or *and the rest*. While you might use *etc.* at the draft stage when you would rather not interrupt the flow of your thoughts by thinking about exactly what *other things* you have in mind, when revising replace each *etc.* with words of substance. In scientific writing, *etc.* makes the reader suspect fuzzy thinking. Ask yourself, "What exactly do I have in mind here?" If you come up with additional items for your list, add them. If you find that you have nothing to add, simply replace the *etc.* with a period and you will have produced a shorter, clearer sentence.

Consider the following sentence and its revision:

 The amount of product formed in a given time depends on a number of factors, such as concentration of reactants, etc.

 The amount of product formed in a given time depends on a number of factors, such as concentration of reactants, temperature, and pressure.

In the original version, the author dodged the responsibility of clear writing and doing the work for the reader by forcing the reader to determine what is meant by *etc.* The sentence, although grammatically correct, is incomplete, waiting for the reader to fill in the missing information. The reader may justifiably wonder if the writer knows what other factors influence the extent of a chemical reaction. The revised sentence clearly indicates what the writer had in mind. Revising for completeness often requires you to return to your notes or the sources upon which your notes are based in order to fulfill your obligation to your reader.

Occasionally, you may be tempted to use *etc.* as a kind of shortcut, to avoid the tedium of listing all of the other things that might be included. Ask yourself why you are doing this. In essence you are saying to the reader "You know what I mean," but can you be sure that the reader does? Or are you perhaps still struggling for understanding and not sure what other items would be included in the group and hoping your reader won't notice? Does use of *etc.* represent laziness or fuzzy thinking? Neither are hallmarks of good writing.

Consider the following sentence in which the writer seems to have a very specific group of elements in mind, but has stopped short of communicating them to the reader:

 Elements with one electron in their outer shell, such as lithium etc., have low ionization potentials.

Again the writer is dodging responsibility for doing the work for the reader. If the writer chooses not to list every member of the group, in this case every element, it is the writer's job to define the group so that the reader still clearly understands what elements the group would include.

Elements with one electron in their outer shell, such as lithium and other members of group 1 in the periodic table, have low ionization potentials.

In contrast to the sentence that contained *etc.* this sentence leaves no doubt in the reader's mind about what other elements belong in the group to which the writer is referring.

## CHECKLIST FOR REVISING

❑  Allow time for revision (pp. 51–52).

❑  Read your paper aloud, slowly, and listen for problems as you read (pp. 52).

### Revise for Content

❑  Make every sentence say something worth saying (pp. 52–54).

❑  Show rather than tell (pp. 54–55).

❑  Be cautious in drawing conclusions (pp. 55–56).

❑  Make the text self-sufficient (p. 56).

## Revise for Clarity

❑ Anticipate the needs of an audience of interested peers (p. 57).

❑ Use acronyms and abbreviations with the needs of your reader in mind (p. 58).

❑ Do the work for the reader (p. 67).

❑ Keep the reader moving forward (pp. 58–60).

❑ Watch out for problems created by modifier placement (pp. 60–63).

❑ Eliminate the ambiguity often created by pronouns (pp. 63–65).

❑ Revise for parallelism (pp. 65–66).

## Revise for Completeness

❑ Anticipate the needs of the reader (pp. 66–67).

❑ Be as specific as possible (pp. 66–67).

❑ Avoid shortcuts like *etc.* (p. 67).

# 5

# EDITING FOR CONCISION AND ACS STYLE

*Less is more.*

## EDITING

Like revision, which literally means "seeing again," editing is best performed after a break from working with a particular piece of writing so that you have a chance to view it with fresh eyes.

Whereas revising might involve real rethinking, reorganization, or deleting or adding material or evidence, editing focuses more on sentence-level issues: word choice, phrasing, tone, voice, correctness, and style—refining what you have written. Having said that, experienced writers know that the lines between revising and editing are difficult to draw and what may begin as surface editing may lead to more substantive changes. Both research studies and the experiences of your authors suggest that editing, like revision, is much more effective if done on hard copy rather than on the computer screen; however, both operations are an essential part of the writing process and both have a common goal: producing the most clear, concise, and correct finished product possible.

## EDITING FOR GENDER-NEUTRAL LANGUAGE

The American Chemical Society and the U.S. Government Printing Office style guides, as well as the style guides published in every academic discipline, now advocate the use of gender-neutral language in place of language that reinforces outdated gender roles and sexist assumptions. Because as a society we are still steeped in sexist language habits that continue to influence us, making your writing gender neutral sometimes requires a conscious effort during the editing stage.

Consider, for example, this quotation by Sir William Osler, one of the most famous physicians in the English-speaking world at the turn of the twentieth century, which eloquently articulates *in the language of his day* the crucial role that writing and publication play in the scientific enterprise:

 In science credit goes to the **man** who convinces the world, not to the **man** to whom the idea first occurs.

Although the use of the word *man* as a generic to refer to both males and females was considered correct in the past, this usage is now viewed as antiquated. Consider Osler's valuable insight recast in gender neutral language that avoids sexism:

 In science credit goes to the **scientist** who convinces the world, not to the **scientist** to whom the idea first occurs.

Avoiding sexism is important when writing about chemistry. Here are some strategies for editing your writing to ensure that your writing is gender neutral.

## Avoid Using Masculine Nouns to Refer to Males and Females

As in the example above, avoid the use of the word *man* as a term to represent both males and females as well as the various compound words formed from it such as *mankind* and *manmade* by substituting neutral alternatives. For example, in place of *man*, depending on the context, you might substitute words such as *people, humans, human beings, scientists,* or *human species.* In place of *manmade*, gender-neutral alternatives include *manufactured, synthetic, artificial, built,* and *constructed.*

## Avoid Using the Masculine Pronouns (*He, His,* and *Him*) to Refer to Both Males and Females

One way to revise this usage is to eliminate the pronoun or replace it with a definite article such as *a, an,* or *the.*

 A **chemist** should acquire the habit of writing down weighings, buret readings, and other practical details **he** might need for subsequent calculations.

 A **chemist** should acquire the habit of writing down weighings, buret readings, and other practical details that might be needed for subsequent calculations.

Every **student** must write a persuasive essay on **his** favorite element.

Every **student** must write a persuasive essay on **a** favorite element.

Occasional use of masculine and feminine pronouns in tandem (*he* or *she* or *his* or *her*) is another acceptable alternative, although this usage achieves gender neutrality at the risk of monotony and wordiness and should be implemented very sparingly.

A **chemist** should acquire the habit of writing down weighings, buret readings, and other practical details that **he or she** might need for subsequent calculations.

Every **student** must write a persuasive essay on **his or her** favorite element.

Another option is to recast the sentence in the plural and change the construction to the plural form (*they* and *theirs*).

**Chemists** should acquire the habit of writing down weighings, buret readings, and other practical details that **they** might need for subsequent calculations.

**Students** must write persuasive essays on **their** favorite elements.

Note: we do **not** recommend using a plural pronoun (*they*) with a singular antecedent (*chemist*) because this results in an agreement error.

 A **chemist** should acquire the habit of writing down weighings, burette readings, and other practical details that **they** might need for subsequent calculations.

 Every **student** must write a persuasive essay on **their** favorite element.

You will encounter this usage in spoken language, but when writing about chemistry, we recommended you choose a means of achieving gender-neutral language that is both politically correct and grammatically correct.

Yet another means of achieving inclusiveness and balance is to alternate between using masculine and feminine pronouns, a stylistic choice we have adopted throughout this book to refer to the students from whom the writing samples were selected to reflect the actual gender balance among our students. We caution against adopting this solution except in texts of substantial length in which it can be implemented in a methodical way; otherwise, the alternating pronouns may be mistaken as carelessness or inattention.

## EDITING FOR CONCISION

Make every word count. Omitting unnecessary words will make your thoughts clearer and more convincing. We have already talked briefly about whole sentences that are really nothing more than instances of throat clearing (Chapter 4, p. 52), especially at the beginning of paragraphs and the purpose they serve in the composing process. Throat clearing, redundancy, wordiness—these are common attributes of the early drafts of even highly effective writers. Experienced, effective writers know, however, that it is essential to allow time to reread methodically what they have written looking for ways to express themselves as economically as possible. To assist you in that process, we offer the following "Four Commandments of Concise Writing."

### First Commandment: Eliminate Throat Clearing

What do we mean by throat clearing? Imagine yourself walking into a class and, without any prior notice, your professor asks you to address the class for 15 minutes on X, a subject about which you have some knowledge but have no prepared remarks. Perhaps you are that rare person for whom this would cause no alarm, but if you are like most people, it might create some anxiety. One strategy you might adopt in order to buy a little time to gather your wits and think of something sensible to say is to clear your throat. In this case, you would begin your "comments" on subject X with something along the lines of "Well, *ahem, ahem,* the situation regarding X, *ahem, ahem,* is a very controversial one, *ahem, ahem, ahem*—and opinions are widely divided, *ahem, ahem, ahem.*" In essence, you are stalling for a few precious seconds to think of what you want to say. Sure enough, your brain shifts into gear, you remember that you do know something about topic X, and you begin to say sensible things in the cadences of normal speech. Hopefully your listeners are so absorbed in whatever you are saying that they have forgotten all the sputtering at the start.

When we write, we do much the same thing for much the same reason: to get started. Getting started makes us anxious and so, metaphorically, we clear our throats, which takes the form of being unnecessarily wordy when we begin to write. Or sometimes, we stop to clear our throat midsentence or midparagraph, until we think of what we want to say next. Just as in a speaking situation, throat clearing during writing serves a practical purpose: it buys us a little time until we get refocused and move on to saying something of substance, When we are writing we insert extra words or mindless little phrases, like *due to the fact that* in place of *because* or *in the not too distant future* instead of *soon*, because that initial wordiness buys us a few seconds to figure out what it is we really want to say.

Here is an example of a sentence in which the writer is using just such vacuous little phrases, as well as unnecessary prepositional phrases and mindless modifiers to get her basic ideas down on paper.

> The importance of this work lies in the fact that the contamination of water by arsenic is a very serious problem as a result of the consequences it has had on the health of people living in Bangladesh. (38 words)

Once she has expressed her ideas, the writer is able to go back and, simply by eliminating the throat clearing, revise it into a much more direct, economical sentence.

> This work is important because arsenic contamination of water is an urgent problem with serious consequences in Bangladesh. (18 words)

Here is a list of classic throat clearing phrases to look for when revising, all of which can be replaced by a single word such as *because* or *since*.

| | | |
|---|---|---|
| as a result of the fact that | because of the fact that | for the reason that |
| the reason for | in light of the fact that | owing to the fact that |
| due to the fact that | the fact that | |

Avoid meaningless modifiers such as the following that add nothing to your writing:

| | | | | |
|---|---|---|---|---|
| kind of | really | sort of | specifically | basically |
| generally | very | for all intents and purposes | | |

And here are some phrases to watch for that work quite well as stand-ins for *ahem, ahem, ahem.*

| | |
|---|---|
| It is interesting to note that | Evidence has shown that |
| It has been documented that | |

Such phrases are common and are to be expected in first drafts, but they should be ruthlessly eliminated when revising. Consider an example:

The data indicate that chromated copper arsenate is toxic and can be found in different types of pressure-treated wood. (19 words)

To revise we merely eliminate those first four words:

Chromated copper arsenate is toxic and can be found in different types of pressure-treated wood. (15 words)

Here is an example of an even longer bit of throat clearing:

Evidence provided by Lenka and Dietrich (1) has shown that analysis using matrix-assisted laser desorption ionization (MALDI) mass spectrometry provides quantitative data, while significantly reducing analysis time by allowing for unpurified environmental samples to be tested. (37 words)

This sentence doesn't really become substantive until we get to "analysis using matrix-assisted laser desorption ionization." Remove the throat clearing to end up with

Analysis using matrix-assisted laser desorption ionization (MALDI) mass spectrometry provides quantitative data, while significantly reducing analysis time by allowing for unpurified environmental samples to be tested (1). (28 words)

Throat clearing often finds its way into sentences presenting the results of statistical analyses, as in this example:

When compared by a *t*-test, it was found that the average rate of reaction in the presence of ultrasound was not significantly different from the average rate of reaction in the presence of microwaves. (34 words)

Everything preceding and including the words *found that* constitutes throat clearing. Spare the reader the hemming and hawing and unnecessary verbiage:

The rates of reaction in the presence of ultrasound or microwaves were not significantly different. (15 words)

The next example requires similar attention:

Another technique that can be used to supercool atoms is with laser trapping, which has also been developed in recent years; however, the fact that this process tends to end up scattering photons makes it not so easy to reach the densities and temperatures that are desired. (47 words)

A good editor would revise the phrases *that can be used to, which has also been developed in recent years*, and *the fact that this process tends to end up*. Here is an improved version of the sentence.

 Atoms can be supercooled by the new technique of laser trapping, but its tendency to scatter photons makes reaching desired densities and temperatures difficult. (24 words)

Notice that the revised sentence is half the length of the original. Editing for throat clearing has removed wordy, unnecessary relative clauses, eliminated reliance on *used* plus the infinitive *to supercool*, deleted *the fact that*, and turned a wordy negative adverb phrase *not so easy* into a one-word positive adverb *difficult*.

The written equivalent of throat clearing is a natural part of the process of thinking and writing—of how people wrestle meaning into words—and it serves a very useful purpose at the draft stage in the writing process. However, once you have found your voice and have begun to say sensible things, you should always go back and revise. Look for instances where you got bogged down with some unnecessary *ahemming* and eliminate any unnecessary words, modifiers, and phrases.

## Second Commandment: Eliminate Unnecessary Prepositions

Prepositions, those (usually) little words that establish relationships between other words, such as *to, in, for, of, on, over,* and *with*, tend to proliferate when we are thinking our way through a sentence, making connections, and putting pieces of information together. Like throat clearing, prepositions serve a purpose in the process of getting our ideas into written form, and also like throat clearing, they contribute to unnecessary wordiness. When revising you should work hard to remove as many unnecessary prepositions as possible.

Consider this example:

Oil of cloves is a product of nature that is extracted from the dried flower buds of a tree from tropical regions of the world. (25 words)

Any sentence containing such a long string of prepositional phrases— *of cloves, from the dried flower, of a tree, from tropical regions, of the world*—is automatically a candidate for the editor's attention. This sentence actually contains a simple thought, buried amid the clutter of unnecessary words. After revision, the thought emerges clearly:

 Clove oil derives from the buds of a tropical tree. (10 words)

Here is another example:

 Oil of cloves is used to provide relief from pain in the treatment of toothache as well as for the inflammation of the skeleton and from muscle strain. (28 words)

Careful excision of the unnecessary prepositional phrases results in a sentence that is not only more concise, but pleasingly parallel.

 Clove oil provides relief for dental, muscular, and skeletal pain. (10 words)

Here is yet another example:

 The cells responded to foreign proteins by rapidly dividing and starting to produce antibodies reactive to protein groups that introduced their production. (22 words)

The reader's head spins, an effect avoided by being more concise:

 In the presence of foreign proteins, the cells divided rapidly and produced antibodies. (13 words)

## Third Commandment: Avoid Weak Verbs

Formal scientific writing is often confusing—and boring—because the individual sentences contain no real action; commonly, some form of the colorless verb *to be* (*is, are, was, were*) is used where a more vivid verb would be more effective. This can easily be addressed after you have a solid draft written. At the draft stage, when the thinker/writer roles are still inseparable, the linking verb *to be* can play a useful role. Just as throat clearing may assist you in the initial articulation of your ideas in the process by buying you a few seconds to figure out what comes next, reliance on forms of the verb *to be* at the draft stage can help a writer link together various fragments of knowledge or insight into language: "*b* is a result of *a*, and *c* is a result of *a*, and *a* and *c* are similar in that both are . . ." and so on. Writing is a tool for thinking and learning, but often this really important thinking results in lifeless, wordy sentences. Writing is hard work, and you cannot expect your brain to do everything all at once. You need to **crank out the ideas and then go back and refine how you express them through careful revision and editing**. Just as you should always be vigilant to eliminate throat clearing when you revise, you should consciously work to eliminate a too heavy reliance on forms of *to be* and pare down and breathe some life into the flat, wordy prose it produces.

For example, consider this sentence from a student's early draft in which we have bolded forms of *to be* to call attention to them.

> The fidelity of DNA replication **is** dependent on the fact that DNA **is** a double-stranded polymer which **is** held together by weak chemical interactions between the nucleotides on opposite DNA strands. (32 words)

In a sentence like this, you can almost see the writer struggling to wrestle a complex idea into words and syntax. The word *is*, a form of the linking verb *to be*, functions as just that. It is a word that allows the writer/thinker to link together something he knows about the relationship between DNA being a double-stranded polymer and the fidelity of replication. Once the writer identifies the relationship, that replication of DNA "is dependent," he can eliminate the wimpy *is* and use the stronger verb *depends*.

> The fidelity of DNA replication depends on the fact that DNA is a double-stranded polymer held together by weak chemical interactions between the nucleotides on opposite strands. (28 words)

Why stop there? Piecing it together also required a bit of throat clearing which really serves no purpose now that the writer has articulated the idea. Eliminate some throat clearing (*on the fact that*) and another weak verb (*is*):

> The fidelity of the DNA replication depends on DNA being a double-stranded polymer held together by weak chemical interactions between the nucleotides on opposite strands. (26 words)

Here are some other examples of sentences in which we can easily see writers relying heavily on forms of *to be* to think their way through complicated ideas. In this sentence, the writer makes good use of throat clearing (*due to the fact that*) as well:

> Due to the fact that water, which **is** what makes up most of the earth's surface and **is** thus a very plentiful chemical, and **is** made up of a lot

of hydrogen atoms as well as some oxygen, it **is** an obvious choice
for the source of hydrogen gas. (49 words)

Ably assisted by no less than four reiterations of *is*, the writer has rea-
soned her way to a conclusion—a laudable achievement—but the resulting sentence is long, monotonous, and meandering. Excising the wimpy
verbs and the throat clearing produces a much more concise, less cumbersome sentence.

Water, which is abundant, accessible, and consists of hydrogen and
oxygen, is an obvious potential source of hydrogen gas. (19 words)

We see the exact same sort of process reflected in the writing in these
sentences.

The first step in this process **is** to find the desired gene that **is** to be
expressed in the DNA. This DNA **is** then cut out of the DNA strand by
a family of proteins that **are** known as endonucleases. (40 words)

The writer is doing exactly what he should be doing at the draft stage:
thinking on paper (or screen or wherever the words are being formed into
sentences). As is often the case, those sentences are neither concise nor
clear when they first spill forth. An active effort to eliminate the forms of
*to be* produces a much more succinct description of the proposed
process.

After identifying the desired gene to be expressed in the DNA,
we can cut it out with endonucleases, a family of proteins.
(22 words)

While there is no harm in exploiting weak linking verbs in the service
of thinking and piecing together ideas at the draft stage, when you revise,
be ruthless about eliminating them as much as possible from the final
product you present to others: your instructors, potential employers, the
scientific community.

## Fourth Commandment: Use Passive and Active Voice Effectively

In English it is possible to describe the same action using two different
**voices**: the **active** voice or the **passive** voice. A sentence written in active
voice is one in which the subject "performs" the action. For example, the
subject in this sentence is *student* and the action is *threw*.

**Active:** The student **threw** the flask out the window.

The passive voice refers to a sentence in which the subject receives the action and the verb is formed with a helping verb (some form of the verb *to be: am, is, are, was, were, being,* or *been*) followed by the main verb's past participle. In this sentence the subject is *flask*, the helping verb is *was*, and the main verb's past participle is *thrown.*

**Passive:** The flask **was thrown** out the window by the student.

The active voice is preferable in most situations for a number of reasons. Passive voice obscures who or what is responsible for the central action in a sentence. Active voice makes it very clear who or what is the agent of the central action—who is doing what—and it is therefore more direct, concise, and economical than passive voice. Although passive voice has its uses, especially in scientific writing, it is often a great enemy of concise writing, which is also highly valued in scientific writing. So which should you use when writing about chemistry? **You need to be able to choose and use the voice that best suits your purpose in a particular situation.**

Passive voice is wordy in part because it always relies on some form of the lifeless verb *to be,* which, as we have discussed, is a useful but wimpy verb. Consider a simple piece of reporting about an unfortunate incident in the lab.

**Passive:** An insulting comment **was made** during a conversation between a student and the TA during our organic lab session yesterday. (20 words)

Not only does the use of passive voice with its reliance on the helping verb *was* make this wordy, but it leaves us wondering who did the insulting, which seems pretty important. In this case, using the active voice not only results in a sentence that is more concise, but a sentence that is more clear and informative.

**Active:** The TA **insulted** a student during a conversation in our organic lab session yesterday. (14 words)

Consider now a different kind of reporting of information, like the kind you would do in the experimental section of your lab report for your organic chemistry lab. You and your lab partner followed your lab manual instructions and successfully synthesized bromobutane. It is possible to communicate your achievement using either the active voice or the passive voice.

**Active:** We **synthesized** bromobutane.

**Passive:** Bromobutane **was synthesized** by us.

The passive voice in this instance takes more words, but it doesn't really matter who did the synthesizing. The words *by us* are not necessary and would not be included. Since what is important in a laboratory experiment is not *who* did what, especially in the experimental section where your goal is simply to describe what you did in sufficient detail to allow another researcher to replicate it exactly, **the established, time-honored convention in chemistry is to use the passive voice in writing the experimental section of lab reports.**

Bromobutane **was synthesized**.

On other occasions when writing about chemistry, you may find that using the active voice is better suited to your purposes because, as we have noted, passive voice contributes to wordiness and often makes the active agent, the doer, anonymous, and a weaker, sometimes, ambiguous sentence may result. Consider the following example describing research on arsenic contamination in soil:

Once every month for two years, soil samples **were collected** from five orchard sites in Hampshire County, Massachusetts.

Whom should the interested reader contact if there is a question about where exactly the soil samples were collected? Was the soil collected by the writer, by fellow students, by an instructor, or by a private company? Eliminating the passive voice clarifies the procedure:

Once every month for two years, members of the class **collected** soil samples from five orchard sites in Hampshire County, Massachusetts.

Similarly, *it was found that* becomes *I found*, or *We found*, or perhaps *Ben-Daat found*. Whenever it is important, or at least useful, that the reader know who the agent of the action is, and whenever the passive voice makes a sentence unnecessarily wordy, use the active voice. Note that it is acceptable to use the pronoun *we* in scientific writing, particularly when switching to the active voice expresses thoughts more forcibly and clearly and eliminates unnecessary words.

## When to Use Active Voice

Use the active voice when both reporting findings and acknowledging the agent are important, but economy of expression is also important. The following is an example of the sort of sentence that relies on passive voice to credit those who did the research and to report their findings. What it sacrifices is economy of expression.

In this experiment, which **was conducted** to study the relationship between vitamin A and iron release from the liver, it **was discovered** by researchers that hemoglobin, hematocrit, or red blood cell counts in humans **were not increased** by medicinal iron supplements alone during deficiency, but the anemic condition **was** only **improved** when vitamin A **was given** in addition to iron supplements.

Although this sentence makes it clear what the researchers did, using the passive voice requires 61 words. By using the active voice, we can accurately describe the study and report their findings in only 43 words:

Researchers **studied** the relationship between vitamin and iron release from the liver and **discovered** that iron supplements alone **did not increase** hemoglobin, hematocrit, or red blood cell counts in humans. The subjects' anemic conditions only **improved** when they **took** iron and vitamin A.

## When to Use Passive Voice

While it is true that the active voice is generally more concise and clear, there are instances, especially in scientific writing, when the passive voice should be used.

**1. When the emphasis is on the action rather than the doer.**

 The beaker was swirled for 30 s.

Who swirled the beaker is of no importance, but it does matter that the beaker was swirled and that the swirling continued for 30 seconds. Therefore, the convention in chemistry is to write the experimental section of a lab report in the passive voice, as shown above.

**2. When the agent is irrelevant or we don't care.**

The Chemistry Department office has been moved.

If the office has been moved and we want to post a sign to let people know, it is unnecessary to include information about who made the decision to move it or who actually picked up the file cabinets and desks and moved them as in "Three nice guys from Physical Plant moved all the Chemistry Department office furniture and equipment to the new location." This information is irrelevant if we just want to direct people to the new office location; therefore, the passive voice suits our purpose and does an efficient job of communicating that information.

3. **When the agent is unknown, or we don't want to say who the agent is.**

 The instrument was damaged over the weekend.

There was no sign of forced entry, and several people have keys to the lab, but no one has come forward to admit responsibility. Therefore it is impossible to use active voice to say who damaged the instrument. Consequently, passive voice suits our purpose here. Or maybe we know who damaged the instrument, but using the passive voice allows us to report the incident without naming names.

4. **When there is no agent.**

Soil is made up of inorganic and organic compounds.

In order to choose between active and passive voice, we have to answer three questions:

- **Do we know who or what is performing the action?**
- **Does it matter who or what is performing the action?**
- **Do we want for some reason to hide who or what performed the action?**

And then we choose the voice that allows us to achieve our objective.

**Do not mix active and passive voice in a single sentence.** Once you have made a decision to write in either active or passive voice in a particular sentence or section of a report, it is important to be consistent.

The distillate was poured into a separatory funnel and washed with about 8 mL of water, and then I collected the bottom layer.

The distillate was poured into a separatory funnel and washed with about 8 mL of water. The bottom layer was then collected.

## EDITING FOR AMERICAN CHEMICAL SOCIETY STYLE: SOME GUIDELINES

What we offer here is by no means a comprehensive discussion of the disciplinary conventions observed within the **profession of chemistry**, merely a sampling of those stylistic and editorial conventions we believe will be of most help to you as you learn to write like a chemist. For more detail, consult *The American Chemical Society Style Guide* itself, which offers extensive information about the editorial preferences and practices of the discipline. You should also be aware that individual chemistry journals have their own preferences regarding conventions, which may deviate from those of the American Chemical Society (ACS) in which case the old adage of "when in Rome, do as the Romans do" applies.

### Abbreviations and Acronyms

As we noted in Chapter 4, *acronym* and *abbreviation* are not synonyms. UV is an example of an abbreviation; FACSS, which stands for the Federation of Analytical Chemistry and Spectroscopy Societies, is an example of an acronym because the letters form a pronounceable "word." Both abbreviations and acronyms are used frequently when writing about chemistry, and it is important to observe the established disciplinary conventions.

**1. Latinate abbreviations.** The following **Latinate abbreviations** should be used **only in tables, figure captions**, and **parentheses in text**. Elsewhere they should be spelled out.

   e.g. which stands for *exempli gratia* which is Latin for *for example*
   i.e. which stands for *id est* which is Latin for *that is* or *that is to say*
   vs. which stands for *versus* which is Latin for *against*
   etc. which stands for *et cetera* which is Latin for *and the rest*
   et al. which stands for *et alii* which is Latin for *and others*

 Real gases have a finite molecular volume; i.e., they are not true point particles.

 Real gases have a finite molecular volume; that is, they are not true point particles.

A plot of absorbance vs. concentration is shown in Figure 1.

A plot of absorbance as a function of concentration is shown in Figure 1.

While it is common practice in scholarly writing to use italic type for foreign words, especially Latin words, **Latin terms or abbreviations such as the following should not be italicized when writing in chemistry**:

a priori   ab initio   ca   de novo   et al.   etc.   in situ   in vitro
status quo   ad hoc   vs.   e.g.   in vivo

Note that in the United Kingdom, the convention is still to italicize Latinate abbreviations.

**2. Genus and species names.** The ACS specifies particular conventions for denoting and abbreviating the names of genus and species.

- Spell out **the full genus and species name** in the **title**, the **abstract**, and **the first time it appears** in the text. After that, abbreviate it, but spell it out with each different species name.
- Always capitalize the genus names, but never species names.

*Escherichia coli*

- Form the abbreviation with the capitalized initial letter of the genus name followed by a period.

*E. coli*

- Always italicize genus and species names and abbreviations.

First use                          Subsequent abbreviation
*Saccharomyces cerevisiae*         *S. cerevisiae*
*Escherichia coli*                 *E. coli*

**3. Symbols for elements.**
- Do *not* treat symbols for the elements as abbreviations. They do not need to be defined.

Cu        Ag        Au

The conventions for writing the names and symbols of elements are discussed later in this chapter (p. 92).

4. **Star-quality abbreviations.** There are some abbreviations used so commonly in chemistry writing that they have acquired a kind of celebrity status and never need to be defined. Here are some of the most common:

| | | | |
|---|---|---|---|
| at. wt | atomic weight | M | molar |
| bp | boiling point | mmp | mixture melting point |
| CP | chemically pure | NMR | nuclear magnetic resonance |
| DNA | deoxyribonucleic acid | RNA | ribonucleic acid |
| GC | gas chromatography | sp gr | specific gravity |
| GLC | gas–liquid chromatography | sp ht | specific heat |
| IR | infrared | sp vol | specific volume |
| *m* | molal | UV | ultraviolet |

5. **Abbreviations in the title of a paper.** As a general rule, **avoid using abbreviations except those with celebrity status** (see above).

Murphy, O. J., III; Yi, X.; Weis, R. M.; Thompson, L. K. SD RR SS NMR Distance Measurements Probe Structure and Mechanism in the Transmembrane Domain of the Serine Bacterial Chemoreceptor. *Biochemistry,* **2001**, *41*, 3025–3036.

Murphy, O. J.; III; Yi, X.; Weis, R. M.; Thompson, L. K. Site-directed Rotational Resonance Solid-state NMR Distance Measurements Probe Structure and Mechanism in the Transmembrane Domain of the Serine Bacterial Chemoreceptor. *Biochemistry,* **2001**, *41*, 3025–3036.

## Capitalization for Chemists

1. Do not capitalize the words *periodic table* or the names of chemical elements.

   calcium   helium   the periodic table   mendelevium

2. Write the symbol for elements with an initial capital letter.

   Au   Ne   He   Hg

3. Do not capitalize the names of chemical compounds.

   ethanol   ferric nitrate   sodium hydroxide   isopropyl iodide

4. For a term derived from the name of a person (an eponym), capitalize the name but not the noun it modifies.

   Graham's law          Einstein's theory    Boltzmann constant
   Avogadro's number  Erlenmeyer flask    Bunsen burner

5. Capitalize adjectives formed from proper names.

   Mendelian          Copernican          Cartesian          Newtonian

6. When surnames are used as units of measure, do not capitalize.

   ampere      dalton      gauss    kelvin    pascal      newton
   angstrom    faraday    hertz     joule     ohm         watt

7. Celsius and Fahrenheit are always capitalized because they are not themselves units; they are the names of temperature scales.

8. When the words *figure, table, chart, or scheme* refer to a specific numbered item, use an initial capital letter.

   See Figure 2               The data in Table 4 and Table 5.

9. Do not capitalize the common names of equipment or techniques.

   electron-diffraction chamber    atomic absorption spectrometry

   Note: be careful to distinguish between instruments and techniques. An atomic absorption **spectrometer** is an **instrument**; atomic absorption **spectrometry** is the **technique** used to determine trace metals.

10. Although debate still continues about whether to capitalize computer terms such as Web site and Internet, the American Chemical Society recommends capitalization of the following:

    **Web** (as in Web site, Web browser, Web server, Web page)

    **Internet**

    **Net** (when referring to the Internet, but use lowercase when referring to any network)

## Hyphens

1. Use a hyphen to join two words that together describe a noun and function as a single modifier.

   thin-layer chromatography  solid-phase extraction
   flame-ionization detection

Do the same with three-word modifiers.

signal-to-noise ratio   root-mean-square analysis
voltage-to-frequency converter

2. Use a hyphen in a spelled-out fraction and a spelled-out number from 21 to 99:

one-fifth       one-tenth       forty-three       seventy-two

3. Use a hyphen in a modifier that contains *well, still, ever, ill or little*.

well-known scientist   little-known hypothesis   ill-fitting stopper

4. Use a hyphen if a word is formed with prefixes such as *anti, cross, no, pro, pre, post, re, semi, sub, and over* ONLY under these special circumstances:
   a. when the second word in the combination begins with a capital letter or a number.

   non-Newtonian  anti-Markovnikov  pre-2000   post-1988

   b. when the second word in the combination begins with the same letter that occurs at the end of the prefix.

   pre-equilibrium      sub-bandwidth       non-nuclear

   c. when the second word in the combination is a chemical term.

   non-alkane       non-metals       non-phenyl

Otherwise, no hyphen is used in a word formed with these common prefixes.

antibacterial       precooled       polypeptide

5. Use a hyphen in a word that is formed from a word and an initial capital letter:

H-bomb      X-ray      U-turn

6. Be sure to use a hyphen—rather than an en dash—to represent the double surnames of those who choose to hyphenate their names.

Elizabeth Davis-Calhoun  Irene Joliot-Curie  Cecil Day-Lewis

7. Do not hyphenate modifiers that are chemical names.

sodium hydroxide solution     acetic anhydride concentration

8. Do not hyphenate multiplying prefixes (e.g., *mono, di, tri, tetra*).

divalent        triatomic        hexachlorobenzene

9. Do not use a hyphen to join an *ly* adverb and an adjective.

clearly defined goals           recently developed technique
accurately measured values

## Spacing

There is almost always a space between a number and the unit. The exceptions are % (percent), ° (angular degrees) and the corresponding symbols for angular minutes (′) and angular seconds (″).

$$10 \text{ kg} \quad 50 \text{ mL} \quad 100 \text{ °C} \quad 20\% \quad 45°20'15''$$

Insert a space before and after a mathematical symbol that has numbers on both sides or has a symbol for a variable on one side and a number on the other.

$$48.3 \pm 0.3 \text{ mg} \quad 6.022 \times 10^{23} \quad n = 3 \quad p < 0.05$$

When units are combined to give compound units, leave a space between the symbols for the individual units.

$$50 \text{ }\mu\text{g L}^{-1} \quad 5.73 \text{ g cm}^{-3}$$

$$2.3 \times 10^{3} \text{ L mol}^{-1} \text{ cm}^{-1} \quad 0.082 \text{ L atm mol}^{-1} \text{ K}^{-1}$$

Notice that temperature on the Centigrade scale is expressed in units of degrees C, whereas on the absolute scale, temperature is expressed in kelvin. An alternative way of dealing with compound units is to use a center dot ( · ) to indicate multiplication and a solidus (/) to indicate division. In this case, there are no spaces around the dot or solidus.

$$2.998 \text{ m/s} \quad 5.73 \text{ g/cm}^{3} \quad 2.3 \times 10^{3} \text{ L/(mol} \cdot \text{cm)} \quad 6.626 \times 10^{-34} \text{ J} \cdot \text{s}$$

Notice that in the case of the units for molar absorptivity [L/(mol · cm)], it is necessary to insert parentheses to indicate that the unit is not though if this were the case, the unit would be more normally written as L·cm/mol.

There are two spaces after punctuation that ends a sentence, and there is one space after a comma, semicolon, or colon.

## Spelling

1. *Proofread for spelling errors.* When it comes to spelling, English is a particularly difficult language. What we have is a hodgepodge of rules, nearly every one of which has some glaring exception. Yet misspellings convey the impression of carelessness or laziness. These are not advisable images to present to instructors, prospective employers, or the admissions officers of graduate or professional programs. It is your responsibility to make sure that the work you submit is **free of spelling errors**.

Using a spell-checking computer program will save you from misspelling many nontechnical words, but it will not catch such spelling errors as *is* versus *if* or *nothing* versus *noting*, and it is unlikely to be of much help in screening technical terms for you. When in doubt use a dictionary.

If you are fortunate enough to be working on your own personal computer, you can add technical terms to your computer-program's dictionary, but be careful to enter the correct spellings. You also need to be vigilant because the terminology you will be using in your writing in chemistry will be expanding rapidly. With each new assignment, you will be adding several new technical terms with challenging spellings, and unless you keep the computer dictionary up-to-date, it can't provide support.

Use the computer for a first pass, but use your own eyes for the second. We recommend **proofreading in hard copy**. Many people find, your authors included, that they catch errors when they read the text in hard copy on paper that they simply miss when reading words on a computer monitor.

2. *Singular and plural spellings.* Certain words, particularly those of Latin origin, are so familiar in the plural form that writers tend to use the plural as though it were the singular form and assign the singular form of the relevant verb. Here are the correct singular and plural forms for a sampling of challenging words that feature prominently in writing about chemistry. In cases where two plural forms are acceptable, we offer the preferred version first.

| Singular | Plural |
|----------|--------|
| alga | algae |
| apparatus | apparatus, apparatuses |
| bacterium | bacteria |
| basis | bases |
| criterion | criteria |
| datum | data |
| equilibrium | equilibria |
| focus | focuses, foci |
| formula | formulas, formulae |
| genus | genera, genuses |
| helix | helixes, helices |
| hypothesis | hypotheses |
| species | species |
| spectrum | spectra |
| vertex | vertexes, vertices |

3. *A note about data and datum.* The use of the plural *data* has been mistakenly used as though it were the singular form so often that it has earned a position of prominence on the pet-peeve list of many chemistry instructors. Some dictionaries, however, now tolerate its use. For example, *The American Heritage® Dictionary of the English Language* acknowledges that *data* is "not always treated as a plural noun in English."

According to the American Chemical Society, *data* can be either a singular or a plural noun. For example, *data* can be used as a plural noun to refer to several different collections of results, as it is in this sentence:

The data from the various research labs are contradictory.

*Data* can also be used as a singular noun when it is used to refer to a whole collection of information as one unit as in this sentence:

As soon as the data from his experiment is available, we will meet to discuss it.

Be aware, however, that for many experienced instructors of chemistry, the use of *data* in the singular still signals carelessness and a disdain for accuracy.

## Chemistry-Specific Conventions

We offer here a quick reference guide for the use of **typeface, super-scripts, Greek letters**, and **special symbols** used specifically in the discipline of chemistry. As we said earlier in this chapter, some individual chemistry journals have their own preferences regarding conventions, which may deviate from those of the American Chemical Society. You should always consult the author guidelines. **Remember that consistency is essential**.

## Chemical Elements and Formulas

Chemists observe specific conventions regarding the use of **typeface, roman type, or *italic type***. The use of different typefaces is yet another tool writers have to assist readers in readily grasping the intended meaning of what they write.

1. Use roman type (not italics) and lowercase (not capitals) to write **the names of elements**.

    silicon        lead        boron        iron

2. Use roman type (not italics) and an initial capital letter to write the symbols for elements.

    Si        Pb        B        Fe

    Distinguishing between capital letters and lowercase letters is particularly important when writing about chemistry because failure to do so can be very misleading.

    CO is carbon monoxide        Co is cobalt.

3. Remember that even when the symbol for an element is used, **the name is pronounced**. Therefore, when the situation calls for an article to precede it, you need to **choose an article (*a, an*, or *the*) that accommodates the pronunciation** rather than the first letter of the symbol. For example,

    a H (pronounced "hydrogen") compound

    a Ag (pronounced "silver") precipitate

    an Sb (pronounced "antimony") property

    Note: **this usage does <u>not</u> apply to isotopes.**

4. Use **roman type** (not italics) and **lowercase** (not capitals) to write the names of **chemical compounds**.

   sulfuric acid    ethyl alcohol    carbon dioxide    calcium sulfate

   Students are mysteriously inclined to use capital letters when they refer to chemicals. This is incorrect.
   **Use a capital letter for a chemical only when**

   a. **it appears at the beginning of a sentence**
   b. **it is part of a title or heading**
   c. **it is a registered trademark, such as Teflon, which is Dupont's trade name for poly(tetrafluorethylene)**

5. Write the **formulas** of chemical compounds in **roman type**:

   $$H_2SO_4 \qquad C_2H_5OH. \qquad CO_2 \qquad CaSO_4$$

   It is acceptable to use the formula for a compound in your text, provided there is no ambiguity about whether the species so identified is really the one in question. For example, if you write,

   The most common arsenic species in surface water is arsenate.

   you would be quite correct, because the term *arsenate* includes the various protonated species. But if you were to write,

   The most common arsenic species in surface water is $AsO_4{}^{3-}$.

   you would not be on such solid ground, because the most common species is probably $H_2AsO_4^-$. Thus you have misled your readers.

   **It is not acceptable to use the symbol for an element in place of the word**, as almost certainly when you are writing about an element, you also mean "and its compounds." For example, in the following sentence, the word "nitrogen" really means "appropriate compounds of nitrogen."

   One of the most important plant nutrients in soil is nitrogen.

   Using the name of the element to mean "relevant compounds of the element" is an accepted convention in chemistry writing.

**Superscripts and Subscripts**    You can easily create subscripts and superscripts with word-processing software and should take the trouble to do so. Your instructor will be irritated if you do not change $H_2PO4-$ to $H_2PO_4^-$, even though it is unlikely that you really meant $H_2PO^{4-}$. Do not forget to include the charge on an ion because this is an important piece of information. The convention is that the number precedes the plus or minus sign and is omitted for unit charges of either sign. Thus the phosphate ion is $PO_4^{3-}$, and not $PO_4^{-3}$.

## Special Symbols

**Greek letters** are commonly used in chemistry writing, and you should ensure that you use them when appropriate. Again, word-processing software will readily do this for you. Often there are several options. For example, you may be able to create the Greek letter $\mu$ by holding down the "option" or "alt" key while typing $m$, or you could type $m$ and then change it to $\mu$, by highlighting and selecting the "symbol" font. You will probably find that you have an option under the "insert" menu called "symbol" that provides many possible special characters and symbols. You should not type a $u$ where you need a $\mu$, especially in material that will form the visual aids for an oral presentation. Almost all of the features that you find in your word-processing software are available in your presentation software. The ability to create Greek letters may not be available from your spreadsheet software; consequently, the captions for graphs that are exported to other applications may need to be fixed. We discuss this in more detail in Chapter 7, Writing Laboratory Reports, in the section dealing with the default formatting of figures that Microsoft Excel produces (see p. 120).

## Quotation Marks

Regarding the placement of closing quotation marks with respect to other punctuation, some years ago ACS declared a position, which they call "logical placement," that differs from the traditional style. According to *The ACS Style Guide*, if the punctuation (the comma or the period) is part of the quotation, then it should be placed on the inside of the quotation marks. If it is not part of the quotation, it should be placed outside the quotation marks. **We will follow this convention in the writing examples for the remainder of this book; however, we will adhere to standard punctuation for the body of the book.** The following example illustrates a situation where the ACS guideline applies:

 In the literature on plasma spectroscopy, there is frequent mention of something called the "Stark effect."

In the literature on plasma spectroscopy, there is frequent mention of something called the "Stark effect".

# CONCLUSION

As far as possible, when you write about chemistry, you should pay attention to the details of the conventions of the American Chemical Society style. No one expects you to remember all of these details, but you should be aware that these conventions exist. Even if you are unable to discover what a particular convention is (e.g., whether *microorganism* has a hyphen or not), you should be consistent in whatever use you select in any particular piece of writing. Your readers will be more impressed by such consistency. The alternate strategy of varying the point of style or convention in the hope that you will be right at least some of the time will be interpreted as not paying attention to detail.

## Correctness: The Conventions of Standard Written English

The language used in academic writing is more formal than the language we use for conversation; the "voice" we use in conversation is more casual. Very few people, including most professors, regard academic writing as their native language. To accommodate a global audience, writing in chemistry conforms to what is referred to as Standard Written English (SWE), a particular variety of English that is governed by specific rules regarding usage, grammar, and punctuation. Knowing and practicing the rules of SWE is not about sounding erudite, but about communicating successfully with a broad audience. We strongly recommend that you work hard to observe and practice the formal **conventions of SWE** as well as the **stylistic conventions of the discipline of chemistry** because writing correctly ensures that your meaning will be communicated clearly and accurately.

## CHECKLIST FOR EDITING

*Editing for Gender-Neutral Language*

❑   Avoid using masculine nouns to refer to males and females.

❑   Avoid using the masculine pronouns (*he*, *his*, and *him*) to refer to both males and females.

*Editing for Concision*

❑   Eliminate instances of throat clearing whenever possible.

❑   Eliminate unnecessary prepositions.

❑   Replace weak verbs with stronger verbs.

❑   Choose and use the voice, active or passive, that best suits your purpose.

### Editing for ACS Style

❑   Avoid using Latinate abbreviations except in tables, figure captions, and parentheses.

❑   Do not italicize common Latin abbreviations.

❑   Observe the disciplinary conventions for handling genus and species names.

❑   Do not treat symbols for the elements as abbreviations.

❑   Avoid abbreviations in the title of a paper.

❑   Except for star-quality abbreviations, define acronyms and abbreviations when first used.

❑   Do not capitalize *the periodic table*, the names of chemical elements, chemical compounds, species, equipment, techniques, or surnames used as units of measure.

❑   Capitalize adjectives formed from proper names, genus names used as formal names, trade names, and surnames when used as modifiers.

❑   Capitalize *figure, table, chart*, and *scheme* only when they refer to a specified numbered item.

❑   Distinguish between singular and plural forms of nouns of Latin origin and use them correctly.

❑   Proofread carefully for spelling, grammar, and word-processing errors.

# II

# *GUIDELINES FOR SPECIFIC TASKS*

# 6

# KEEPING LABORATORY NOTEBOOKS

*Laboratory instruction should give students hands-on experience with chemistry, the self-confidence and competence to keep legible and complete experimental records, and to communicate effectively through oral and written reports.*

COMMITTEE ON PROFESSIONAL TRAINING,
AMERICAN CHEMICAL SOCIETY

## THE ROLE OF LABORATORY INSTRUCTION

The laboratory component of an undergraduate chemistry program has a number of functions in addition to those highlighted in the quotation above. Some functions are related to the acquisition of manual skills (handling apparatus for synthesis, operating instruments for analysis), some are related to the acquisition of critical thinking skills (interpreting experimental results, designing experiments), and some are related to the acquisition of transferable skills (working collaboratively in a small group, managing your time, multitasking).

In addition to laboratory courses designed to teach you chemistry that is already known, a well-designed undergraduate curriculum should provide research experiences that will offer you the opportunity to discover something that is not already known. These research experiences should give you a taste of how the science of chemistry is conducted. Chemistry involves observing and recording, asking questions, formulating hypotheses, devising experiments to test those hypotheses, presenting data, analyzing and interpreting data, formulating new questions and

hypotheses, and telling the relevant community what you have done and what you have found.

Whatever your career plans, be assured that learning how to keep a laboratory notebook and how to write research reports is an investment in your future. Even if you are taking chemistry courses as preparation for a career in medicine or pharmacy or some other career, recording the results of observations and writing a report about them at a later date are valuable skills. The laboratory notebook is an extremely important feature of the chemist's workplace, and undergraduate programs are designed to give you plenty of practice in developing the ability to keep a laboratory notebook so that you are able to function in a real, as opposed to a teaching, laboratory setting. Many real laboratories operate within legally prescribed codes of practice that require entries in laboratory notebooks to be made in a particular way, and many companies rely on the laboratory notebooks of their employees as evidence that can be produced in court in the event of an intellectual property dispute over, for example, who was the first to discover a new process or create a new formulation.

Acquiring the skills of writing in your lab notebook and producing a report of the results will help you today, as an undergraduate, to be better organized and more productive, to spend less time writing lab reports, and to get better grades.

We will start by discussing the kind of notes you will write in a teaching laboratory notebook and then say a few words about keeping a notebook for an independent study or research project.

## THE TEACHING LABORATORY NOTEBOOK

Your instructor is modeling the world of the professional chemist, so that you can learn the skills needed to be successful in your chosen career. The entries made in your notebook are crucial, because they represent the only evidence that you really did invent this process or make that compound before anyone else did. The evidence in the lab notebook forms the basis of many patent applications; therefore, the notebook must withstand the scrutiny of a patent official.

**Your lab notebook should be an accurate record so that the work can be repeated at a future date. This is vital: important discoveries must be reproducible. If you fail to keep a proper lab notebook, you will find your employment in most chemical- and chemistry-related industries will be brief.**

Your department probably has guidelines for keeping a chemistry laboratory notebook, and quite possibly, your laboratory instructor will give you detailed instructions for the particular course. Make sure that your notebook conforms to the requirements. Most instructors of laboratory courses will give you critical feedback about your lab notebook. This feedback may be informal (the instructor chats with you in the lab) or it may be formal (notebooks are collected and graded). One way of giving you constructive feedback, while allowing you to keep your notebook so that you can enter material relevant to the next experiment, is to ask you to submit a copy of the relevant pages of your lab notebook for grading. Some instructors will require a notebook that contains carbon paper and will ask you to submit the duplicate pages for grading immediately after the lab class is over or, depending on the instructor's preference, along with your report of the experiment.

Because it is essential that you learn to **record everything that is relevant at the time you make the observation or measurement**, a place for the notebook must always be available in your workspace. Put the book on the bench first; then assemble your apparatus around it. Take the notebook to the balance room and record the weights directly in your book.

**Never write anything related to your experiment on scrap paper**, the sleeve of your lab overcoat, your hand, or anywhere other than your lab notebook. The risk of losing a scrap of paper is very high, as is the probability of making a transposition error when copying the numbers into your lab notebook. Some lab instructors have been known to seize any scraps of paper they encounter and destroy them.

## WHAT TO RECORD

The following list illustrates the types of information that should be included in a laboratory notebook.

1. **The specific goals of your experiments (this may be in the form of a hypothesis statement or a statement of purpose)**
2. **The proposed design, including any relevant safety information about the potential hazards of the experiments you are about to perform (this is known as a "safety audit")**
3. **What you actually did, as you did it**
4. **When you did it and with whom**
5. **Your observations and numerical data**

6. **The location (computer file name) of any measurements recorded**
7. **Your thoughts about the interpretation of the results and what you are planning to do next**
8. **The signature of a knowledgeable witness**

In a teaching laboratory class, you may be assigned some pre-lab exercises. Not all instructors do this, especially for upper-level labs, because by this time you are expected to be able to prepare for a laboratory session without the formal prompts of pre-lab exercises. Your responses should be written under the heading of items 1 or 2 in the list above. Even if there are no pre-lab exercises, you will use your time much more efficiently if you make some notes about what you will be doing. We will have more to say about this later. You may have some questions that you want to ask the instructor; record them here. You may not be required by your instructor to make entries relating to item 7, but if you are having ideas about your results, you should write these down, as they will help you enormously in preparing your report. You may not need a signature (item 8), although sometimes instructors will ask to see your lab notebook at the end of the lab class and sign off on it.

In summary, here are some general instructions about the lab notebook.

### Basic Guidelines for the Teaching Laboratory Notebook

1. **Use a bound book and write legibly in blue or black ink, not in pencil.**
2. **Leave several pages at the front for a list of contents.**
3. **Make sure the pages are numbered.**
4. **Record facts (dates, titles, aims, procedures, measurements, and observations), reasons (for doing something you did not plan to do), and ideas (conclusions, speculations, suggestions, plans for the next experiment).**
5. **Use the first person, *I* (or *we*, if working in a group).**
6. **Enter data directly into the notebook (not on scraps of paper) while the procedure is being carried out.**
7. **Cross out mistakes neatly; do not hide them. Initial any changes or corrections.**
8. **Indicate clearly where supporting material is to be found.**
9. **Use standard terminology. Do not write in your own personal code.**
10. **Do not spill anything on the notebook.**

11. **Never tear out any pages.**
12. **Be careful not to lose the notebook.**

## Pre-lab Assignments and Preparation

Write your responses to any pre-lab questions in your notebook and be sure to distinguish this material clearly from the real experimental data. Most likely, the material you generate will be helpful while performing the experiment. Plan ahead for what you will do in the lab. Often there are operations that can be done in parallel, thereby saving time or allowing you to finish within the allocated time. By planning ahead, you will know, for example, when the procedure calls for the addition of 10 mL of dilute sulfuric acid, whether to (a) just pour it out of the bottle, (b) use a measuring cylinder, or (c) use a calibrated transfer pipet. You will also discover whether an instrument you will use needs to warm up for a significant period of time before you can make a reliable measurement. By planning ahead, you will get more out of the exercise and will finish your work sooner.

If you are part of a group, plan who will do what *before* the lab period starts. Do not use the first half hour of the lab period to decide this. If your instructor has assigned roles to each member of the group, when it is your turn to be "manager," you will need to be thoroughly familiar with the upcoming experiment so that you can assign tasks to the various members of your group.

It may help to sketch a simple flowchart of your planned activities ahead of time, as illustrated in Figure 6. In fact, you might be asked to do this by your instructor as a pre-lab exercise. It is also a good way to plan experiments in an independent study or other research experience. We also strongly suggest that you draw some pictures of what you are going to do. This can be particularly helpful if you are going to assemble a synthesis apparatus.

You can also set up the results tables, thereby demonstrating your outstanding organizational skills, by preparing entries such as those shown in Table 1 and Table 2. Your instructors will be very impressed with this level of preparation. Never underestimate the value of creating a favorable impression with your instructors.

## Examples of Notebook Entries

Two pages of a lab notebook are shown in Figures 7 and 8. The experiment in question is an investigation of some of the characteristics of molecular fluorescence with application to the determination of quinine in

| Lab Handout | Student flowchart |
|---|---|

### Determination of Calcium and Magnesium in Water by EDTA Titration

**February 29th 2007**

In this experiment the "hardness" (i.e., the calcium and magnesium content) of a water sample is determined by titration with standard EDTA solution.

Goal: to determine the hardness of a water sample. Units? $mg \, L^{-1}$ of calcium. Note that both Mg and Ca are determined. Prepare EDTA, standardize, and analyze tap (?) water.

↓

1. Prepare approximately 0.006 M EDTA solution by dissolving about 1.2 g of the reagent grade disodium salt of EDTA in 500 mL of distilled water. Add about 0.5 g (6 pellets) of sodium hydroxide and about 0.1 g of magnesium chloride hexahydrate. Mix well and store in a glass bottle. Retain this solution for possible use in later experiments.

Weigh 1.2 g EDTA sodium salt (top loading balance). Transfer to beaker and add 500 mL water (measuring cylinder) + 6 pellets NaOH + 0.1 g $MgCl_2 6H_2O$ (top loader). Stir with glass rod to dissolve. Put in glass bottle. (Maybe plastic better as EDTA could leach metals from glass?). Note that some EDTA will react with Mg ($5 \times 10^{-4}$ mol). For values here EDTA concentration will be 0.0055 M.

↓

2. Obtain primary standard calcium carbonate by exchanging a clean, dry weighing bottle for one containing approximately 0.5 g of calcium carbonate. Note and record its purity. Weigh accurately (to 4 decimal places) approximately 0.5 g into 20 mL of distilled water in a 250-mL beaker. Add about 1 mL of concentrated hydrochloric acid, in drops, down the side of the beaker, and cover with a watch glass placed directly on top of the beaker. When the calcium carbonate has dissolved, rinse the watch glass into the beaker and boil for 5 min to expel most of the carbon dioxide. Add 50 mL of distilled water, transfer to a 500-mL calibrated flask, and rinse the beaker into the flask with a wash bottle. Dilute to the mark. Mix thoroughly by repeated inversion.

Put 20 mL (measuring cyl) distilled water in 250-mL beaker.

↓

Weigh (by difference) 0.5 g (analytical balance) $CaCO_3$ (NOTE purity), add to beaker. Cover with watch glass.

↓

Add 1 mL (glass dropper) Conc. HCl (careful!) slowly. Rinse underneath watch glass back into beaker. Boil for 5 min.

↓

Add 50 mL water (measuring cyl).

↓

Transfer to 500-mL flask. Pour down glass rod into small funnel, break seal with piece filter paper, catch last drop, rinse and repeat (2-3 times), rinse funnel. Dilute to mark (watch parallax error), invert (hold stopper) to mix, shake well.

Figure 6.   Part of a flowchart based on a laboratory exercise handout.

Table 1. Mass of Sodium EDTA Taken to Make Standard Solution.

| Item | Mass in g |
|------|-----------|
| weight of weighing bottle + Na EDTA | |
| weight of weighing bottle | |
| Weight of Na EDTA | |

Table 2. Volume of EDTA Solution Equivalent to Standard Calcium Solution.

| | Rough | 1st replicate | 2nd replicate | 3rd replicate |
|---|-------|--------------|--------------|--------------|
| Final buret reading | | | | |
| Initial buret reading | | | | |
| **Volume added** | | | | |

tonic water. The pre-lab exercises asked for the structural formula of quinine, the likely concentration of quinine in tonic water, and an explanation of the instruction, given the formula of quinine, "to weigh out 120.7 mg to make 1 L of a 100 mg $L^{-1}$ solution." Notice that in the notebook entries the student has not written complete sentences but has made notes.

Record your data clearly. Each number should be accompanied by the appropriate unit of measurement. You should get into the habit of noting the make and model number of every instrument that you use as well as the name and version number of the instrument's software and any data-processing software you use.

In an undergraduate course, if you are following a detailed, step-by-step written procedure, it may not be necessary to copy this into your notebook (be guided by your instructor), but it is very, very important that you get into the habit of recording any variations you may make on the "standard" procedure. In short, you should **record what it is you are doing at the time you are doing it**.

Because it is important to know who did what, you should write in the first person (*I* or *we*) in your lab notebook, for entries relating to what you did. When one of your partners performed part of the experiment, record this appropriately. Remember, when it comes to writing the formal report, the convention in chemistry is to shift into the

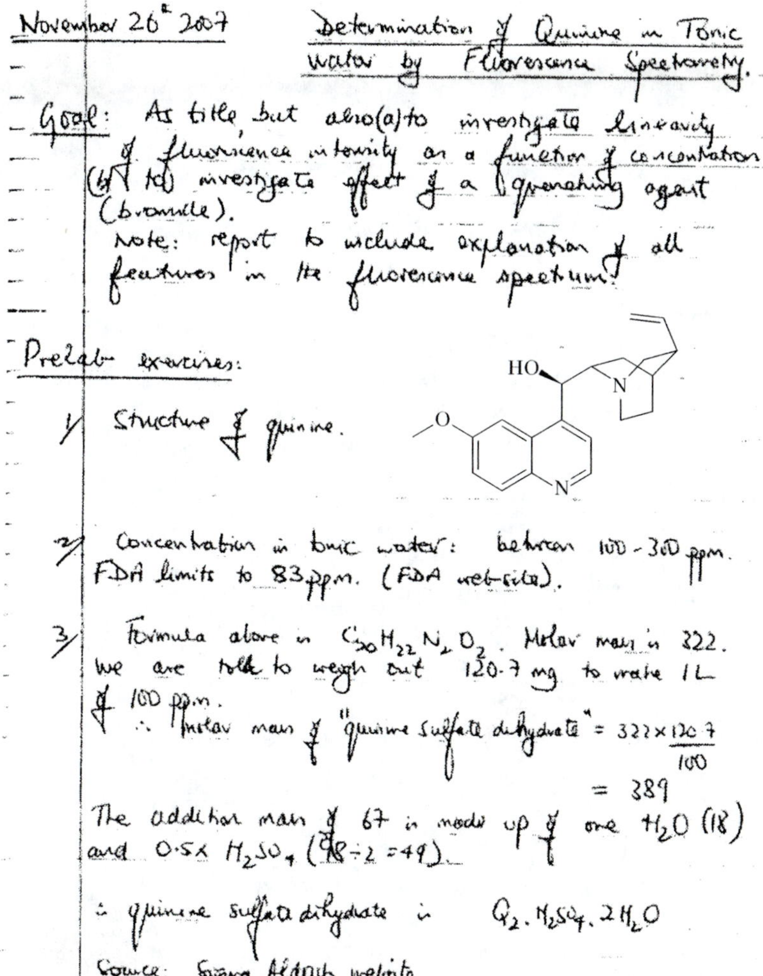

November 26ᵗ 2007          Determination of Quinine in Tonic
                          water by Fluorescence Spectrometry.

Goal:  As title but also (a) to investigate linearity
       of fluorescence intensity as a function of concentration
       (b) to investigate effect of a (quenching) agent
       (bromide).
       note: report to include explanation of all
       features in the fluorescence spectrum.

Prelab exercises:

1/  Structure of quinine.

2/  Concentration in tonic water: between 100 - 300 ppm.
    FDA limits to 83 ppm. (FDA web-site).

3/  Formula above in $C_{20}H_{22}N_2O_2$. Molar mass in 322.
    We are told to weigh out 120.7 mg to make 1 L
    of 100 ppm.
    ∴ Molar mass of "quinine sulfate dihydrate" = $\frac{322 \times 120.7}{100}$

                                              = 389

    The addition mass of 67 is made up of one $H_2O$ (18)
    and 0.5x $H_2SO_4$ (98÷2 = 49).

    ∴ quinine sulfate dihydrate in  $Q_2 \cdot H_2SO_4 \cdot 2H_2O$

    Source: Sigma Aldrich website

Figure 7. Example of entries in a student lab notebook. This page shows the first
entries for this experiment with the answers to the pre-lab questions. Notice that
the student did not indicate where the value of "100–300 ppm" came from nor
that this range is at odds with the Food and Drug Administration (FDA) limit of
83 ppm. Although the student did not record the URLs for the FDA and Sigma
Aldrich, she will have them bookmarked and will be able to copy and paste them
into her report.

Nov 26th 2007          Determination of Quinine

Preparation of 100 ppm quinine solution

$$
\begin{aligned}
\text{Mass weighing bottle + quinine sulfate} &= 12.3456\ g \\
\text{Mass weighing bottle} &= 12.2249\ g \\
\text{Mass quinine sulfate taken} &= 0.1207\ g
\end{aligned}
$$

Preparation of 1L of 0.05 M $H_2SO_4$

Given 1 M $H_2SO_4$  ∴ volume needed is given by
$$0.05 = \frac{1 \times V}{1000} \quad \therefore V = 50\ mL$$
(used measuring cylinder)

Preparation of 100 mL of standards.
Conc$^n$ of stock = 100 ppm.

| Conc required/ppm | vol of stock taken /μL | Device used |
|---|---|---|
| 0.1 | 100 | ⎫ |
| 0.2 | 200 | |
| 0.3 | 300 | Variable vol micropipet |
| 0.5 | 500 | ⎭ |
| 1.0 | 1000 | 1 mL bulb transfer pipet |
| 10.0 | 10,000 | 10 mL bulb transfer pipet. |

Selection of emission wavelength

Used 1 ppm std. Set λ to 350 nm (selected from abs spectrum in handout). Scanned $\lambda_{em}$ from 200 to 800 nm. Emission max at 450 nm.

Figure 8 Example of entries in a student lab notebook. This page shows the first entries during the experimental work. The student will have prepared the tables in advance and just recorded the weighings. Note that the student should have recorded the filename where the emission spectrum is stored; it may be difficult to find it again.

impersonal passive voice, at least for the experimental section where the emphasis is on the action (**what was done, rather than who did what**). For more detailed discussion of active and passive voice, see pp. 79–84 of Chapter 5. A fundamental feature of both the lab notebook and of any formal report of experimental work is that the information recorded will allow someone who is familiar with basic laboratory procedures to repeat the work.

## Making Drawings

It is unlikely that, in a chemistry lab, you will need to make drawings of your observations. Chemists have developed a vocabulary to describe pretty much every chemical phenomenon and property you are likely to come across (for example, "When I added the sodium hydroxide solution, a gelatinous blue-green suspension formed"). However, if you assemble an apparatus for preparative work, for example, you should sketch it (if you did not already do so as part of your pre-lab activities), as this is the easiest way to record what you actually did.

## Computers in Labs

We expect that eventually teaching laboratories will become all-electronic environments and the lap-top computer, or its equivalent, will replace the handwritten notebook; nevertheless, such a shift will change nothing in terms of what you need to record. In research labs, whether in a university or college or in an industrial organization, it may be some time before the handwritten notebook is replaced by an electronic notebook, because it is harder to demonstrate that electronically recorded information has not been changed at some later date.

## THE RESEARCH LABORATORY NOTEBOOK

Many undergraduates participate in research, either as an on-going activity over several semesters in a particular faculty member's lab, or as a one-semester independent study, or maybe through one of the many summer research experiences for undergraduates (REU) sites around the country. We strongly suggest that you get as much research experience as you can while an undergraduate, and the sooner you start the better. Not only is such experience vital for your subsequent career, whether it be in industry or academia (as we discuss in Chapter 14), but research is fun!

Everything in the preceding section describing the teaching laboratory notebook also applies to the research lab notebook, though there are some differences.

## Basic Guidelines for the Research Notebook

**Be sure to include the following:**

1. the specific goals of your experiments
2. the proposed design
3. what you actually did, when you did it, and with whom
4. observations and numerical data
5. location (file name) of instrumental measurements
6. your thoughts about the interpretation of the results, and what you are planning to do next
7. the signature of a knowledgeable witness (may not be needed at some colleges and universities, but will be in an industrial situation).

Don't forget to leave several pages at the front for the list of contents. Almost certainly you will start your research project by finding out what has been done previously. Prior work may have been carried out by other researchers in the lab in which you are working or by researchers at one or more other institutions. You may begin your research by reading reports and lab books of other students as well as papers in the original literature and then writing an account of the prior work and setting out some ideas about what the goals of your project are and what you are going to do. You should record in your notebook what you do in terms of reading and the results of any literature searching. You should record any comments or questions for your adviser. You should also write a statement about the goals of your work, which may be in the form of a hypothesis statement. For example, your goal may be to test the hypothesis that the formation of protein fibrils is catalyzed by copper ions. Your goal may be presented in the form of a statement of purpose. For example, your goal may be to devise a procedure to determine caffeine in chocolate.

As you will not be given a handout with detailed instructions for experimental procedures, you will be, for the most part, writing original material for items 1 and 2 in the above list. However, your introduction to the laboratory work of a project may take the form of repeating experiments described by another research group. Often, because the act of writing down what you plan to do helps you design the experiments, your research lab notebook will also function as a journal. It will help you interpret the results of the experiment as well. Writing about **what you think your results mean** and **what you need to do next** is an important part of the research process. Writing these ideas in your notebook also means that you will not forget anything when you find yourself in a particularly creative phase and are having lots of ideas. It also means that you will not mislay information, because **you are not going to lose your lab notebook**.

**Take your notebook with you when you meet with your adviser**. Not only can you write down any suggestions and ideas that the two of you may come up with for (a) interpretation of the results of completed experiments and (b) the design of new experiments, but you will be able to refer to your notebook to answer questions about your work (thereby demonstrating to your adviser that you are keeping a good lab notebook).

If you are working on an extended research project, such as a senior or master's thesis, or even a Ph.D. dissertation, you certainly do not want to repeat experiments because the entries in your notebook concerning early experiments are incomplete or confusing. You will be surprised by how quickly you forget the details of what you do; consequently, even if you are an undergraduate working on a semester-long independent study, you need to keep an appropriately detailed lab notebook.

Your institution may have guidelines about keeping a research lab notebook that you should follow. Legal issues related to intellectual property, patents, and commercial exploitation are important, and creating the paper trail needed to prove when and where the groundbreaking work was done is a vital component of this process. Many universities and colleges can be quite aggressive in pursuing the possibility of making money from your discoveries. Everyone hopes you'll come up with the next "Gatorade," which, since 1973, has garnered more than $80 million for the University of Florida. It is, therefore, quite appropriate for your adviser to ask to see your laboratory notebook on a regular basis. Monitoring your notebook doesn't mean that your advisor doesn't trust you to do a good job. It means that your adviser is meeting one of his or her responsibilities to the institution.

In keeping your notebook, assume that you are doing something worthwhile, that you might well discover something remarkable (it does happen), and that you will suffer complete amnesia while you sleep that night. In other words, take the time to write down—in your own words—everything you are about to do, everything you actually do, and why you are doing it. You can't always tell what will turn out to be important later. You *can* write down too little, but **it's difficult to write down too much**.

Write legibly and clearly, and if you use abbreviations in your notebook, be sure to indicate what each stands for, so that when the time comes for you to construct the report for grading, the end of semester report, or a senior thesis, you are in no doubt as to what you did and what the results were. It is also possible that you and your adviser will write a report for publication.

Unlike the situation in the teaching lab, where (probably) you get to keep your notebook, **your research lab notebook stays with the lab** and will be read by the next researcher to continue the project. You want to ensure that this person does not have to repeat your experiments unnecessarily. If you build a unique piece of apparatus, make sure you label the components so that someone else, working only with your lab notebook, could assemble the same apparatus. A digital photograph of your apparatus, labeled with the help of appropriate software, taped into the notebook is helpful.

It is likely that many of your results will be in electronic form. In addition to **ensuring that all the files are properly labeled and backed up**, you should print out the most important charts, spectra, and tables and glue them securely in your notebook at the appropriate places. Keep your backed-up files somewhere else, not just in the lab.

## CHECKLIST FOR THE LABORATORY NOTEBOOK

❑   Conforms to instructor's guidelines (hard-backed, bound, duplicate pages).

❑   Occupies a designated space on the lab bench.

❑   Has several pages left blank at front.

❑   Is written in ink.

❑   Provides dates for all entries.

❑   Has numbered pages.

❑   Contains all of the following:

    ❑   Relevant pre-lab material (answers to questions, literature searches).

    ❑   Details of experiments done, including departures from any method being followed.

    ❑   Names and models of instruments and software.

    ❑   Results obtained as the experiments were performed.

    ❑   Information regarding the location of instrumental electronic data (filenames).

    ❑   Ideas about results.

    ❑   Suggestions for next experiments.

    ❑   The signature of a knowledgeable witness.

# 7

# WRITING LABORATORY REPORTS

*Laboratory instruction should give students hands-on experience with chemistry, the self-confidence and competence to keep legible and complete experimental records, and to communicate effectively through oral and written reports.*

COMMITTEE ON PROFESSIONAL TRAINING,
AMERICAN CHEMICAL SOCIETY

## THE ROLE OF LABORATORY INSTRUCTION

All laboratory instruction requires that students write regular laboratory reports and submit them for grading. The laboratory reports that you write as an undergraduate are models of the writing that professional chemists and other scientists do as an integral part of their jobs. Professionals in most career fields find that the ability to write reports that communicate concisely and unambiguously is a key to advancement and promotion.

As we are sure you realize by now, communicating research findings to other members of the chemistry community is a fundamental feature of the way that chemistry develops. Chemists publish new findings to those working in their own areas in the form of a journal article, which, as discussed in Chapter 2, is something you must know how to read. There are other forms of written research reports that are important in chemistry, and we discuss these in Chapter 10. As a student, however, writing laboratory reports presents you with an opportunity to practice and develop your skills at a writing task that is essential to success in a scientific career.

Reports of experimental work—lab reports and journal articles—are mostly put together in the same way: according to an established, time-honored format with particular components, each of which has specific objectives and conventions. Learning how to write a report of experimental work goes something like this:

a. Your instructor explains how to write the report and shows you some examples.
b. You try to do it yourself for a situation in which you won't do much damage if you don't get it quite right.
c. Your instructor gives you critical feedback, which you internalize.
d. You try again.
e. You repeat steps (b), (c), and (d) until you are competent.

Although writing a lab report may not seem to be a task that would require skill and practice (it's not like playing the violin), many students find it a quite difficult task to master. It does require skill, and like any skill—take, for example, swimming—you don't learn to do it well by watching someone else do it or by reading or hearing a lecture about it. You learn to swim by getting into the water and practicing doing it. The more you practice, the better you get. If you have the benefit of a coach, an instructor who provides you with feedback, you will improve that much faster.

We offer the following advice.

- Approach writing lab reports as learning a basic skill, analogous to typing, which once mastered, will save you many hours during your career both as an undergraduate and beyond. Exploit the opportunities to hone your skills in this regard.
- Recognize that thinking and writing are intimately intertwined and that writing the lab report represents an opportunity not only to learn to write but also to write to learn.
- Pay attention to the differences between what your instructors in, say, organic chemistry want, and what your analytical chemistry instructors ask for. Not all branches of chemistry employ identical formats.

As we emphasized in Chapter 1, the ability to communicate effectively and accurately is essential to a successful career in any field. Make the most of the opportunities presented by your chemistry lab classes to learn to write well.

## WRITING REPORTS OF TEACHING-LABORATORY EXPERIMENTS

There is considerable variation among instructors in regard to what they expect from you in terms of a lab report. There may also be variations during any particular course: some reports may only be "partial" reports; others are "full" reports. Study the information from your instructor carefully and ask for clarification if needed. Instructors are often reluctant to give you examples of model reports for your particular lab course because they feel that students may be tempted to copy the model and not generate their own original report. Before writing your first report for a particular course, look at a few short papers published in relevant chemistry journals, such as the *Journal of the American Chemical Society* or *The Journal of Organic Chemistry*. Your instructor may provide you with a few especially good models. Reading these journal articles for content is unnecessary; you do not need to understand the topic of a paper to appreciate how the article is constructed. Note the way the Introduction is constructed, the amount of detail included in the Experimental section, and the format of figures and tables in the Results section. You should note that, for some synthetic laboratory courses, the convention may be to put the Experimental section after the Results and Discussion section. Just as in journal articles, each section of your report should be written in complete sentences.

For reports of syntheses, you will almost certainly be required to draw chemical formulas and, possibly, suggest mechanisms, which requires access to chemical-drawing software. You may be able to obtain such software free. Ask your instructor for advice, and check the course or department Web site for links to "useful" sites.

## COMPOSITION OF THE REPORT

The various sections of a research report are as follows:

**Title**
**Authors**
**Abstract**
**Introduction**
**Experimental Details or Theoretical Analysis**
**Results**
**Discussion**
**Conclusions and Summary**
**Acknowledgments**
**References**

We suggest that you write the **Experimental Section** first, then the **Results Section**, then the **Discussion Section**, and, only after you have written all these components, write the **Introduction**. Then and only then can you write an **Abstract** that distills it down to its essence. We will examine the sections in this order and will discuss the specific details required in a teaching-laboratory report. As a general rule, **never write anything in your report that you do not understand**.

## TITLE AND AUTHORS

Give the title as it appears in the laboratory handout, or, if this was a more open-ended, project-type experiment, create an appropriate title, such as "Investigation of the chloride content of calcium chloride," rather than "Report on calcium chloride project." Give the names of all your group members (if this was a group effort) and, assuming that each member of the group writes an individual report, indicate that this is your individual report. Also give the date(s) on which the experimental work was performed. Write the month in letters to avoid any ambiguities.

## EXPERIMENTAL SECTION

One educational goal of a lab class is to teach students how to design the experiments themselves. To this end, you will probably find that as you advance from first year to senior classes, the instructions in the lab manual or handout become less detailed, because your instructors expect you to know or work out what you need to do. By writing a complete experimental section in your report, you show that you were able to decide on the course of action appropriate for the experiment.

Another educational goal for this activity is for you to practice writing about standard laboratory procedures in the concise language and voice used by chemists. Report what you did in sufficient detail so that another student could repeat your work. Often the difficulty in writing this section of a lab report is in selecting the right level of detail; it is hard to hit it just right, but keeping your fellow students in mind as your audience will help.

### Ten Guidelines for Writing the Experimental Section

**1. *Use subheadings.*** In general, an experimental section has several subsections; therefore, consider creating subheadings that are relevant to your particular lab experiment. For example, in the determination of the hardness of water experiment, you might have subheadings such as "Preparation of EDTA standard solution," "Standardization of EDTA," "Analysis of water samples," and "Statistical evaluation of results."

**2. *Give specific details.*** Provide details of operations that are variable, such as the length of time the reaction mixture was heated under reflux, but omit details of standard procedures, such as weighing, using a buret, or measuring a melting point.

**3. *Write in the past tense and passive voice.*** For example, you would write,

The reaction mixture was heated under reflux for 20 min, cooled and transferred to a 100-mL separatory funnel. Hexane (25 mL) was added and the flask shaken for 30 s. After separation, the UV-vis absorption spectrum (190–800 nm) of the hexane layer was measured.

You would not write,

You reflux the mixture as per the lab manual, and then we extracted some of the stuff we made into hexane and ran the UV-vis.

**4. *Use formal language.*** In addition to problems with voice and tone, the negative example above illustrates some other common problems. Scientists, including your instructors, are bilingual when it comes to communicating science. They will speak in an informal language in the teaching lab and lecture classroom, but they will speak in a formal language at a conference and will certainly write about their science in formal language. In writing your lab report, you must adopt the formal language. Words like "stuff" are not appropriate. Nor is it acceptable to use the name of a technique as shorthand for making a measurement with an instrument. Although your instructor may say, "OK, now run the IR and see if there's a carbonyl stretch," in your report you will write, "The product was examined by IR absorption spectrometry" or "The IR absorption spectrum of the isolated product was obtained." Watch out for similar issues with gas chromatography (GC), nuclear magnetic resonance spectrometry (NMR), and mass spectrometry (MS). Ask for guidance from your instructor regarding abbreviations. It is acceptable to use some abbreviations such as GC and NMR without defining them since they are so widely recognized (see Chapter 5). Other abbreviations are context dependent: "FIA" could stand for either "flow injection analysis" or "fluorescence immunoassay."

**5. *Avoid ambiguity with formulas, phases, and formulations.*** If you were to write "$CH_3OH$ (50 mmol) was added," there is no doubt that about 2 mL of methanol was added; however, if you were to write "NaOH (50 mmol) was added," it is not clear how this was done: was the additive solid sodium hydroxide or was it a solution of sodium hydroxide? To remove this ambiguity, write either "Sodium hydroxide (2.0 g) was added," or "Sodium hydroxide solution [20.0 mL, 10.0% (m/v)] was added." For reports of syntheses, you may be asked to include the number of moles in addition to the mass of the chemical added. Most instructors will discourage the use of abbreviations such as EtOH for ethanol and similar nonstandard abbreviations or shorthand.

**6. Avoid ambiguity with numbers.** The numbers of digits you include is important. If you write, "The mixture was refluxed for 22.5 min," there is no doubt, to the nearest 0.1 of a minute, about the length of time involved. However, if you write, "The mixture was refluxed for 100 min," does this mean any time between 95 and 105 minutes or any time between 99.5 and 100.5 minutes? We are talking about significant digits here (all the digits known with certainty plus the first uncertain digit), and you should not be ambiguous about how many digits are significant. To remove this kind of ambiguity, write numbers in standard format. For example, if three digits were significant, write the number as $1.00 \times 10^2$. Don't forget to include zeros at the end of the number if they are significant. A mass of 25.00 g is known with much greater certainty than one of 25 g. Remember that you a creating a document that, in principle, would allow someone else to repeat the work.

**7. Pay attention to chemist's style.** Note that the numbers are written as numerals and not as words, but it is considered unacceptably poor style to start a sentence with numerals. So you would *not* write,

25 mL of hexane were added.

You would write,

Hexane (25 mL) was added.

Note the change from the plural to singular form of the verb, and note that there is a space between a number and its unit (see page 89).

**8. Avoid relying heavily on the verb to use.** This construction results in dull and tedious writing, as in the following example illustrates.

A top-loading balance **was used** to obtain approximate weights, then a four-place analytical balance **was used** to determine the precise weight of the potassium hydrogenphthalate. Bulb pipets **were used** to transfer aliquots of the sample. A hot plate **was used** to heat all ten sample solutions simultaneously. Watch glasses **were used** to cover the beakers while heating. A 50-mL buret **was used** for the titration.

In place of the monotonous *a* _____ *was used to* _____ formula, you might, by identifying the action and substituting more specific verbs, write instead,

Approximate weights of potassium hydrogenphthalate were **obtained** with a top-loading balance followed by precise weighing, to four decimal places, on an analytical balance. Solutions were **transferred** with bulb pipets and titrations were **performed** with a 50- mL buret. All 10 samples, in beakers covered with watch glasses, were simultaneously **heated** on a hot plate.

The present participle, *using,* can get you into trouble. If you write, "The precipitate was clearly seen using a microscope," you would elicit a wry smile from your reader who might conjure up some image of a crystal trying to manipulate a microscope to examine something more closely. You could avoid this kind of problem by writing "The precipitate was clearly observed with the aid of a microscope."

**9. *Include information about computation.*** You should describe any mathematical treatment of quantitative data, and, if you performed statistical analysis with the help of a computer, you should provide information about the identity of both the software and the statistical technique(s).

**10. *Remember to note the make and model of any instruments.***


## RESULTS SECTION

For the purposes of a lab report, it is probably a good idea to **deal with the results and the discussion as separate sections, but be guided by the instructions for your particular course**. You should write an account of the results in a way that guides the reader and does not just present a series of tables and figures with no explanatory narrative. You will also need to establish the level of detail your instructor wants to see in your report. Does he or she wish to see the individual weighings or just the information that so many grams of disodium EDTA were weighed out? Do you need to include the initial and final buret readings or just give the average value together with some indication of the spread of the results such as the standard deviation? Remember, of course, that all these details will be in your laboratory notebook. If you obtained an IR absorption spectrum as part of the process of confirming the identity of the product, should the spectrum be included as part of the report? If it is, then you need to give it a figure number and refer to it in the text. For example, you would write, "The IR absorption spectrum of the product is shown in Figure 2" and not "See the attached IR spectrum." **Charts, graphs, diagrams, spectra, and pictures are all called "figures" in the context of a report of work in a chemical laboratory**.

The figures and tables are numbered and presented in numerical order; the first ones you present are called Figure 1 and Table 1, respectively. Figures and tables are called out, that is, **refer to them by number and not as "the table below."** Avoid trying to insert the tables or figures into the text so that you do not have to refer to them. You should draw the reader's attention directly to the figure or table and point out the feature(s) of interest. You would not write,

> The fluoride concentrations were all below the detection limit of 0.1 mg L$^{-1}$ (Table 1).

The writer of this example puts the work on the reader. An effective writer guides the reader to the table, to what is there, and to what is important. For example,

> As can be seen from Table 1, the concentration of fluoride in all samples was below the detection limit of 0.1 mg L$^{-1}$.

Note that when you refer to a specific table or figure, the words *Table* and *Figure*, as well as the abbreviation *Fig.*, begin with a capital letter.

If the goal of the experiment was to investigate the trend in chloride concentrations in soil as a function of distance from a highway, you need to consider whether a graph of chloride concentration as a function of distance is needed. The decision about how to display results is a judgment call for you (unless the lab handout specifically tells you to plot the data). If there are only three data points—for example, 0 m 100 mg L$^{-1}$, 10 m 50 mg L$^{-1}$, and 25 m 10 mg L$^{-1}$—a plot is not necessary; a table will do very nicely. On the other hand, if you sampled 20 locations, it will be difficult to visualize the profile unless you create a plot. In a lab report, you will also need to show any instrumental calibration plots. In this case, assuming that ion chromatography was the technique involved, you

Table 3. Concentration of Arsenic Species ($\mu g\ g^{-1}$ as elemental arsenic) in Soil Spiked with As(III) Sequentially Extracted with 100 mmol $L^{-1}$ $H_3PO_4$ and 100 mmol $L^{-1}$ NaOH.

| Species | $H_3PO_4$ extract[a] | NaOH extract[a] | total[b] |
|---|---|---|---|
| As(III) | $3.0 \pm 0.2$ | $2.6 \pm 0.2$ | $5.6 \pm 0.3$ |
| DMA | ND[c] | ND | ND |
| MMA | ND | ND | ND |
| As(V) | $12.7 \pm 0.9$ | $2 \pm 2$ | $15 \pm 2$ |
| Total[b] | $15.6 \pm 0.9$ | $5 \pm 2$ | $21 \pm 2$ |

[a]mean $\pm$ standard deviation (n = 3), [b]$\pm$ term is square root of sum of squares, [c]not detected

should include a plot of detector response as a function of chloride concentration. In a lab report, it is quite acceptable to include both a table and a plot of the same data, but this is something for which your instructor will provide guidance.

## Tables

Pay close attention to the numbers of digits that you quote in a table, especially if you have copied the table from a spreadsheet. Present information about units the minimum number of times and use footnotes to provide additional information (such as what the $\pm$ term means and the number of replicate measurements in the calculation). An example is given in Table 3. The numbers presented in the table are given to the number of significant digits as specified by the value of the $\pm$ terms that indicate which digit is the first uncertain digit. In calculating the numbers in the "Total" column, more digits will have been carried in the calculation, and then the result would have been rounded appropriately. The format of this table is a close approximation to that which you would see in an American Chemical Society journal.

If the entries in a table do not all have the same units, label the top of the column appropriately [for example, density (g $mL^{-1}$)]. When writing about these results, it is helpful to match up items with their values by using a convention in which the units are given only once followed by "a comma and the word *respectively*." For example,

The concentrations of As(III) and As(V) found by extracting with phosphoric acid were $3.0 \pm 0.2$ and $12.7 \pm 0.9$ $\mu g\ g^{-1}$, **respectively**.

## Figures

Avoid having multiple figures when several similar graphs could be included in the same plot. Be sure that you have the axes in the correct orientation. The $x$-axis (the horizontal axis or abscissa) is assigned to the independent variable, whereas the $y$-axis (the vertical axis or ordinate) is assigned to the dependent variable (the one you measure in your experiment). Usually this also means that the values on the $x$-axis are known with (much) greater certainty than are the $y$-axis values. Assigning the axes in this way is important, because to fit a mathematical function to your data you will, almost certainly, use a procedure that assumes that that the $x$-direction error is negligible compared to the $y$-direction error. Do not subtract the instrument response to the blank (the solution with no analyte) before processing the data, and even if the response is 0.00, still include this (0, 0) point in the data set to which the best line is fitted. Be sure that you can enter the appropriate number of significant digits into the cells in your spreadsheet or other program. A detailed discussion of the statistics behind fitting mathematical functions to data points is beyond the scope of our book. For further explanation, we suggest that you consult "Statistics for Analytical Chemistry" by J. C. and J. N. Miller. This text also explains why the "correlation coefficient" value (calculated by the software you used) doesn't really tell you very much about whether the underlying relationship is a straight line or not.

## Dealing With Spreadsheet Software Output

When copying and pasting figures from a spreadsheet program such as Excel, you will need to edit the figure so that it conforms to the appropriate format. Look at the figures in a relevant journal article. An example of a figure that the spreadsheet software typically produces is given in Figure 9, together with commentary on how to modify this output so that the figure appears as shown in Figure 10. Bear in mind that **there are differences between the different branches of chemistry regarding the formatting of figures, and be guided by your instructor**.

You will notice that the student who produced this graph has used µ for micro (and not u) and has found a way to make the $-1$ a superscript. One way to fix the limitations of the formatting of text in the spreadsheet program is to create a text box in the word-processing program and overwrite the label after the plot has been copied into the word-processing document.

For the situation described in Figure 10, it is appropriate to fit a trend line because the underlying relationship between the two variables is expected to be linear, but this is not always the case. Consider the experiment mentioned earlier in which the concentration of chloride was

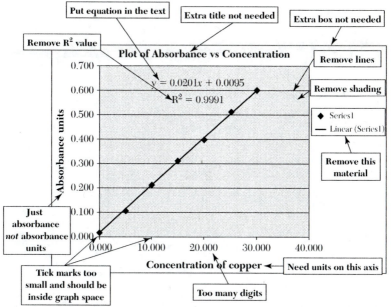

Figure 9.  Typical plot from a spreadsheet program with comments about what needs fixing.

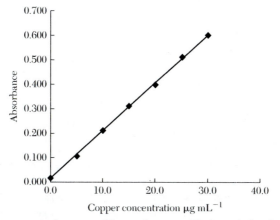

Copper concentration μg mL$^{-1}$

Figure 1.  Flame atomic absorption calibration for copper. The line, which is the best fit by least squares regression, is $y = 0.0201x + 0.0095$, where y is absorbance and x is concentration in μg ml$^{-1}$, with correlation coefficient 0.9996.

Figure 10.   Figure showing the result of fixing the problems shown in Figure 9.

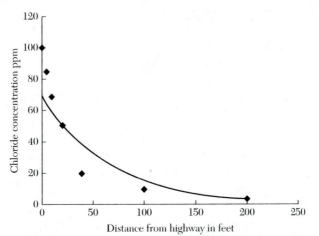

Figure 11. Chloride concentration in soil as a function of the distance from the highway. The trend line is the best exponential fit to the data points.

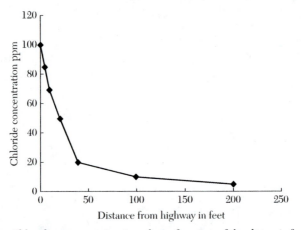

Figure 12. Chloride concentration in soil as a function of the distance from the highway.

monitored as a function of the distance from the highway. The results of this experiment are shown in Figure 11.

As there is no reason to expect that the relationship between the chloride concentration and the distance from the road is exponential, some instructors will consider that it is not appropriate to give the impression that this is the case by including this trend line on the plot. In a case such as this, the graph space should simply display the points, or you should create some simple visual aid, such as joining the points by straight lines, as shown in Figure 12.

Other instructors may disagree. If you are not sure which format is acceptable, ask your instructor.

## DISCUSSION AND CONCLUSIONS SECTION

Most instructors will ask that in a teaching-lab report you include your conclusions in the discussion section. In this section of the report, you must interpret your results in the context of the specific goals of the experiment and in the light of any specific questions that you were asked in the lab handout. Make sure that you know what these are; otherwise, if you do not answer all of them, you will not receive full credit for your report. In general, you should consider the following issues:

1. What did you expect to find and why?
2. How did your results compare with those expected? If you set out to test specific hypotheses, do your data support one hypothesis more than another or allow you to eliminate one or more of them? Explain your logic.
3. How might you explain any unexpected results?
4. Based on your results, what question or questions might you logically want to ask next?
5. How can your conclusions be generalized to other systems/reactions?
6. Did you answer all the questions posed by the instructor?

You should assume that the discussion is the one place in the report where you can show that

- You have understood why you did what you did (in the context of the goals of the experiment)
- You understand the reason for what you observed in terms of the behavior of the atoms and molecules of the materials involved
- You understand how your results compare with what is already known
- You have thought about and understand any discrepancies in your data (either internally or with respect to what is already known)
- You have suggestions for further interesting experiments that would resolve some of the problems you encountered
- You can make some comments about the broader implications of your results.

In other words, **you can show that you have been thinking like a chemist**.

In discussing your results, you should start from the premise that most teaching-laboratory experiments are based on reproducible phenomena that have been studied and reported previously. Therefore, there is relevant material in the literature about your topic. It may well be in the textbook for your course, or it may be in the original primary literature. You should make an effort to find some further information to include in your report. As we have said elsewhere (see page 35), Internet sources are acceptable places to start your search, but any citations you include in your report should be to validated sources, such as articles in research journals.

## Errors in Chemistry Experiments

There are three sorts of error: **random errors, systematic errors**, and **blunders**. **Random errors** are unavoidable; they are consequences of the natural uncertainties of operations, and they are just as likely to be positive as negative. A **systematic error**, on the other hand, causes a unidirectional bias in your experiment, and, if it can be identified, it can be compensated for or corrected. Systematic error is always present, but it may be insignificant. For example, the purity of any chemicals used to make standards will be less than 100%. On the other hand, a systematic error may be significant: for example, the additional amount of titrant needed to cause a detectable change in color of the indicator. In this case, you can determine this volume experimentally by titrating a solution containing no analyte and correct all of your values by this amount. A **blunder** is a mistake (such as spilling some of the chemical you have just weighed out while transferring it to a beaker for dissolution) that causes your results to be inaccurate. For experiments that result in the calculation of a numerical value, you should estimate the overall ± term based on the propagation of errors throughout the procedure. If you know the true value, you can comment on the accuracy of your result. If your value is significantly different from the true value, based on some appropriate statistical test, then you should discuss possible reasons for this. Go easy on the blunder-type explanation as this does not gain you many points with whoever is grading your work. Everybody makes mistakes, but you should not be offering this type of error as the explanation for every result that is not in agreement with what you expect.

Now for some comments about chemical reactions: although reactions used in teaching experiments may be **reproducible**, they may not be **robust**, meaning that the course of the reaction is sensitive to small changes in the conditions. You should recognize that many reactions do not go to 100% completion with the formation of just one product, and therefore yields may well be less than the theoretical value and that your target compound may be contaminated with the products of side reactions and unreacted starting materials. Not all reactions are instantaneous and are therefore subject to a variety of kinetic effects. Small concentrations of catalysts (or inhibitors) can have quite dramatic effects on reaction rates, as can changes in temperature. Also small variations in starting conditions can lead to variations in the relative amounts of products of the primary reaction and the side reactions.

You should also recognize that when instruments are being used near the limit of their performance, the ± terms will be quite large. This does not necessarily mean that you are dealing with very low concentrations. It may be, for example, that for the wavelength at which you are measuring, very little light intensity is reaching the detector.

Here are some extracts from the discussion and conclusions sections of a report of an experiment involving the measurement of chloride as a function of the distance from the highway. Note that the writers have used *we*, as this was a joint report on behalf of all of the group members. If you are solely responsible for the report, it is quite permissible (we think) to write in the first person singular (*I*) in this section; however, not all instructors agree with us and you should ask for clarification from yours. These extracts do not make a complete discussion section, but they are meant to illustrate the kind of material you should include, as we described on page 123.

1. The writers show that they understand why they did what they did.

1.1 The writers show that they understand how quantitative information is obtained from a calibration curve.

As can be seen from Fig. 4, the peak-area calibration for chloride was linear over the range 0.1 to 80 ppm, but the response to the 100 ppm standard was 8% lower than would be expected on the basis of the sensitivity established by the lower concentration standards. This part of the calibration is still useful, but would require additional standards to establish the curvature beyond 80 ppm.

1.2. The writers show that they understand the concept of detection limit, and they show that they know that a further experiment could be performed.

The detection limit, that is the concentration that would give a signal-to-noise ratio of 3, is estimated based on the expanded scale trace shown in Figure 5, to be 0.06 ppm. Not enough replicate measurements were made to estimate the detection limit based on the IUPAC definition (the concentration giving a signal equal to three times the standard deviation of the responses to a blank), as sufficient time was not available. We conclude that ion chromatography is a suitable technique for incorporation in an instrumental method for the determination of chloride in soil extracts, as the instrumental detection limit is considerably lower than values typically encountered in real samples.

1.3. The writers show that they understand the idea of method validation by spike recovery measurements, and that they are aware of what is already known about this aspect of the experiment.

 The results of our attempts to validate the procedure by adding a known amount of chloride to a soil sample prior to analysis (a spike and recovery study) showed that we may not be extracting all the chloride, as the recovery values varied from 85 to 105% with an average of 92%. This is within the acceptable range of 80–110% specified by the International Soil Contamination Society [4].

2. The writers show that they have looked for the results of other similar experiments with which to compare their results. They discuss the differences.

 If road salt were the source of the chloride contamination, then it might be expected that the concentration would decrease with distance from the roadway. We did observe this general trend, though the roughly linear decrease is not in agreement with the findings of Sparrow and Thrush [7], who found that the chloride concentration first increased with distance and then decreased. They explained their results as due to the ejection of liquid and solid particles by vehicle tires and snowplow activity. The profile at our site is probably influenced by the drainage ditch, which is approximately 15 m from the road.

3. The writers make some critical evaluative comments about the technique they used, showing that they are aware of some limitations, such as interference effects and time needed.

3.1. The writers show that they understand a possible interference effect (that is, a source of systematic error).

 Of the common inorganic anions that might also occur in soil samples, only sulfate is a possible interference as the peak is not fully resolved from that of chloride in the chromatogram. This partial overlap was not a problem in the analyses reported here, but for samples with a high sulfate concentration, some further chromatographic method development would be needed. A good starting point for such experiments would be the conditions reported by Hawk et al. [6] who showed that with an IONSEP column, good resolution between sulfate and chloride could be obtained.

3.2 The writers show that they have made an effort to discover if anything can be done to overcome another limitation, and that they understand the implications of switching to another measurement technique.

Another limitation of the overall procedure is the time taken for each analysis. One chromatographic run takes 20 min and thus, even if the instrument could be run 24 h per day, the throughput would only be 72 analyses per day. If chloride were the only analyte of interest, for large numbers of samples an alternate procedure such as flow-injection spectrophotometry would be preferable. Ruzicka and Hansen showed [8] that such a system could process up to 30 samples per hour. Under these circumstances, the extraction of the analyte from the sample would be the rate-limiting step and investigations of the possibilities of accelerated extraction procedures would be warranted.

## INTRODUCTION

The introduction should follow this structure: first "big picture," then "small picture," then "reason for doing the work" (i.e., the goal of the experiment). Writing the introduction is an opportunity for you to learn about the subject of the experiment. You may be able to base your introduction entirely on your own lecture notes, but more likely you will want to use both the course textbook and other sources. You may be directed to some literature sources by your instructor. The material you find will also be useful for your discussion. Make sure that any citations conform to the conventions for chemistry (numbers, not names and dates). The first citation should be number 1, the next number 2 and so on. **You should use the present tense for writing about the reasons for doing the work** (for example, "the goal of this experiment is to synthesize bromobutane"). **This section is best written after the results and discussion sections have been written.**

You should define specialized terminology. Your instructor probably knows the meaning of the terms you will use, but by defining them in your own words in your report, you can convince the instructor that you also know what these words mean. **Write to illuminate, not to impress.** Even though your instructor is grading the report, write for an audience of your peers. Here are two examples of extracts from introductions that illustrate this rule.

Alkyl halides may be prepared from the corresponding primary alcohol by reaction with a hydrogen halide HX, where X is Cl, Br, or I. The reaction, which is reversible, is an example of an $SN_2$, i.e., a bimolecular nucleophilic substitution, reaction. In this case, the nucleophile is the bromide ion, $Br^-$, and the leaving group is water, the first step in the reaction being the protonation of the hydroxyl group of the alcohol.

Metals in aqueous solution may be determined at concentrations of a few tens of $mg\ L^{-1}$ by flame atomic absorption spectrometry (FAAS). Atoms are formed in an air-acetylene flame when the aerosol, produced by a nebulizer and spray chamber, is introduced in the premixed gases. The radiation from a special light source, the hollow-cathode lamp, characteristic of the element to be determined passes through the cloud of atoms in the flame. The decrease in intensity is converted to absorbance by the instrument signal-processing electronics.

**Never set out to prove, verify, or demonstrate the truth of something**. Rather, set out to **synthesize, analyze, determine, measure, test**, or **describe**. In chemistry and other sciences, truth is elusive, and one experiment will never prove anything conclusively; it will add further evidence that the phenomena you are observing are well understood. It is not uncommon to repeat someone else's experiment and obtain a different result. But one such experiment does not necessarily overturn current thinking. There are many uncontrolled factors that may be capable of changing the outcome of an experiment. You want to show that you understood this when you did your experiment, so you would *not* write,

The goal of our experiment was to prove that hydrogen halides react with alcohols to form alkyl halides.

or

For this experiment, our aim was to verify that calcium can be measured in orange juice by flame atomic absorption spectrometry.

or

This experiment was designed to show that the ionization constant of a weak acid can be obtained from conductivity measurements.

The first example, which contains a grandiose and unwarranted generalization, might be modified to read,

The goal of our experiment is to synthesize bromobutane from the reaction between 1-butanol and bromide ion in concentrated sulfuric acid solution.

Note that the writer uses the present tense.

**Be brief.** Although every sentence should be designed to prepare the reader for the statement about the goal of the experiment that will appear at the end of the introduction, you should explain the wider context of the chemistry that you are studying. If, for example, your study was undertaken to determine the calcium content of tap water by titration with EDTA, you should explain why the "hardness" of water is an issue. Or, if you set out to measure the rate constant for the basic hydrolysis (saponification) of ethyl acetate, you might mention the use of saponification in the manufacturing of soap or the use of ethyl acetate for flavoring.

### A Sample Introduction

When coal is burned, any sulfur it contains is converted to sulfur dioxide. If this is released into the atmosphere, it can be further oxidized to sulfuric acid [1]. Rain containing sulfuric acid is harmful to plants and can leach toxic elements, such as aluminum, from soil into surface waters endangering aquatic life [2]. It is important, therefore, to know the sulfur content of the coal used for the generation of electricity. The goal of this experiment is to determine the sulfur content of coal. The procedure involved the conversion of sulfur to sulfate by heating the powdered coal with sodium carbonate and magnesium nitrate. After dissolution in water, the sulfate was determined by high-performance ion-exchange chromatography.

Note that in this introduction, the material progressed from a rather general statement, "burning coal releases sulfur dioxide," to more specific statements, "acid rain can mobilize aluminum from soils," and finally to the specific objectives of the experiment, "to measure the sulfur content of coal." You will see the same progression in the Introduction sections of most published reports. Your instructor should also see it in yours.

## ABSTRACT

An abstract is a summary of the report that includes the quantitative results. Leave writing the abstract until last. Include your quantitative results together with a statement about errors and whether the results are in agreement with what you expected. If they are not, then you need to include a statement as to why this might be the case. Here is an example from a report of an experiment in which students investigated the determination of copper in tap water by the technique of flame atomic absorption spectrometry.

Copper was determined in aqueous solutions by atomic absorption spectrometry with an air-acetylene flame atomizer, following optimization of the instrument parameters (fuel oxidant ratio and burner position) for the highest absorbance for a 10 mg $L^{-1}$ solution. Data for calibration of the instrument over the range 0 to 20 mg $L^{-1}$ were obtained. Unknown solution number 5 was analyzed, after a 10-fold dilution, against this calibration and found to contain $1.4 \times 10^2$ mg $L^{-1}$ copper, but when analyzed by the method of standard additions, the concentration found was $1.0 \times 10^2$ mg $L^{-1}$. In a separate experiment, it was found that the presence of ethanol (50% v/v) caused the absorbance value to increase by about 40% compared with that for a pure aqueous solution. This enhancement is attributed to the greater number density of ground state atoms formed when ethanol is sprayed into the flame due to the increase in flame temperature and more favorable aerosol formation and transport. It is concluded that unknown 5 contains a matrix component that increases the atom number density. The instrumental detection limit, determined on the basis of spraying solutions containing 1.0, 0.1, and 0.01 mg $L^{-1}$ of copper, was estimated to be 0.1 mg $L^{-1}$. As was expected, all of the samples of Gordon Bennett residence tap water examined contained less than 0.1 mg $L^{-1}$ copper. To determine copper at this concentration by flame atomic absorption spectrometry, sample solutions would need to be preconcentrated.

Note also that **the sample abstract is informative**. The writer does not simply say that "copper was measured by atomic absorption spectrometry." Rather the writer provides a specific summary of the results and what they mean. Be sure that your abstract is equally informative. Clearly, this section of your report will be easier to write if you save it for last.

## ACKNOWLEDGMENTS AND REFERENCES

For a teaching-lab report there will, most likely, be no need for any acknowledgements, and your references should be collected in numerical order in the appropriate style. For a discussion of the formatting of references see Chapter 3.

# CHECKLIST FOR A LABORATORY REPORT

- ❑ Conforms to the general guidelines provided by the instructor.
- ❑ Conforms to the specific instructions for this experiment.
- ❑ Anticipates the needs of an audience of peers.

### *Title*

- ❑ Gives specific indication of what the experiment was about.
- ❑ Consists of no more than 20 words, ideally fewer.

### *Abstract*

- ❑ Briefly (in one or two sentences) summarizes background.
- ❑ Clearly, succinctly states the question addressed and the hypothesis tested.
- ❑ Concisely reports major finding.
- ❑ Includes quantitative results (numerical values).
- ❑ Consists of a single paragraph of 200–500 words.

### *Introduction*

- ❑ Offers a clear statement of the specific issue or question addressed in the present tense.
- ❑ Clearly describes the big picture, then the small picture, then aim of experiment.
- ❑ Articulates clearly why the question is being addressed or the purpose of the experiment.

### *Experimental Section*

- ❑ Is divided into subsections relevant to the particular experiment.
- ❑ Provides a continuous narrative in the passive voice, in the past tense (*the beaker was swirled*).
- ❑ Includes details of chemicals, instrument(s), and software.
- ❑ Mentions all factors likely to have influenced the outcome.
- ❑ Provides sufficient detail to enable someone else to repeat the work.
- ❑ Does not contain any results or discussion.

### Results Section

❑   Provides a continuous narrative.

❑   Summarizes important findings in the data; does not simply repeat raw data.

❑   Presents results in the past tense and in active voice whenever possible.

❑   Includes tables and figures that are properly formatted, numbered, and called out (referred to by number in the text).

❑   Includes data that have been subjected to statistical analyses and ± terms calculated.

### Discussion and Conclusion Section

❑   Contains answers to all the questions posed by the instructor.

❑   Shows understanding of molecular-level behavior.

❑   Offers interpretation of statistical analysis.

❑   Compares results obtained with expected results and discusses differences.

❑   Offers evaluative comments and addresses broader implications.

❑   Cites and discusses other relevant work in the literature.

### References Section

❑   Cites references in ACS (or other appropriate) format.

# 8

## WRITING SUMMARIES AND CRITIQUES

### PREPARING TO WRITE THE SUMMARY

For assignments in writing summaries and critiques, you are asked to read a paper from the original scientific literature (the primary literature) and then summarize and assess that paper, usually in fewer than two double-spaced typewritten pages. *Brief* in this case does not mean *easy*. In fact, producing that one- or two-page summary or critique will probably require as much mental effort as that involved in preparing a full essay or review paper.

On the other hand, when you can write good summaries of individual papers, you will have a much easier time writing introductions, discussions, and term papers incorporating multiple references. Indeed, **until you can write clear and convincing summaries of individual papers in your own words, synthesizing material effectively from different sources is virtually impossible**. To do well in these assignments, you must fully understand what you have read, which usually means that you must read the paper many times, slowly and thoughtfully.

Follow the same procedures whether you are asked to write a summary or a critique; indeed, a critique begins as a summary, to which you then add your own evaluation of the paper. To begin, read the paper at least twice, following the advice given in Chapter 2 (pp. 18–33). It is often difficult to distinguish the important from the not-so-important points during the first reading of a scientific paper. Skim the paper once for general orientation and overview. Don't try for detailed understanding in the first reading, but do jot down or highlight (different methods work for various kinds of learners—figure out what works for you) any unfamiliar terms or the names of unfamiliar techniques so that you can look them up before you reread the paper.

After you have read the entire paper once, write down what you remember about the paper, what you don't understand about what you read, and any questions that come to mind as you write. This will help you focus your attention on some of the major points for a second reading.

During the second, more careful reading of the paper, pay special attention to the Experimental, Results, and Discussion sections.

As you read, pay special attention to the following:

- What was the goal of the work reported?
- Did the researchers achieve this goal?
- What evidence is presented to convince you that the goal was achieved?
- Do you believe the evidence and the author's interpretation of that evidence? (Examine the tables and figures carefully.)
- Are numerical results accompanied by appropriate statistical evaluations of errors?
- Are there any results presented that are not discussed?
- What questions remain unanswered?

Try to develop your own interpretations of the data before rereading the researchers' interpretations. We are readily influenced by the opinions of others, especially when those opinions are well written by "experts." Keep an open mind when reading the researchers' words, but try to form your own opinions about the data first: you may see something that the researchers did not. You may also notice features of the results that are NOT discussed by the researchers; this is useful material for the "critique" part of your assignment.

## WRITING THE FIRST DRAFT

You will know that you are ready to write your first draft of the assignment when you can distill the essence of the paper into a single, intoxicating, summary sentence—or, at most, two summary sentences. These sentences should include all the key points, present an accurate summary of the study, be fully comprehensible to someone who has never read the paper, and be expressed in your own words. As a general rule, **do not begin to write a review until you can write such an abbreviated**

**summary**. This exercise will help you discriminate between the essential points of the paper and the extra, complementary details. An example of a good summary sentence is given later (see page 137).

If you cannot write a satisfactory one- or two-sentence summary, reread the article; you'll get it eventually. After your summary sentence has been committed to paper, ask yourself these questions:

1. Why was the study undertaken? To answer this, draw especially from the information given in the Introduction (check that last paragraph) and Discussion sections of the paper.
2. What were the specific goals of the work undertaken? Summarize each goal in a single sentence.
3. What experiments were done? How did they relate to the goals on your list?
4. What assumptions about prior work were made by the researcher(s)? Might any of them be wrong? Are they testable? How might they be tested?
5. What were the major findings?
6. What is particularly interesting about the study? The questions asked? Some aspect of the methodology? Some particular result or set of results?
7. What aspects of the results are not dealt with satisfactorily in the article?
8. What questions remain unanswered? These may be questions addressed by the study but not answered conclusively, or they may be new questions arising from the findings of the study under consideration.

## WRITING THE SUMMARY

When you can answer these questions without referring to the paper you have read, you are ready to write. Writing without looking at the original paper will help you avoid unintentional plagiarism (see pp. 28, 148, 156) and will test your understanding of the paper. You can (and should) always go back to the original paper later to double-check and fill in specific factual details.

Instructors often specify a maximum number of words or pages, and you should take that directive seriously. Economy of expression is highly valued in scientific writing, and the ability to write to a target length is a useful skill to develop. Chemists frequently encounter rigid word constraints in their writing: an abstract submitted for consideration in a conference program is commonly limited to 250 words, the summary of a grant application may be capped at one page, or the contents page entry in a journal may be limited to one sentence of no more than 30 words. If your instructor asks for text to be double-spaced, in 12-point font with 1-inch margins all the way round, you will only be able to get about 300 words on one page. Even in the absence of such specifications, it is a mistake to think that creative tinkering with margins or use of alternative fonts will fool the instructor into thinking that you have achieved the kind of economy of expression a word limit clearly demands. If you exceed the word limit, keep revising for concision (see Chapter 5) until you achieve your target length.

At the top of the page—below your name, the course designation, and the date—give the complete citation (in ACS format, see Chapter 3) for the paper being discussed, beginning at the left-hand margin: names of authors, title of the paper, title of the journal in which the paper was published, year of publication, and volume and page numbers of the article. On a new line, indent five spaces and begin your summary with a few sentences of background information. Your introductory sentences must lead up to a statement of the specific goals the researchers set out to achieve. Next, tell (1) what approaches were used and (2) what major results were obtained.

**Present the researchers' results using the past tense**    Be sure to state, as succinctly as possible, exactly what was learned from the study. **Use the present tense to describe the contents of the article.** As you will also use the present tense to make your own evaluative comments, you need to make sure that readers know when you are summarizing the contents of the article and when you are making your own comments. To do this, credit the researchers when they are the source of the idea.

 The results show that the electrochemical procedure has a lower limit of detection than that of the spectrophotometric method used currently by the brewing industry.

The sentence above creates ambiguity by failing to clarify the source of this observation: is it your own original observation or simply a summary of what the researchers themselves reported in the article? A few carefully placed words serve to avoid such ambiguity, as in the following example:

The researchers point out that their electrochemical procedure has a lower limit of detection than that of the spectrophotometric method used currently by the brewing industry.

To condense the contents of a journal article into one printed page is no small feat, but it can be done if you fully understand what you have read. Consider the following example. Before writing the summary, the student condensed the paper into these two sentences:

> By building on previous work showing the benefits of the dual-pulse pretreatment of the platinum working electrode, Fung and Mo determined the ethanol content of beer by using an optimized flow injection voltammetric method that they validated by comparison with a reference method. They improved the detection limit with a staircase waveform, so that they only needed to pretreat their samples by diluting them with sodium hydroxide solution, thereby avoiding the usual requirement of removing the dissolved oxygen.

Note that the two-sentence distillation contains considerable detail despite its brevity, implying impressive mastery of the paper's contents; it is complete, accurate, and self-sufficient. When you can write such sentences, pat yourself on the back and proceed; the hardest work is over.

## A Sample Student Summary

B. John Barleycorn

Chem 391A

October 6th 2007

Fung, Y; Mo, S. Determination of Ethanol in Beer by Flow Injection Dual-Pulse Staircase Voltammetric Detection. *Analyst* **1996**, *121*, 369–375.

As the production of alcoholic beverages is subject to taxation, rapid, automated methods for measuring ethanol content are needed. Fung and Mo have developed a flow injection (FI) voltammetric method for determining ethanol content in beer based on measuring the oxidation current at a platinum electrode in a thin-layer flow-through cell. The goal was to develop an interference-free method, with a large linear range, for which it was not necessary to remove dissolved oxygen. A major problem of previous studies, namely the rapid loss of electrode activity, was overcome by a dual-pulse pretreatment, which LaCourse and coworkers had shown to allow detection of alcohols and sugars separated by high-performance liquid chromatography. Fung and Mo found that, under alkaline conditions, it was not necessary to remove dissolved oxygen, and that the detection limit could be improved with a staircase potential waveform.

Fung and Mo identified optimum conditions to achieve useful sensitivity, throughput, and precision by varying the pretreatment-step potentials, pH, voltage scan rate, staircase-potential step height, flow rate, and injection volume. Under optimum conditions, the sensitivity was 26 $\mu$A mmol$^{-1}$ L$^{-1}$, the throughput was 60 h$^{-1}$, and the precision was 1% relative standard deviation at 0.5 mmol L$^{-1}$. Although aspartame interfered (contributed more than 5% of the analytical signal from a 1% ethanol solution) at 100 mg kg$^{-1}$, up to 10,000 mg kg$^{-1}$ of sucrose and all other potential interferents (tested at 1000 mg kg$^{-1}$) could be tolerated. The researchers conclude, therefore, that the method should be interference free when applied to beer samples. The linear range was from 0.01 to 10 mmol L$^{-1}$. Beer samples were filtered and degassed (i.e., the carbon dioxide was removed), and then diluted 1 + 999 with 0.1 mol L$^{-1}$ sodium hydroxide solution. A 100-$\mu$L subsample was then injected into the FI system. Neither the carrier (0.1 mol L$^{-1}$ NaOH solution) nor the diluted samples were degassed; both contained dissolved oxygen.

The researchers compared the results of the new method for determining the ethanol content of four beer samples with those using a method endorsed by the Association of Official Analytical Chemists (AOAC); they found no statistically significant differences between the results.

## Analysis of Student Summary

Note that the writer of the summary introduces the topic and summarizes the purpose of the experiments and the major outcome of the work in the first three sentences. The remaining sentences in the first paragraph show the relationship to previous work and show specifically how the limitations were overcome. The next paragraph summarizes the experiments conducted to develop the method, including the various parameters that were optimized and how possible interferences were investigated. The paragraph concludes with a sentence that summarizes the sample pre-treatment. The final paragraph explains how the procedure was validated, that is, how it was shown to give the right answers when applied to analyses of real samples. The summary contains 360 words.

Note that the writer **used the past tense in describing the work** done by the researchers in their laboratory, but uses **the present tense** to describe the big picture: "as the production of alcoholic beverages *is* subject to taxation, rapid, automated methods for the measurement of the ethanol content *are* needed." The writer also uses the present tense to refer to a feature of the paper, namely a conclusion drawn by the researchers ("The researchers *conclude*, therefore, that the method should be interference free when applied to beer samples"). Note also that there are **no evaluative comments**. The summary writer's job is to produce a concise, accurate account of the important features of the research.

## WRITING THE CRITIQUE

A critique is much like a summary, except that you add your own assessment of the paper you have read. The opportunity to assess does not mean you should tear the paper to shreds. **A critical review is a thoughtful summary and analysis, not an exercise in character assassination**. Most chemical studies have shortcomings, which often become obvious only in hindsight. Yet every piece of research contributes some information, even when the original goals of the study are not attained. Emphasize the positive: **focus on what was learned from the study**. Although you should not dwell on the study's limitations, you should point out those limitations toward the end of your critique.

When the manuscript of a paper is submitted to a journal, the reviewers are often asked to respond to a series of questions that might be summarized as

(1) **Is it new?**
(2) **Is it true?**

Unless you have encyclopedic knowledge of the research already published, it will be hard for you to answer the first question; you would need to search the literature independently. This is more than your instructor has in mind, but you should examine the results obtained in the light of the material contained in the introduction to the article in question. In writing a critique of the article, you should concentrate on answering questions such as these:

- Were the conclusions reached by the authors completely in line with the data presented?
- What information is missing?
- What questions remain unanswered?
- How might these questions be addressed?
- How might the study be expanded or improved for the future?

Keep in mind as you write that you wish to demonstrate to your instructor (and to yourself) that you understand what you have read. Do not comment on whether you enjoyed the paper or found it to be well written; stick to the science unless told to do otherwise. It is permissible, however, to comment on the paper's organization. Many articles in chemistry journals are poorly organized, with a considerable amount of experimental work described in the Results and Discussion sections. If you had difficulty following exactly what the researchers did, you should mention this in your critique and indicate why you were confused. In order to write a good critique, you need to know something about the area of chemistry that is under discussion; the criteria that you might invoke in evaluating a paper in organic chemistry, for example, would not be exactly the same as those for a paper in analytical chemistry.

## A Sample Critique

The first stage in writing a critique is to write a summary; therefore you should start by summarizing the contents of the paper as in the previous example. By demonstrating through a succinct and cogent summary of what is in the paper, you establish your authority. Then critically evaluate the material.

Here is a critical evaluation of the paper that was summarized earlier:

> Fung and Mo have devised a rapid method, which, because of the FI format and the minimal sample pretreatment, could be completely automated. Consequently, the method is probably more cost effective than many previously described methods. As they were able to obtain a low detection limit, they could dilute the samples by a large factor (1000 times), thereby decreasing interferences from other components of the beer. However, as a result, the precision, 6–12% RSD, they report for their method is poor. They also report

poor precisions, 19–30% RSD, for the AOAC method. These values, which are rather large for an analyte present in percent concentrations, are partially responsible for the positive outcome of the statistical tests indicating that the results of the methods were not significantly different. I think further work on the validation of the method is needed. In addition to the comparison of the results with those of another method, the recoveries of spike additions of ethanol to several real samples could be measured. In addition, I suggest that the slope of the standard additions plot be compared with that of the external calibration plot as further evidence that the new method is, in fact, free from interferences in real samples. As the composition of beer varies widely in terms of the matrix components, more than four different real beer samples should be analyzed.

## Analysis of the Critique

Note that the student starts the paragraph by accentuating the positive, answering the question "is it new?" Then the writer points out a limitation of the results (the ± terms are rather large) and a consequence of this, namely that the data will pass a significance test (such as the *t*-test) of whether the means of the results obtained by the new method and a reference method are significantly different. In answering the question "is it true?" the writer has indicated that the answer is "yes, but . . ." Then the writer goes on to suggest some further experiments that could be done to remove the "but," namely spike recovery and standard additions. Finally the writer draws on his or her general knowledge of the sample materials and points out that just four beers are unlikely to represent all beers adequately. Note also that the writer has clearly differentiated his or her thoughts from those presented in the paper by the judicious use of the present tense for writer's comments and by use of the word *I*.

## CONCLUDING THOUGHTS

Clearly, writing good summaries and critiques is hard work, but it is an excellent way to learn how research in the various branches of chemistry is done and what constitutes a publishable piece of research. Being able to critically evaluate accounts of the work of other researchers is a skill needed by all professional chemists, not just those who work in universities or government research establishments. It is equally important that educators and industrial chemists be able to write critically about the relevant literature. Preparing good summaries and critiques propels you toward a true understanding of what you read—and of the nature of scientific inquiry.

## CHECKLIST FOR SUMMARIES AND CRITIQUES

### Preparing to Write the Summary
- ❑ Follow the guidelines presented in Chapter 2 on reading and note-taking.
- ❑ Skim the paper once for initial understanding.
- ❑ Takes notes as you read on what you don't understand and look up terms that are unfamiliar.
- ❑ Read the paper again focusing special attention on the Experimental, Results, and Discussion sections.
- ❑ Reread the article until you are able to summarize the essence of the paper in a sentence or two.
- ❑ Once you have a general summary sentence, go back and ask specific questions regarding the assumptions that informed the research, the goals that shaped it, the questions asked, the results reported, and the questions that may or may not have been answered.

### Writing the Summary
- ❑ Observe the specified target length and revise for conciseness rather than tinkering with margins or font size to achieve it.
- ❑ Use the present tense to describe the contents of the article.
- ❑ Use the past tense to describe what the researchers did in the lab.

### Writing the Critique
Complete all the steps necessary for a summary and then
- ❑ Ask whether the work reported is new.
- ❑ Ask whether the work reported is true.
- ❑ Concentrate on questions regarding the thoroughness, the soundness, and the success of the work itself.
- ❑ Comment on the organization and clarity of the paper only if they impede understanding.
- ❑ Use the present tense to make your own evaluative comments.

# 9

# WRITING ESSAYS AND REVIEW PAPERS

## WRITING TO LEARN

**Good writing is writing that achieves a particular objective.**
When you are given a writing assignment, you must first assess the goal and then make sure that all the various choices you make—what you say, how much you say, how you say it, and in what order you say it—support that goal. Most of this chapter is devoted to writing essays and reviews that have been assigned by an instructor as part of a chemistry course.

Essays are short exercises in which students are expected to write clearly, concisely, and logically. Depending on the topic of the assignment, you may also be learning to evaluate and organize the material you find in the research literature. In preparing an essay, you synthesize information, explore relationships, analyze, compare, contrast, evaluate, and organize your own arguments clearly, logically, and persuasively, gradually leading up to an assessment of your own. A term paper is really just a long essay; its greater length reflects a more extensive treatment of a broader issue and typically incorporates more references. Although practicing chemists don't write term papers, they often write reviews that appear in the scientific literature, either as stand-alone review papers or as chapters within books.

In addition to asking you to find and summarize suitable material, by assigning short essays and longer term papers, your instructor is asking you to present critical evaluations of what you have read. A good essay, term paper, or review is a creative work; **you must interpret what you have read in a thoughtful and logical way and then come up with**

**something that goes beyond what is presented in any single article or book you have consulted**. Your goal is to articulate some new thoughts based on what others have already done. This may seem a rather daunting task to ask of a student, but we confidently predict that you can do it if you give yourself enough time. Often we don't know what we really know until we write about it; the process of writing is itself a process of discovery. As you write, you will find that ideas come to you that would not have come if you were not writing. One of the goals that instructors have when assigning writing in college and university courses is to make you aware that **writing to learn is as important as learning to write**. This capacity of writing to generate new ideas is one reason why the strategy of creating a term paper based on a detailed preliminary outline is not very productive and is also why revising is an integral part of the writing process. What we write at the beginning of the process will need not just polish but also significant change before it is ready to present to a readership. The first draft is mostly an opportunity to get ideas down on paper, where they can't escape and where they can be evaluated, developed, and, ultimately, shared.

Essays and term papers are based mainly on readings from the primary scientific literature—that is, the original research papers published in such scientific journals as *Analytical Chemistry*, the *Journal of the American Chemical Society*, and *Environmental Science and Technology*. Textbooks and review articles (such as those published in *Scientific American* or *Chemical and Engineering News*) comprise the secondary and tertiary literature, which gives someone else's interpretation and evaluation of the primary literature.

## WHY BOTHER?

Writing an essay or review paper benefits you in several important ways. For one thing, you teach yourself something relevant to the course you are taking. **The ability to self-teach is essential for success in graduate programs and academic careers, and it is a skill worth cultivating for almost any profession**. In addition, you gain experience in reading and evaluating the primary scientific literature. Textbooks and lectures present you with facts and interpretations. By reading the papers on which these facts and interpretations are based, you come face to face with the sorts of data and interpretations of data on which the so-called facts of chemistry are based, and you gain insight into the true nature of scientific inquiry. **The data collected in an experiment are always**

**real; interpretations are subject to change**. Preparing thoughtful essays and term papers will help you move away from the unscientific, blind acceptance of stated facts toward the scientific, critical evaluation of data and ideas. These assignments are also superb exercises in logical organization, effective presentation, and discussion of information—skills that can only ease your career progress in the future.

There is another reason why instructors ask their students to prepare essays and longer papers. One can simply summarize a dozen papers in succession without understanding the content of any of them. We call this the "book report" format, in which the writer merely presents facts uncritically: the researchers did this, the researchers did that, the researchers found this, the researchers suggested that. By evaluating and synthesizing, rather than simply paraphrasing and listing what others have already done, you can show your instructor that you really understand what you have read and that you have actually learned something and not simply paraphrased the information presented to you.

All graduate programs in chemistry require that students write review articles, usually in the context of program requirements relating to original research proposals. Most graduate programs require students to review the literature relevant to their dissertation research as part of a longer document in which the original research to be done is proposed. Students are sometimes also required to create original research proposals in areas outside of their dissertation area. We discuss the writing of research proposals in more detail in Chapter 11, but you should note that the skills you develop in writing essays and term papers will be helpful when you write these higher-stakes documents. Most graduate programs will evaluate students' progress based on these written proposals and the students' ability to defend them in oral examinations.

## GETTING STARTED

You must first decide on a subject of interest. Often your instructor will suggest topics that you can use as guides, but do not feel compelled to select one of those topics unless so instructed. To get started, you need only a general subject, not a specific topic. Stay flexible. As you research your selected subject, you will usually encounter an unmanageable number of pertinent references, and you must therefore narrow your focus. You cannot, for instance, write about the entire field of trace elements in biological systems because the field has many different facets, each associated with a large and growing literature. In such a case, you will need to find a smaller topic, such as metalloenzymes. As you continue your literature search, you might even find it necessary to restrict your attention further to only those enzymes that contain nickel.

Alternatively, you may find that the topic originally selected is too narrow and that you cannot find enough information on which to base a substantial paper. You must then broaden your topic, or switch topics entirely, so that you will have something to discuss. Don't be afraid to discard a topic for which you are unable to find sufficient information.

**Choose a topic you understand.**   You can't possibly write clearly and convincingly about something beyond your grasp. Don't set out to impress your instructor with complexity; instead, dazzle your instructor with clarity and understanding. Simple topics often make the best ones for essays and papers. Be sure to choose or develop a subject that interests you. It is much easier to write successfully about something that genuinely interests you than about something that bores you.

## RESEARCHING YOUR TOPIC

The college or university library has a number of functions, one of which is to store printed material so that users can efficiently find and view it. The shelves of the chemistry section of the library will contain textbooks, reference books, and the current and past issues of printed journals, typically bound in volumes that contain all of the issues that were printed in a given calendar year. The librarians employed by your institution are there to help students and faculty use the library facilities effectively; they are an extremely valuable resource and people you should get to know. As you will quickly discover, there are many possible sources of information, most of which can be accessed on-line. We already made some comments about these sources in Chapter 3, which you should review. As a scientist, your job is not just to select sources of information that are relevant to your chosen topic, but also to work with sources that are reliable. Many Web sites contain reliable scientific information, but you should avoid heavy reliance on these in selecting the sources whose contents you are going to write about in your essay or review. Almost certainly one of the goals that your instructor has in mind for this exercise involves giving you experience in identifying relevant articles in the original primary literature and synthesizing a coherent account of their contents.

Fortunately, the original primary literature is extremely well catalogued, and the databases can be searched by a number of Web-based services. For example, the American Chemical Society has created a database known as **Chemical Abstracts**, which dates from well before the age of computers (around 1907), which can now be searched electronically by **a research tool called SciFinder**. There is a version for colleges and universities to which your library may subscribe called **SciFinder Scholar**. These research tools are not available to just anyone with a computer, Internet service, and browser software; however, while you are a student, you may be able to get almost unlimited access to the service. The same applies to **Web of Science**, another very powerful resource for scientists wishing to search the original literature. On the other hand, there are research tools that are in the public domain, such as **PubMed** and **Google Scholar**. The tools that are available through your library will contain links to enable you to find out whether the journals and articles are in the library and whether you can obtain an electronic version of an article in the form of a pdf file. Even if the journal is not available to you electronically, your library may be able to obtain a copy for you through an interlibrary loan procedure. In this case, the document may be a pdf of a scanned image of the original. Perhaps, following your visit to the library, if you can connect to your library Web site from an on-campus computer (or via an appropriate password from off the campus), most of your literature searching can be done from your own desk.

Your institution's library may also be able to help with the management of material that you wish to extract from the various databases that you search by providing a personal database, such as RefWorks. Depending on the word-processing software you are using, you may be able to link your text with the material in RefWorks to create the reference list at the end of your essay in an appropriate chemistry-specific format. There is commercially available software, such as EndNote, that will act as your personal database and will link to your word-processing software to create appropriately formatted reference lists. A significant advantage of such software is that it will automatically take care of renumbering should you decide to insert or remove a reference.

Before you begin your research, reread Chapter 2 carefully on the subjects of reading and taking notes. You are not setting out to regurgitate mindlessly what others have done and found, and you will not be reading to memorize anything. Instead, **your aim is to evaluate and synthesize information from a number of sources to come up with something new to say about the topic**. You are setting out to make a specific point (called a thesis statement) and to convince readers that that point is valid. You will also need to start researching your general topic (for example, arsenic contamination of groundwater) many weeks before the first draft is due to give yourself time to read carefully and, especially, to digest the materials that you have read.

Begin by reading the appropriate sections of any textbook suggested by your instructor to get an overview of the general subject of which your topic is a part. Then consult at least one recent review article before tackling the primary literature. Now you are ready to locate and read research reports on your topic, following the advice presented in Chapter 2 on reading and taking notes. The goal is to select a number of interrelated papers and to read these carefully. You do not want to accumulate a huge number of references that receive only cursory attention. You will need to survey what has been published and then, based on some criteria that you impose, select a few suitable sources from the undoubtedly large number available. This process of sifting and filtering can take some time, which is another good reason to get started early on your term paper.

**Be sure you understand thoroughly what you have read.**   As we pointed out in Chapter 2, most journal articles are structured so that you can find key features easily. The Title, Abstract, and Conclusions should be carefully scrutinized, as well as the last paragraph of the Introduction, which is where you will find a statement about what is new in the paper or what the specific goals of the research were. One of the best ways to assess your understanding is to summarize the material in your own words as you read along, paragraph by paragraph, section by section. When you have completed the entire paper, try writing a one-paragraph summary of what you have read and then a one- or two-sentence summary (see Chapter 2, pp. 18–33). You cannot evaluate or use information until you can first write a clear, concise, accurate summary of that information in your own words (this is discussed more fully in Chapter 8). Later you may be able to incorporate some of these summary sentences directly into your essay or paper. Such summary sentences, in your own words, help avoid any problems with possible plagiarism (see page 28).

## DEVELOPING A THESIS STATEMENT

It takes a fair amount of mental effort to come up with a useful thesis statement. Continually ask yourself while taking notes:

- Why am I writing this?
- What is especially interesting about this particular information?

- What puzzles me about what I have read?
- Can I see any relationship between this information and what I have already read, written, or learned?
- What evidence do the researchers present to support the conclusions drawn?
- Am I convinced that this evidence is reliable?

Also look for apparent contradictions in the results of different studies and in the interpretations of different researchers.

As you finish each paper, jot down some ideas about topics you would like to know more about. As you start developing opinions about what you have read, jot those thoughts down as well, and ask yourself what those opinions are based upon. Writing down such thoughts will help to fuel intellectual engagement with the material, an essential ingredient in the recipe for success. Eventually you will begin coming up with original ideas, interesting things you hadn't thought about before; then you will be ready to draft a thesis statement that both you and the reader will find interesting.

**A thesis statement needs support to be convincing.**    You might, for example, suggest that while many researchers assume that arsenic is toxic at even very low concentrations, there is reason to question this assumption. Or you might suggest that the continual leaching of arsenic from pressure-treated wood will eventually contaminate local well water. Or you might argue that many diseases can be diagnosed by measuring the chemicals in exhaled breath or that materials fabricated from blends of polymers and carbon nanotubes will have exceptionally high mechanical strength. Or you may not reach any definitive conclusion at all. Your argument might just be that the evidence for the anticancer properties of selenium is not as convincing as some people think and that there are specific, important issues that need to be studied further.

Refine your draft thesis statement as you keep reading and as you keep writing until you are able to articulate a statement that is arguable, that is, it is not self-evident and it requires support. This statement will fuel the entire project. **You will present this statement near the beginning of your paper and devote the rest of the paper to supporting it**.

As you continue to read and think and write, you will, we predict, be gratified to find that you begin to formulate a thesis statement; that is, you *discover* the thesis as you work. If you start well in advance of when your assignment is due and if you spend several hours a week reading and thinking and writing about your topic—following the methods advocated in Chapter 2—we can almost guarantee that it will happen for you. If you wait to begin reading and thinking until a week or so before the report is due, we can almost guarantee that it will not, and you will have missed the opportunity to learn how to do something really useful.

## WRITING THE PAPER

### Getting Underway: Taking and Organizing Your Notes

Some instructors will help by monitoring your progress, such as asking to see your notes, lists of papers read, summaries of those papers (see Chapter 6), and partial drafts. This is splendid for you because it puts you on a schedule. Otherwise, you must schedule yourself. **Start on the project as soon as possible** and allocate at least a few hours a week to it, every week, until it is done.

As soon as you have at least a draft of a thesis statement, begin the formal process by reading all of your notes. After reading your notes to get an overview of what you have accomplished, sort your ideas into categories. Many of us who did not grow up with personal computers may have made notes on index cards; these are very easy to sort, provided that only one idea is written on each card. If you made your notes on full-sized sheets of paper, you may need to annotate with pens of different colors, with each color representing a particular aspect of a topic. Alternatively, you might snip out sections of the notes with scissors and then group the resulting pieces of paper into piles of related ideas. This is how one of the authors of this book used to work. Another of the authors, who contributes to a major review article every year, organizes the material by printing the titles, authors, and abstracts of the relevant articles onto individual sheets of paper, which he then annotates in handwriting with the help of highlighter pens of two or three different colors. He then organizes the individual sheets into piles that correspond to the major subsections of the article. He says he finds it easier to deal with the several hundred possible articles this way rather than to work entirely electronically. For some jobs, a large table or even the floor are more effective work surfaces than the computer's virtual desktop.

Most of these activities can, of course, be done entirely electronically. If you have made notes directly on your computer, you can highlight and cut, copy, and paste to group together notes on related issues. You should experiment to find a system that works well for you. Be sure to back up electronic material regularly to some storage location that is independent of your personal computer. Most colleges and universities allocate to each student several megabytes of storage space on a server that can be accessed via the Web. Inexpensive and highly portable flash drives are also useful for this purpose. Be sure to use a sensible system for naming files that readily indicates which is the latest version of a document. It can be difficult to retrieve your latest version if you inadvertently overwrite that file with an earlier version. We usually include the revision date in our file names.

At this point, you must eliminate any notes that are irrelevant to your specific topic. No matter how interesting a fact or idea is, it has no place in your paper unless it clearly relates to your thesis statement and therefore helps you develop your argument. Some of the notes you took early on in your exploration of the literature are especially likely to be irrelevant to your essay, because these notes were taken before you had developed a firm focus. Put these irrelevant notes in a safe place for later use; *don't* let them sneak into your paper.

You must next decide how best to arrange your categorized notes so that your essay or term paper progresses toward some conclusion. Again, ask yourself whether a particular section of your notes seems especially interesting to you and, if so, why. Look for connections among the various items as you sort.

## The Crucial First Paragraph

The direction your paper will take must be clearly and specifically indicated in the opening paragraph, as in the following examples written by student A:

Many researchers consider that not only has arsenic no biological function in humans, but also that there is no exposure that can be considered safe.[1-3] Our efforts to control our environment and improve the quality of life through the application of appropriate science and technology have resulted in the accumulation, in both rural and urban areas, of considerable amounts of various arsenic compounds that have been widely distributed as pesticides, herbicides, and timber preservatives.[4] However, arsenic, mostly as simple inorganic oxoanions and the various mono through tetra methyl derivatives, is widely distributed in the environment due to natural processes of mineral weathering, water movement, volcanic activity, and microbiological activity.[5] Concentrations of a few mg

$kg^{-1}$ in soil and a few $\mu g\ L^{-1}$ in waters are common.[5] I will argue that, as we have evolved in an environment that has always been contaminated with arsenic, humans, in common with microorganisms, plants, and other animals, have developed a tolerance to the daily intake of a few $\mu g$ of various forms of arsenic in our diet. I will examine the human metabolism of arsenic and compare it with the metabolism of that substance by other organisms, especially those that have developed tolerances to very high concentrations in their immediate environment.

The nature of the problem being addressed is clearly indicated in this first paragraph, and student A tells us clearly why the problem is of interest: (1) arsenic is toxic and is widely distributed due to human activity, (2) but arsenic has for a long time also been widely distributed in the environment through natural processes, and (3) many living organisms have a high tolerance toward arsenic, (4) so humans might also tolerate low concentrations of arsenic. Note that the use of the pronoun *I* is now perfectly acceptable in scientific writing, but be aware that not all instructors will find it acceptable.

In contrast to the previous example, consider the following weaker (although not horrible) first paragraph written by student B on the same subject:

Arsenic, element 33 in group 5A of the periodic table, is poisonous and it is generally accepted that high concentrations of arsenic compounds are toxic to all life forms.[1,2] This is the reason that arsenic compounds are widely used as pesticides, herbicides, timber preservatives, and even embalming fluids.[3–6] However, some species of fern have the ability to tolerate and accumulate high concentrations of arsenic as compounds with sulfur-rich peptides,[7] and some microorganisms can convert arsenic to the volatile trimethylarsine gas.[8] Humans, in common with many other living organisms can methylate arsenic compounds, thereby decreasing their toxicity.[9] The tetramethyl arsonium compounds found in many marine organisms, including several that we eat, are completely harmless.[10] The beneficial effects of the ingestion of small daily doses of arsenic were known to the inhabitants of the Austrian Tyrol[11] well over a hundred years ago, and as arsenic has been in our environment since life first evolved, living organisms are tolerant to low concentrations of this element as they are to many other elements. Examples of such tolerance will be presented.

In this example, the opening sentence contains a certain amount of throat clearing and redundancy and could be edited to the following:

> It is generally accepted that high concentrations of arsenic compounds are toxic to all life forms.

Student B weakens the paragraph by prematurely referring to the ferns and microorganisms that can handle high concentrations of arsenic in sentence three. Since student B has not yet articulated a thesis, the reader is likely to be puzzled by the introduction of a situation that seems to contradict the opening two sentences. The reader is further puzzled by the reference to compounds that are, apparently, harmless and present in the seafood we commonly consume, when the paragraph started with an assertion that all arsenic compounds are toxic. While the reader is still trying to absorb the startling news about seafood containing arsenic, which is "toxic" yet "harmless," student B cites the "beneficial effects" of arsenic enjoyed by a community of people living in the Austrian Tyrol a century ago who apparently ingested arsenic intentionally. When the reader arrives at the end of the opening paragraph, where we expect to see the thesis articulated, student B offers a fuzzy observation that falls far short of making sense of the preceding string of seemingly contradictory statements. This is not the sort of writing likely to elicit a comprehending nod from the reader; the more likely response is a puzzled grimace.

The first paragraph of a paper must be an introduction, not a summary. It must set the stage for all that follows. Although the last sentence of student B's paragraph does clearly state what is coming, the reader must ask, "To what end?" The writer has set the reader up for a book report, not a critical evaluation or a persuasive argument.

Reread the paragraph written by student A and notice how the same information has been used so much more effectively, introducing a thoughtful essay rather than a tedious recitation of facts. Student A's paragraph was written with a clear sense of purpose, with each sentence carrying the reader forward to the final statement of intent, the argument on which the rest of the paper will be based. You might guess (correctly as it turns out) from reading student B's first paragraph that the rest of the paper was somewhat unfocused and rambling. In contrast, student A's first paragraph clearly signals that what follows will be well focused and tightly organized. It might take three or four revisions, but get your papers off to an equally strong start.

Another example of a typical, but not especially effective, first paragraph might be helpful:

Proteins are complex organic molecules that have biological function because of their three-dimensional shape as well as their functional group composition. Many enzymes are proteins with shapes that are specific for the substrates in the reactions that they catalyze. The study of protein folding is currently one of the most important areas of research at the chemistry-biology interface, and recent developments will be discussed in this term paper.

What is wrong with this introductory paragraph? The author is certainly off to a strong start with the first sentence. The second sentence, however, begins by repeating information already given in the first sentence and ends by saying nothing of substance (enzymes are proteins that are catalysts). The last sentence sets up a book report even though the author calls it a term paper.

Why will protein folding be discussed? More to the point, why should the reader be interested? The reader will more readily be drawn into your net if you indicate not only where you are heading, but also why you are undertaking the journey.

The first paragraph of your paper must state clearly what you are setting out to accomplish and why. Every paragraph that follows the first paragraph should advance your argument clearly and logically toward the stated goal.

## Supporting Your Argument

State your case, and build it carefully. Use your information and ideas to build an argument, to develop a point, to synthesize. **Avoid simply summarizing the papers one by one**: the researchers did this, then they did that, and then they suggested the following explanation. Instead, set out to compare (point out what is similar), to contrast (point out significant differences), to illustrate, and to discuss.

As described more fully in Chapter 3, you must back up all statements of facts or opinion with supporting documentation; this documentation may be an example drawn from the literature you have read or a reference to a paper or group of papers that support your statement, as in the following example:

According to Haraguchi,[1] metallomics is a new scientific area that integrates the various research fields related to metals in biological systems. Several researchers have determined[2-5] that certain metals play key roles in such systems. There are several enzymes whose active sites contain a metal ion; for example urease, which catalyzes the conversion of urea to ammonia, contains nickel.[6]

Similarly the opening sentences in the student examples on pages 151 and 152 are supported by references. In contrast, the statement by student C on page 154 has no such support, weakening considerably the authority of the writer.

In referring to experiments, **don't simply state that a particular experiment supports some particular hypothesis**, or that a researcher reached a particular conclusion. Describe the relevant parts of the experiment, and **explain how the results relate to the hypothesis in question**. For example, how potent are the following sentences?

> Many researchers[1-4] appear to have accepted the suggestion by Humphrey and Davey[5] that, in aqueous acid solutions, the tetrahydroborate anion, $BH_4^-$, hydrolyzes to release nascent (or atomic) hydrogen. This highly reactive species then reacts with other solutes, such as selenite, to form volatile hydrides.[5]

There is nothing in these sentences to convince readers of anything, not even that their author has read more than the title and abstract of the papers cited. In contrast, look at how much more convincing the following paragraph is:

> D'Ulivo and coworkers[1-3] studied the mechanism of the formation of volatile hydrides, such as those of antimony, arsenic, bismuth, germanium, and selenium, by the reaction of tetrahydroborate with the relevant ion in aqueous acid solution. They determined the identity of the reaction products by gas chromatography with mass spectrometry detection in a systematic study in which water, tetrahydroborate, and the acid were replaced by the deuterated counterpart. They showed that the absence of hydrides containing mixtures of hydrogen and deuterium was consistent with a reaction mechanism in which hydrogen was transferred directly from the borohydride; however, if nascent hydrogen was formed, both hydrogen and deuterium would be incorporated into the final product.

**In all your writing, avoid quotations unless they are absolutely necessary; in writing about chemistry they almost never are** appropriate. Rely on your own words and your own understanding of what you have read.

## The Closing Paragraph

At the end of your essay, summarize the problem addressed and the major points you have made, as in the following example:

> There seems little doubt that chemical vapor generation, particularly hydride generation, as a means of sample introduction in atomic spectrometry is a successful procedure with several advantages over conventional nebulization, including improved detection limits and elimination of spectral interferences. Recent developments in characterizing the mechanisms of the relevant tetrahydroborate reactions have brought closure to a long-running debate over the role of nascent hydrogen in such reactions. However, it seems likely that hydrogen atoms or radicals are involved in both the electrochemical generation of hydrides and the generation at the surface of the zinc powder used in the well-known Gutzeit reaction that forms the basis of a widely adopted field test kit for the estimation of arsenic in groundwater. In the case of the generation of volatile derivatives by the UV irradiation of solutions containing low-molecular-weight carboxylic acids, further work is needed to resolve the differences between the free-radical mechanisms proposed by Guo et al.[4] and those involving the formation of carbon monoxide or ketene proposed, on the basis of computational modeling, by Takatani et al.[6]

**Never introduce any new information in your summary paragraph.** Bear in mind that this will probably be the last part of your paper that your instructor will read before assigning a grade, so make your closing statements as strong as possible.

## PLAGIARISM

There is zero tolerance in academic communities for academic dishonesty. It is very important, therefore, that in creating an original essay or review that you will present as your own work, you neither present someone else's ideas as though they were your own, nor fail to acknowledge the sources from which you obtained the information.

As an example, consider this sentence from the review by Francesconi and Pannier mentioned in Chapter 2 (see page 26):

> Furthermore, although there are no demonstrated health benefits from having selenium intake above physiologic requirements, there is a general perception that increased selenium ingestion is beneficial, which has led to a flourishing market in selenium supplements.

Now consider this sentence based on the paragraph:

 In addition, although **health benefits from having selenium intake above physiologic requirements** have not been demonstrated, **there is a general perception that increased selenium ingestion is beneficial,** and this **has led to a flourishing market in selenium supplements**.

The degree of similarity between this paragraph and the original paragraph renders this a clear example of plagiarism. We have placed in bold the words that are taken verbatim from the original to show that all the writer has done is replace one or two words with synonyms and changed the word order a little, without crediting the source. It is easy to commit this sort of plagiarism accidentally if you copy the exact words from a source into your notes without indicating that these are the author's exact words, or if you simply copy and paste the original text into your notes electronically without recording the source.

Here is an acceptable way to incorporate this material into your own writing.

 Francesconi and Pannier [1] point out that although no one has demonstrated any benefits to taking selenium above the minimum needed to stay healthy, selenium supplements are widely available as people think that taking additional selenium is good for them.

Always present the results of previously published work in a way that makes it clear who is responsible for the ideas.

Consider the following two paragraphs:

 Kearns [1] found that in the flow injection determination of arsenate by the molybdenum blue method, phosphate interfered to an extent that depended on the residence time. Ben-Daat [2], however, indicated that the interference was related to the solution pH downstream of the confluence point and that residence time had no effect if the pH was below 2.5.

In the flow injection determination of arsenate by the molybdenum blue method, the phosphate interference might depend on residence time. However, Ben-Daat [1] showed that this was not the case. It is likely that the interference is dependent instead on the pH of the solution after the reagents have merged.

The first example is fine; every idea is clearly associated with a source. In the second example, however, the writer has not taken care to attribute the ideas to their sources and takes credit for the ideas of Kearns (who is not even mentioned) and Ben-Daat. In doing so, the writer has plagiarized.

**Plagiarism is theft.**   It is one of the most serious offenses that can be committed in academia, where original thought is the major product of one's work—often months, sometimes years, of work. Most colleges and universities have clearly articulated policies regarding plagiarism, and they make a considerable effort to educate students about the issues; thus, most institutions will consider any act of plagiarism to have been deliberate. Typically, at the very least, an act of plagiarism will result in an F on the assignment. Some instructors may respond by assigning an F for the entire course. In addition, you may be reported to the institution's honor board, who may maintain a record of infractions. Such a record could seriously jeopardize your chances of admission to, for example, law school. Repeated plagiarism (but sometimes even a single offense) can result in expulsion from college.

Computer programs designed to detect plagiarism are now being used at more and more colleges and universities (and by more scientific journal editors). Such programs, like Turnitin, search enormous databases that include millions of papers available on the Internet. In adopting the use of such software, the institution is not trying to catch cheaters but is simply acknowledging that, because electronic text is so easily accessed, copied, cut, and pasted, it is very easy to plagiarize inadvertently. The software provides feedback to students and instructors about the extent to which the text you have submitted is identical to previously published text.

To help you crystallize your ideas about just what exactly constitutes plagiarism or may be considered dishonest, there is a short quiz at the end of this chapter.

## CITING SOURCES

Cite only sources that you have actually read and would feel confident discussing with your instructor. Unless told otherwise, cite sources directly in the text by the appropriate number, either in superscript form or placed in brackets or parentheses. **Whichever system you use, be consistent**.

At the end of your paper, include a references section that lists all the publications referred to in your paper. Your instructor may specify a particular format for preparing this section of your paper. For more detailed information about both citing sources and preparing the references section see Chapter 3. The quiz at the end of this chapter will test your knowledge about the responsible citing of sources.

# CREATING A TITLE

By the time you have finished writing the paper itself, you should be ready to title your creation. Give the essay or term paper a title that is appropriate and interesting, one that conveys significant information about the specific topic of your paper. Again anticipate the needs of your reader and think about what the reader will be able to deduce from the title. Here are some examples, both positive and negative:

 Mechanisms of the formation of hydrides

 The mechanism of the formation of hydrides of group 5A and 6A elements by reaction with tetrahydroborate in aqueous acid

 The determination of arsenic in water

An evaluation of field test kits for determining arsenic in groundwater

Biological transformations of arsenic

The role of methylation and demethylation reactions in the biological transformations of arsenic released from timber pressure-treated with chromated copper arsenate

In your enthusiasm to make your title specific and informative, don't also make it unnecessarily wordy. How could you improve the following title?

An evaluation of the efficacy of organoselenenium compounds as cancer chemopreventative agents as demonstrated by animal studies and clinical trials concerned with the particular effects of supplementation with selenomethionine on males with a propensity for prostate cancer compared with a placebo group

Since only males can get prostate cancer, we can remove the information that only men are involved. Because clinical trials always involve a placebo group, we can omit this information in the title. Several other words do not really convey any useful information, such as *agents*, *particular*, *concerned*, *evaluation*, and *supplementation*. A better title might be

 How effective are organoselenenium compounds against cancer: what have we learned from animal studies and clinical trials of selenomethionine and prostate cancer?

## REVISING

Once you have a working draft of your paper, you must revise it, clarifying your presentation, removing ambiguity, eliminating excess words, and improving the logic and flow of ideas. We discuss revising in Chapter 4. **Always leave time to revise your work**. You may be fortunate to be studying at an institution with a writing center whose staff will offer constructive feedback on the draft of an essay or term paper before you submit it to your instructor. We strongly suggest that you avail yourself of such a service. You should also **leave time to edit your work** (i.e., to check for spelling, grammatical, and typing errors). We discuss editing in detail in Chapter 5.

## CHECKLIST FOR WRITING ESSAYS AND REVIEW PAPERS

❑   The opening paragraph indicates the specific direction that the paper will take, and it articulates a clear thesis statement that drives the rest of the paper.

❑   All statements of fact and opinion are supported by references or examples.

❑   In place of summary and simple reportage of research findings, the essay provides a clear explanation of how the results support the hypotheses.

❑   The final paragraph introduces no new information, but summarizes the thesis.

❑   The title is accurate, concise, and informative.

## THE PLAGIARISM CHALLENGE

Even when you have taken care to distinguish your words and thoughts from those of your sources and to record all the detail necessary for citation accurately, you may occasionally find yourself unsure about what the boundaries are and what would be viewed as dishonest. Read each of the following scenarios and decide whether you think it represents plagiarism or ethical academic practice. Enter **Yes** if you think the actions described represent plagiarism. After you have completed the challenge, see Answer Key (p. 255) for the correct answers and explanations.

1. Your professor has cautioned you against having too many quotations in your paper. In order to minimize the amount of text quoted, you place quotation marks around some, but not all, of the text you copied directly from a source. You are careful to cite the source at the end of the paragraph and provide full bibliographic detail on your references page. *Is this plagiarism?*

2. You are writing an original research proposal on transmembrane signal transduction. The department seminar program features a speaker on the topic who says that the availability of two-dimensional Fourier-transform NMR spectroscopy has revolutionized chemists' ability to determine not only the structure of complex biomolecules but also the conformational changes that occur when a ligand is bound. You jot this down in your notes and use it in the introduction to your proposal. As you didn't take it from a written source, and as you could have come up with this summary statement yourself, you don't cite a source. *Is this plagiarism?*

3. You are taking the class on "Spectroscopic Identification of Organic Compounds" and have been assigned a homework exercise that will count toward your overall grade involving writing about the applications of mass spectrometry. Since you already wrote a paper on mass spectrometry for your "Instrumental Analysis" class last semester, you save yourself some time by submitting this same paper. You wrote both papers entirely on your own. *Is this plagiarism?*

4. You have been given a take-home examination in your "Environmental Chemistry" class that has four meaty questions, and you have only 48 hours to complete it. You know you can do a better job if you focus all your time and energy on just one of these tough questions, so you and three other students decide to split the questions up and each answer only one question. You are, of course, careful to ensure that the work is split evenly among the group and that each person does a fair amount of the work. Then you all share your answers with one another. *Is this plagiarism?*

5. You are writing a research proposal for your "Writing in Chemistry" class, and over Thanksgiving dinner your Uncle Jack, who lives in Cincinnati and works for a well-known chemical company, tells you about some of the products his company

would like to develop. He is a fount of useful information about the importance of surface chemistry and micellar media, so you make a few notes on your laptop the following day. You then develop a research proposal based on his description of the development of a new product, but don't cite your uncle as the source of some of your information. You could, you argue, quite easily have come up with the ideas yourself. *Is this plagiarism?*

6. As part of your "Writing in Chemistry" class, you are expected to write an original research proposal (most graduate programs in chemistry have this requirement as well). You find an article about using Coca Cola to extract nutrients as a way of assessing soil status, and you develop a proposal based on using several other widely available household products, whose chemical composition is also quite well controlled, to extract nutrients from soils. You cite several sources to establish the reliability of the chemical composition of the particular household products you include in your proposal, but don't cite the Coca Cola article since that soft drink is not one of the household products you propose to use. *Is this plagiarism?*

7. In your ecology course, you are given an assignment to write about the importance of wetlands in remediating contaminated surface water. Since you have been involved every summer since you started middle school in a number of wetlands projects in your hometown, you are already so knowledgeable about your topic that you find it unnecessary to do any library research and you do not cite any sources. *Is this plagiarism?*

8. You are a second-year graduate student preparing the written portion of your qualifying exam. You're pressed for time so you incorporate some sentences and paragraphs from several published papers. Although you do not place these passages in quotation marks, you are careful to suggest the sources by statements like "(see reference 3 for more details)." *Is this plagiarism?*

9. Your professor reads a draft of your paper on climate change and says you have a sound argument, but you need to support it with more facts and statistics. You don't have time to find the necessary additional material statistics, but you are able to invent some that you are sincerely confident are "in the ball-park" and could be corroborated if you had the time to do it.

You cite them as if they came from the sources you have already cited. *Is this plagiarism?*

10. You are writing a review on nickel-containing enzymes for your "Metals in Biology" course. You perform a Web of Science search and create a Word file that contains the abstracts of the journal articles as well as the bibliographic information (authors, title, journal name, year of publication, volume, and page numbers). You then create your own text by copying and pasting from this file, with suitable adjustments to the verb tenses and any inconsistencies in nomenclature. You are careful to identify the authors by name and to include a reference to each paper that you describe. *Is this plagiarism?*

## THE CITING SOURCES CHALLENGE

How much do you know about handling and citing sources responsibly? Read each of the following scenarios and decide whether the actions described represent ethical and responsible academic practice. Enter **Yes** for acceptable and responsible practice or **No** for unacceptable academic practice. After you have completed the challenge, see Answer Key for the correct answers.

1. You are writing a short paper for your introductory chemistry course about the use of silver nanoparticles, whose bacteriocide properties improve clothes washing. You know a lot of factual information about silver from an excellent high school AP course, but you no longer have the textbook you used, so you don't cite any source. *Is this acceptable practice?*

2. The assignment specifies that you make use of at least five sources in your paper. You locate five different sources that seem promising, but after you have read them you realize only one of them is really relevant and helpful. You are careful to list all five sources in the references but, even though all the information comes from a single source, you make it appear that the information comes from all five sources in order to satisfy the requirements specified by your professor. *Is this acceptable practice?*

3. You read *Newsweek* magazine every week and notice that the magazine writers never cite their sources. You make considerable use of an article about current issues related to renewable

energy sources for a paper for your first-year seminar course on Chemistry and Society. Since the magazine writers do not cite their sources, you quote them without feeling obliged to cite your sources either. *Is this acceptable practice?*

4.  You are writing the introduction for a paper on the role of trace elements in biological systems. You find from a government source (Office of Dietary Supplement Information, part of the National Institutes of Health) that the recommended adult dietary allowance (RDA) of vitamin B12, which contains cobalt, is 2.4 µg per day. Since tables of RDA values are in the public domain, you don't cite the source. *Is this acceptable practice?*

5.  For a term paper in your Environmental Chemistry course, you do most of your research on-line and find many interesting Web sites from which you quote several useful passages. Since Web sites are in the public domain and constitute common knowledge, you don't cite them. *Is this acceptable practice?*

6.  You are writing a paper on arsenic pollution and because you know that arsenic is toxic and has no beneficial function, you state this without citing a source to back up your assertion. *Is this acceptable practice?*

7.  In doing the research for a chemistry paper on plasma spectroscopy, you come across reference to something called the "Stark effect." The term is new to you. However, since none of the six articles you have read that refer to this effect cite a source defining the effect, you don't cite a source either. *Is this acceptable practice?*

8.  In doing the research for a paper on separation of chiral compounds, you come across repeated reference to "Pirkle phases." This term is new to you and it has never been discussed in class, but you have encountered references to it in several articles. You notice that each author actually cites an original article by Pirkle, the chemist for whom it was named, but since you are just a student you don't cite that article. *Is this acceptable practice?*

9.  You are a first-year graduate student applying to the National Science Foundation for a predoctoral fellowship. In the summer of your junior year, you worked in a lab on a project that was later carried on successfully by others, and you are certain that a manuscript will be prepared for publication by the end of the fall

semester. Since the submission deadline for the fellowship is November 1, you make up a plausible title and are careful to list all those who worked on the project as authors and list this in your resume as a "submitted" paper. *Is this acceptable practice?*

10. You are starting an independent study project for your senior capstone experience, and your adviser suggests that you read the introduction to a recent Ph.D. dissertation written by a student in her group as part of your initial work in becoming familiar with what has been done previously. You download a pdf file from the library and are delighted to find that the first chapter is just what you need for your own background paper that is due in a few weeks. You copy and paste material from the dissertation, carefully citing the references, but because you think a Ph.D. dissertation is not a peer-reviewed publication, you don't include a reference to the dissertation in your background paper. *Is this acceptable practice?*

# 10

# WRITING RESEARCH REPORTS

## THE NATURE OF SCIENTIFIC RESEARCH

Many undergraduate chemistry programs include an "independent study" or research experience in which you work on a project for an extended period of time and then write a report. Such an experience is considered an important part of your education and training, because it gives you an insight into how science is done. We strongly suggest that you seek out multiple research experiences as part of your undergraduate degree program. You should start as early as you can and think of the summers as opportunities to get research experiences, possibly at other institutions. There are many summer research experiences for undergraduates (REU) programs around the country that will pay you a stipend as well as cover the costs of food, housing, and transportation. No matter whether you intend to go to graduate school, to work in industry, or to enter a career not primarily related to chemistry, you will find that research experience is extremely helpful. Solving problems, while working in a team of diverse individuals, is what most of us with scientific education and training do during our careers because, broadly speaking, most jobs can be described in this way.

Research is carried out by scientists working in industry, government labs, and universities and colleges. Typically these organizations have a large number of research groups whose members collaborate. In some areas of science, such as astronomy or particle physics, research groups may be very large with many tens or even hundreds of members. In other sciences, groups may be relatively small with fewer than ten members.

Research groups in chemistry in universities and colleges typically comprise a faculty member as the leader and students (both graduates and undergraduates), postdoctoral research workers, and technicians. Group size varies from just one professor and one undergraduate to much larger groups with more than twenty members and maybe several collaborators at other institutions. Research group membership is dynamic: new members join, older members move on, and students graduate. When you first join a group, you will learn about the background to the problem being studied (big picture), the hypotheses to be tested, the plan of action (experimental design), and the techniques to be used. You may be taught how to find out what is already known (i.e., how to use the library resources available on your campus), and you will discover what is expected of you in terms of communication of your findings both orally and in writing, the topic of this chapter. Because participation in a research group as an undergraduate extends over a significant period of time, it affords students many rewarding and invaluable opportunities. These include the following:

- Becoming familiar with the relevant big picture, detailed background, and previous work done.
- Conducting a series of experiments in which the results of the earlier ones will inform the designs of later experiments.
- Drawing conclusions, summarizing the findings, and making suggestions for further work.
- Creating a written document containing the material of interest to the broader community.

Other advantages of joining a research team include the following:

- Working alongside more experienced, more knowledgeable workers from whom you can obtain guidance and information as needed.
- Participating in an active community of scholars, who regularly come together to discuss their interests and findings and to examine critically relevant new knowledge.
- Taking some responsibility for the design and implementation of the experiments and having some say about the direction of the work.

In addition to writing your laboratory notebook, which will remain with the research group after you have finished, you will be expected to write a report of your work. This report may be used, in part, by your instructor/adviser in awarding a grade. Even if you are not taking an independent study course, for which you will receive academic credit, the research group leader will want a record of what you have done (and found) in a format that is more readily accessible than a 100-page notebook. Usually you will be asked to create a report in the form of a journal article since, after all, this is how research findings are communicated to the broader community of scientists. Even if you are planning to write a longer document, such as a senior thesis, it is likely that it will be constructed in the same way as the journal article report. Each of the major sections (Introduction, Experimental, Results, Discussion, Conclusions, and Suggestions for Further Work) may be a separate chapter in such a thesis. Your institution will have guidelines (maybe even rules), and your instructor/adviser will be able to show you examples produced by other students.

Attention to detail is essential to writing well about chemistry in general; this is particularly important when writing about the results of your experimental work. You should pay particular attention to being consistent in situations in which there are several possible choices of units or symbols or formatting. For example, if you start with "M" for molar, do not switch to "mol $L^{-1}$" partway through. If you use superscript numbers to indicate your cited references, do not later use numbers in brackets or parentheses.

Much of what we have written about the laboratory report also applies to the research report, and you should read the relevant sections of Chapter 7 in conjunction with what we say in this chapter about each of the sections of a report.

## COMPONENTS OF A RESEARCH REPORT

The contents of most scientific research reports, regardless of the field, parallel the method of scientific reasoning: the problem is defined, a hypothesis is created, experiments are devised to test the hypothesis, those experiments are conducted, results are recorded and evaluated, and conclusions are drawn. A research report is typically divided into ten sections.

**1. Title:** In the title, you try to distill the essence of the contents of your report. It should include essential key words; however, it should be short (10 to 20 words).

**2. Authors:** The authors' names should follow the title on a separate line, followed by the addresses of the authors' workplaces (affiliations), and the date.

**3. Abstract:** In the abstract, you summarize your approach to the problem, the major findings (together with relevant quantitative information), and the conclusions of your study. This is probably the most difficult part of the report to write well; save it for last. The abstract should be all one paragraph and between 200 and 500 words. You should ensure that the abstract contains more information than the reader could deduce from the title of the paper. For example, consider the following report title:

> Determination of arsenic in soil by flow injection hydride generation electrothermal atomization atomic-absorption spectrometry: evaluation of sample pretreatment by accelerated solvent extraction and supercritical fluid extraction

Now compare the information communicated in the title with the information communicated in this abstract:

> Following optimization of the instrument operating conditions for which the figure of merit was the sensitivity, the two different extraction systems were compared. A systematic evaluation of the relevant operating parameters (time, temperature, pressure, and the nature of the solvent) was made, and the percentage recoveries from a number of soil samples (including some standard reference soils) were measured. Differences in recoveries were tested for significance by appropriate statistical procedures. The effect of the nature of the arsenic species was also studied.

The reader is not really any better informed by the abstract than the title. A moment's thought after reading the title would lead the reader to deduce that any sensible study with this title must have involved the work described in the abstract. **The abstract should contain the results of the experimental work.** The values of the operating parameters should be given together with the composition of the solvent, the numbers of samples, the identity of the standard reference materials, and the values for the percent recoveries. It should not be necessary for the reader to look in the paper to find important results or any novel features of the experimental work, and it should be quite clear what instrumentation or instrumental techniques were used, though the convention is that you would *not* give the make and model of the instrument in the abstract (or in the title for that matter).

**4. Introduction:** The introduction sets the scene for why the study was undertaken. Typically you will start with the "big picture" and then describe a "small picture" (i.e., the area in which you have been working).

You would summarize the relationship between the current project and the scope and limitations of earlier work, as well as any conflicts among the previously published results, so that the reasons for the project and the approach can be understood. The last paragraph of the introduction should tell the reader what is new.

**5. Experimental Details:** In this section, you describe what you did: an account of the experiments that you have recorded in your lab notebook. Depending on the nature of the work and the particular journal format, you may subdivide this section into several subsections with headings such as "Instrumentation," "Reagents," "Procedures," "Method Development," and "Method Validation." In reports of theoretical work, this section would include sufficient mathematical analysis to enable derivations and numerical results to be checked, and you would outline any new software and cite software from the public domain that was used. You should provide sufficient details so that other researchers, familiar with the area, could repeat your work. If the chemicals you worked with are not routinely available from several suppliers, you should provide information about the sources of chemicals (manufacturer's name and location). If there is only one commercial source, you should provide the number of the batch with which you worked. You should provide details of the instruments (manufacturer and model number) and software (name and version number) that you used.

**6. Results:** In this section you report the major findings of the study, presenting the data or summarizing your findings using equations, figures, and tables. Schemes to show reaction sequences may be presented here. You would avoid interpretation of the results in this section (note, however, that in published journal articles, this section is often combined with the discussion section).

**7. Discussion:** This section, the centerpiece of your report, features the analysis and interpretation of the results. What do the results mean? How do they relate to the objectives of the experiments? This section should also include a discussion of random and systematic errors. If your results contain substantial quantitative data derived from measurement with chemical instruments, you should establish ± terms for relevant numbers in accordance with accepted statistical practices (such as calculating 95% confidence intervals). You would discuss whether your results support or argue against the hypotheses presented in your introduction. If this involved a comparison of numerical values, you would present the results of appropriate significance tests.

You would avoid writing statements containing subjective evaluations. For example,

 There is excellent agreement between the concentration of the selenomethionine found by the new method and that given in the certificate for the standard reference wheat flour.

Rather you would write statements along the lines of the following:

 As the 95% confidence interval about the value found for the selenomethionine content of the reference wheat flour included the certificate value, we concluded that there was no significant difference between the value found and the certified value, and that our new method was accurate.

**8. Conclusions, Summary, and Suggestions for Further Work:** This section may not be necessary if the outcome of the discussion of results is that a conclusion is drawn and the conclusions have already appeared earlier. However, if a number of conclusions have been drawn, it is useful for the reader to be able to find them all collected together, and if the report is lengthy, or is one in which the findings are unusually complex, it is useful to include a paragraph summarizing the objectives and the findings, as well as the conclusions. This section is also the place to make suggestions for additional experiments, which may be an important feature of your report, even though it appears almost right at the end. This is where you can show that you can think "like a chemist." If your report is being evaluated for grading purposes, this section could make the difference between an "A" and an "A minus."

**9. Acknowledgments:** Whether you include such a section depends on the type of report. In a report that models a journal article, you might well include an acknowledgment of help from other members of your group, an instrument technician, or another faculty member. You might acknowledge the source of the money used to conduct your research (normally referred to as "financial support"), especially if this came from some external granting agency, such as the National Science Foundation, or from a former student of your department who has given money to support summer research by undergraduates. Acknowledgments in a thesis or dissertation may be placed near the front of the document, typically following the title page.

**10. References:** This section includes the relevant details of all sources, including textbooks, laboratory handouts, and Web sites, that you have cited in your report. They will be presented in the format appropriate for the particular report. Often the format is that of a designated journal. More information on how to format references is given in Chapter 3.

## LONGER REPORTS

A report of an extended piece of work, such as a senior or honors thesis, might also have a table of contents in which the major section headings and subheadings are listed, together with the page number on which they start. Sometimes separate lists of tables and their page numbers and figures and their page numbers are required as well. These lists would typically appear near the front of the document, often between the Abstract and the Introduction. The Acknowledgments section also customarily appears near the front.

## PUBLICATION OF RESEARCH RESULTS

Work not published is work not done, at least as far as advancing your particular area of science is concerned. However, it is unlikely that as an undergraduate or even as a graduate student you will be solely responsible for the creation and submission of a manuscript describing your research findings. Usually the faculty member in whose lab you have been working will submit the manuscript, but it is quite likely that material in your report will be included. You need to bear this is mind when writing your report (and keeping your lab notebook).

In addition to communicating new knowledge to the broader community, publications play an important part in the career development of scientists, especially those who work in universities and colleges. The terms of employment at many of these institutions stipulate that the faculty will engage in scholarly activities to the advancement of their discipline, and that continued employment, promotion, merit raises, and awards are directly linked to research productivity. Two indicators of research productivity are the number and impact of a faculty member's publications. Many institutions also look at publications for evidence that faculty members are meeting some of the educational goals of the institution: the senior administrators expect that undergraduate students will be listed as coauthors.

You should also be aware that publications are extremely effective in building your own résumé. Your application to graduate school, for a

National Science Foundation Fellowship, or for employment is much more impressive if you can show that your contributions to a research group have been included in a published article (or an article about to be published, or even a manuscript that has been submitted for consideration for publication). Of course, if it takes the contribution of several undergraduate researchers before sufficient work warrants creating a report of the work for publication, it may be several months, or more than a year, before your adviser incorporates your particular contribution into a larger document. At that time, there should be no difficulty in understanding your report (or the entries in your lab notebook); otherwise, your work may not be included. In this case, your name will not be included in the list of authors, and you will have lost out on an opportunity to give an important boost to your résumé. You will still be able to list your participation in the independent study experience, but you will not be able to demonstrate the high quality of participation that comes from listing the work as published or "in press."

Even though you will not be solely responsible for the creation and submission of a manuscript for publication, you should understand the process to which you are contributing. When your adviser considers that a sufficient body of work has been done, with new information that is of interest to the broader community, he or she will write a report in the exact format required by the particular journal. This manuscript (as the document is still known, even though it may be entirely in electronic form) is sent to the editor of the journal. If you look at the front pages of an issue of a journal, you will find a list of people who are involved in the production of the journal issues. In addition to the names of the support staff working for the publisher, it is likely that the names of the editor and the members of the editorial advisory board will be listed, all of whom will be well-known scientists in the discipline. The job of the editor is not to edit the report, in the sense of making changes to the text before the material appears in a particular issue of the journal, but to decide if the contents of the report (i.e., the new science) are of sufficient novelty to warrant publication. To do this, he or she will send the report to two or more scientists (known as referees or reviewers) who are knowledgeable about the particular topic of the report with a request that they evaluate the suitability of the report for publication and write a report. These reports are returned to the editor, who first reviews them, and then communicates the result of the review process to the person who submitted the original document. The result can range from "congratulations, your report is accepted for publication" to "sorry, the work is not sufficiently novel, the experimental design is flawed, and the interpretation of the results is incorrect." Some criticisms can be addressed, and the report can be revised in the light of the comments made by the reviewers. The revised version is sent back and is usually accepted after further review by the editor (or by the reviewers, depending on the extent of the revisions).

## PREPARING A MANUSCRIPT AS THOUGH FOR PUBLICATION

If you are asked to prepare a report of your research in the form of a journal article, your first step is to visit the Web site of the particular journal. There you will find the "Instructions for Authors," and you may be able to download a template that will help you with the format of the entire document, including the figures and tables. It also helps to study similar papers published in recent issues of the targeted journal. How are references cited in the text? How are they listed in the references section? Does the journal permit (or require) subheadings in the Experimental or Results sections? Many journals these days are slightly lax in enforcing uniformity, especially in the way in which figures are presented. The practice now is to print whatever the researchers have provided (at one time, the editorial staff redrew the figures). Thus you may notice that the formatting adopted in one article is not followed in another article in the same issue of a journal. There are sometimes inconsistencies in capitalization: some journals don't insist on an upper case " L" for "liter" and also allow lower case "l." Your goal should be to be consistent in your usage and formatting throughout. If you fail to do so, or fail to follow the relevant instructions, your report may be downgraded by your instructor, which is equivalent to adverse criticism by the editor and reviewers. In extreme cases of failing to follow the journal format, a manuscript may be returned without review.

If you do not incorporate the tables and figures in the body of the text, put them (in numerical order) after the Acknowledgments and References sections. Precede the collections of figures and tables with a page containing a list of figure captions (in numerical order, with multiple captions per page), and finally, include the figures themselves, with the authors' names and the figure designations (e.g., "Tyson et al., Fig. 2") at the bottom of the page. The tables, also in numerical order but with their titles, should follow the figures. It is not necessary to include a separate page of table titles as you have done with the figure captions.

# CHECKLIST FOR A RESEARCH REPORT

### Title
- ❏ Gives a specific indication of what the study is about.
- ❏ Consists of no more than 20 words.

### Abstract
- ❏ Summarizes the background in one or two sentences.
- ❏ Clearly states the specific question addressed and the specific hypotheses tested.
- ❏ Summarizes methods in no more than three or four sentences.
- ❏ Reports major findings in no more than two or three sentences.
- ❏ Concludes with a statement that relates to the specific question addressed.
- ❏ Consists of a single paragraph of 200 to 500 words.

### Introduction
- ❏ Offers a clear statement of specific question or issue addressed.
- ❏ Articulates clearly and logically why the question or issue was addressed.
- ❏ Provides the specific hypotheses, if appropriate, and a rationale for expectations.
- ❏ Includes references to support all statements of fact or opinion.
- ❏ Progresses smoothly from big picture to small picture to what is new.
- ❏ Describes what is new in the concluding paragraph.

### Experimental
- ❏ Is written in the past tense.
- ❏ Provides clear and complete design of study or experiment.
- ❏ Includes details of chemicals, instruments, and software.
- ❏ Indicates clearly the rationale for each step.
- ❏ Mentions all factors likely to have influenced the outcome.
- ❏ Includes a brief description of how data were analyzed (calculations made, statistical tests used).

## Results

❏ Summarizes important findings in the data; does not simply repeat raw data.

❏ Presents results in the past tense and in active voice whenever possible.

❏ Reports major results without discussing their implications (which should be in the Discussion).

❏ Includes only tables or figures that make important contributions to the report.

❏ Provides informative, correctly placed headings (tables) and captions (figures).

❏ Numbers tables and figures in the order to which they are first referred in the text.

## Discussion

❏ Clearly relates data to the expectations and hypotheses raised in the Introduction.

❏ Carefully distinguishes facts from speculation.

❏ Discusses unusual or unexpected findings logically, based on chemistry.

❏ Supports all statements of fact or opinion with references to literature, data, and examples.

❏ Describes further studies, or ways that the present study could be modified in the future.

## Acknowledgments

❏ Notes first and last names, and specific contributions for all those acknowledged.

## References

❏ Is formatted according to the style of the particular journal.

❏ Provides citations in correct format for every reference included in the report.

❏ Avoids any references that are not explicitly cited in the report.

❏ Includes names of authors, title, year of publication, and page numbers in each citation.

## General Format

- ❑ Contains numbered pages and text that is double-spaced.
- ❑ Shows the name of authors and date submitted on the first page.
- ❑ Presents all information in the appropriate section of the report (no experimental details appear in the Results).
- ❑ Statistical significance tests are applied where relevant.

# 11

# WRITING RESEARCH PROPOSALS

## THE RESEARCH PROPOSAL: AN EXERCISE IN PERSUASION

Research proposals are sometimes assigned in advanced chemistry classes in place of the more standard review paper or "term paper." These assignments have much in common, **and you should read, or reread, Chapter 9 before proceeding with this chapter**. Research proposals, essays, and review papers all require evaluation and synthesis of the primary literature—that is, papers presenting original research results rather than articles and books that only summarize and interpret those results. In addition, a research proposal includes a written argument in which you propose to go beyond what you have read; you propose to address a new research question and seek to convince readers that what you propose to do should be done, can be done, and should, in fact, be done in exactly the way you propose it. The comments that we have made previously about plagiarism and responsible handling of sources with appropriate citations also apply to the writing of research proposals. However, as we will mention later, it is acceptable in a research proposal to include direct quotations (plus citation) from other scientists' writings in making a case for the need for the work you are proposing.

Proposals are written to obtain the money and other resources needed to conduct the proposed research, and so they are often called "grant applications." Because more proposals are submitted to any agency or foundation than can be funded, your proposal must not only present a clear and detailed description of a useful contribution to science, it must also present a compelling, persuasive argument. At the National Science Foundation (NSF), for example, typically only 10 to 20 percent of proposals are funded. In this chapter, we explain how to make an effective argument in order to write a successful proposal.

Writing research proposals is part of the job of all scientists, not just chemists. Even scientists in industry will write to persuade others in the organization that funds should be expended on a new project or to sustain an existing one. School teachers are also able to obtain funds for special projects from a large number of funding agencies, provided that they can write convincing proposals. The writing of proposals, which features quite prominently in most graduate programs, can even be a way for you to obtain funding that will give you considerable independence as a graduate student.

The NSF has a fellowship program to which you can apply in the fall of your senior year as an undergraduate and in the first year of a graduate program. You are not expected to be an expert in research at this stage of your career, but you are expected to be able to write persuasively about your ideas for a research project.

Even if you never apply for a grant, research proposals are excellent vehicles for developing your reasoning and writing skills. This assignment, more than any other, gives you a chance to be creative and to participate in the process of scientific investigation. Writing a good research proposal is difficult, which is one of the reasons your instructor is giving you a chance to practice; however, as with other creative work, the sense of accomplishment you feel once you are finished is very satisfying.

Research proposals have a number of components, but there are two major parts:

**1. A review of the relevant scientific literature.**
**2. A description of the proposed research.**

In the first part, you review the primary literature on a particular topic, but you do so with a particular goal in mind: **you want to lead your reader to the inescapable conclusion that the scientific question you propose to answer follows logically from the research that has gone before.** Writing a research proposal, rather than a review paper, thus helps you avoid falling into the "book report" trap. After you have developed a research question to ask, you should have an easier time focusing your literature review on the development of a single, clearly articulated theme. Developing that theme will take some time and thought, but your writing will then have a clear direction.

In addition to providing you with a convenient vehicle for exploring and digesting the primary scientific literature and focusing your discussion of that literature, you may find that the research you propose to do can actually be done—and can be done by you. Your proposal could turn out to be the basis for a summer research project, a senior thesis, or even a master's thesis or Ph.D. dissertation.

As in other pieces of writing, you need to bear in mind the needs of your audience. Most granting agencies operate what is known as the "peer review" system. Proposals are sent to reviewers—members of the proposer's scientific community—who evaluate the proposal against a list of specific criteria and write a report. The reports are sent to program officers within the agency who coordinate the responses from the reviewers. In some programs, the reviewers may meet together as a committee to discuss the proposals further. Typically, each reviewer will also assign a one-word description to the proposal: excellent, very good, good, fair, or poor. If a committee reviews the proposal, the committee will write a report and make a recommendation as to whether the proposal should be funded. The program officers then review all the evidence and make decisions as to which proposals will be funded. In evaluating your research proposal, your instructor is acting as a one-person panel of reviewers.

## WHAT ARE REVIEWERS LOOKING FOR?

Imagine that you have agreed to read from 10 to 15 research proposals and recommend 2 or 3 for funding. Without funding, the proposed research can't be done, so your decisions are important. How would you make them? Here are some of the things reviewers—and instructors—look for in evaluating a proposal:

1. Does the applicant thoroughly understand the relevant literature?
2. Is the applicant asking good, interesting questions?
3. Do the questions follow logically from what is already known about the topic?
4. Are there specific hypotheses to be tested?
5. Can the hypotheses be tested?
6. Can the hypotheses be tested successfully with the methods proposed?
7. Are potential problems anticipated? If so, does the researcher have plans for dealing with them?
8. Is the proposer an appropriate person to carry out the work?
9. Does the work fall within the designated mission of the funding program?

Much like prospective employers reviewing job applications (see Chapter 14), reviewers of grant applications are looking for reasons *not* to fund the proposals they are reading as least as much as they are looking for reasons to fund them. If your writing is not clear, knowledgeable, focused, logical, and careful, why would reviewers think that you would be clear, knowledgeable, focused, logical, and careful in your research?

## RESEARCHING YOUR TOPIC: HOW TO CHOOSE AND READ PAPERS

Usually the first time you are asked to write a proposal, you will get a lot of help from your instructor or faculty adviser. Deciding on a topic for a proposal is difficult, but your instructor will probably provide some guidelines, or a framework, within which to operate and may even have a list of suggestions or ideas for you to consider. You may be directed to investigate the research of a particular faculty member at your institution or elsewhere, or, if you are already working in a research group, you may be asked to propose the next stages of the work in which you are already involved. This is a realistic scenario, because most reviewers will want to see the results of some preliminary work in a proposal.

Our advice is to proceed as you would for researching a term paper or essay. For this assignment especially, you must have a firm grasp of your subject before plunging into the primary scientific literature. so **read a recent review before you look elsewhere and then examine carefully any cited papers that look especially useful or intriguing**. You might then browse through recent issues of appropriate scientific journals, looking for relevant recent findings; your instructor can suggest journals that are particularly relevant to your topic of interest. Scientific databases, such as Web of Science, are extremely useful in finding potentially relevant articles quickly. As soon as you have selected a new journal article to read—probably on the basis of the title—read the abstract carefully. Look up any terms you don't understand before continuing. Look at the end of the Introduction section to discover what the researchers state as the problem of interest, and look especially carefully at the end of the Results and Discussion section or any Conclusions section for statements about unresolved issues and suggestions for further work that is needed.

For example, if your proposal is about a new portable technique for determining arsenic concentrations in the field, you would want to include a recent review article by Dan Melamed[1] in which he wrote, "Accurate, fast measurement of arsenic in the field remains a technical challenge. Technological advances in a variety of instruments have met with varying success. However, the central goal of developing field assays that reliably and reproducibly quantify arsenic has not been achieved."

Before you roll up your sleeves and prepare to wrestle in earnest with a published scientific paper, read it through once for general orientation. When you begin your second reading of the paper, don't allow yourself to skip over any sentences or paragraphs you don't understand. Keep a relevant textbook by your side as you read the primary literature so that you can look up unfamiliar facts and terminology. The goal of your reading is to be able to decide what might be the next logical step(s) in this line of research, or what question should be asked, and how this question might be addressed. We discuss reading papers and taking notes in more detail in Chapter 2.

In addition to the sections mentioned earlier, you should look critically at the methodology reported in the paper. In many areas of chemistry, several research groups are trying to achieve the same goal, and it is quite possible that their published results do not agree. Thus a possible research topic would be to resolve such conflicts through a deeper understanding of the relevant underlying chemical processes. Advances in measurement capabilities can also change the picture. For example, in their article "Selenium metabolites in urine: a critical overview of past work and current status," Francesconi and Pannier[2] write, "This area of research has an untidy past, and perusal of the literature over the last 35 years presents an unclear picture of the important selenium species. Many of the problems arise from loose analytical chemistry and poor interpretation of the ensuing results." These two sentences clearly indicate that some further work is in order, and thus this paper is a good one to cite in the first part of a proposal on this topic.

Electronic resources are particularly useful in determining how many papers have been published on a particular topic in recent years and who the major research groups might be. You can then show that you are aware of the activity, even though you won't have read all of the papers on a particular topic. For example, you might write, "Although the first publication describing a sensor based on nanoparticles appeared in

---

[1]Melamed, D. Monitoring arsenic in the environment: a review of science and technologies with the potential for field measurements. *Anal. Chim. Acta,* **2005**, *532*, 1–13.

[2]Francesconi, K. A.; Pannier F. Selenium metabolites in urine: a critical overview of past work and current status. *Clin. Chem.* **2004**, *50*, 2240–2253.

1999,[2] the growing interest in the topic was not evident until 2003, when 7 papers were published. In 2005, 23 papers were published in which work by 21 different research groups was described."

You will recognize that you have completed the library component for your proposal when:

1. **You can articulate your research question.**
2. **You have a sound grasp of why you are asking the question.**
3. **You are confident you know what has been done already.**

## WHAT MAKES A GOOD RESEARCH TOPIC?

You should have some "big picture" topic in mind. This does not necessarily have to be related to some pressing humanitarian problem. It is quite acceptable to propose research that will lead to a greater understanding of the underlying chemical processes. You need not propose to cure or even prevent any particular disease, rid the world of hunger or parasites, or single-handedly solve any other major problem. Rather, your goal is to pose a specific question that follows in some logical way from what has already been published in your area of interest, that can be addressed by available techniques and approaches, and that can be accomplished in a reasonable amount of time. Reaching such a goal can be a bit tricky. On the one hand, you might ask a perfectly valid question but not be able to come up with a way to address it convincingly. On the other hand, you may pose an addressable question that is difficult to justify. A question such as "Does music influence the rate of chemical reactions?" can certainly be addressed, but you will have great difficulty convincing reviewers that the question is worthwhile, because it has no foundation in the scientific literature. **What you propose to do must not only be doable; it must seem like the next logical question to ask in the area in which you are proposing to work**, based on previously published research.

The trick to asking a good question is to write down lots and lots of questions as you read and think about the topic. As Einstein is supposed to have said, "The way to have a good idea is to have lots of ideas." Many of the questions you come up with won't lead anywhere that interests you, but eventually you will come up with something that fills the bill. The question you propose must also be within your realm of expertise. You cannot write a convincing proposal on a topic that you do not fully understand.

## WRITING THE PROPOSAL

All funding agencies have rules that they strictly enforce about the length and format of the various parts of a proposal. If you break the rules, they won't review your proposal. Consequently, any exercise in which you are asked to write a research proposal will be accompanied by fairly detailed instructions about the number of words, font size, margins, and page length. You must not exceed these limitations, but you should not fall noticeably short either, because this gives the impression that you don't have enough substance to your proposal. As you will discover when you write your first proposal for submission to a granting agency, keeping within the boundaries set can be a problem.

Let us imagine that your instructor has described your research proposal exercise as follows. The total length should not exceed five double-spaced pages (not counting figures). There should be three narrative sections: Introduction (one paragraph), Significance and Background (one–two pages), and Research Design (three–four pages). References should be collected at the end in a separate section and should adhere to full ACS format; that is, you must include the article's title.

You must make some decisions immediately, because these rules are not sufficient for you to decide how many words you can write. The best course of action is to ask for clarification, but in the absence of any further information, you should adopt one-inch margins all the way round and use a 12-point font that is typical of science documents, such as Ariel, Times, or Times New Roman.

In general, there will be three main parts to your proposal: Introduction, Background, and Proposed Research. Most funding agencies will require a separate summary section and will sometimes give quite detailed instructions, such as that it must not exceed one page, it must be written in nontechnical language, and it must specifically address the intellectual merit and broader impact of the proposed work.

### Introduction

Your instructor is serving as a reviewer and, because he or she may not have an in-depth knowledge of the topic of your proposal, which is often the situation with real proposals (including the NSF graduate fellowships mentioned earlier), your introduction has to grab the reader's attention right at the start. In the Introduction, you provide a brief overview of the relevant big picture, outline the research area being considered, and describe the nature of the specific topics you will address. Here is an example:

Arsenic is widely distributed in the environment as a result of both natural processes and our use of arsenic-containing chemicals.[1] Most compounds containing arsenic are toxic, a fact which forms the basis of many of their applications, and the possible accumulation of unsafe concentrations in soils and waters is of concern.[2] Although the timber preservation industry has phased out the production of timber pressure-treated with chromated copper arsenate (CCA),[3] there is a considerable legacy with which to deal, as millions of cubic feet of this material, used to make decks, docks, fence posts, telegraph poles, and even children's playground equipment, are still distributed throughout our communities.[4]

High concentrations of arsenic have been found in soil in contact with CCA-treated wood,[5] and although it has been shown[6] that arsenic is continually removed from this material by abrasion and the action of precipitation, there is little research on the fate of the arsenic once it is in the soil. The aim of the proposed research is to investigate what happens to arsenic that is leached from CCA-treated wood. Three hypotheses will be investigated: (a) the arsenic compounds are water-soluble and are washed away by surface runoff, (b) the arsenic compounds react with components of the soil (such as iron oxides and humic acids) to form insoluble products, and (c) soil bacteria convert inorganic arsenic compounds into volatile organic compounds (such as trimethylarsine oxide) that evaporate into the atmosphere.

Notice that the author of this proposal has not used the introduction to *discuss* the question being addressed or to describe how the study will be done. The introduction provides only (1) general background to help the reader understand why the topic is of interest and (2) a brief but clear statement of the specific research topic that will be addressed. A detailed discussion of prior research belongs in the Background section of the proposal, and a detailed description of the proposed study belongs in the Proposed Research section of the proposal.

**It helps to write the last sentence, which states the specific question(s) to be addressed, of your introduction first**. Then write the rest of your introduction, giving just enough information for the reader to understand why anyone would ask such a question. Limit your introduction to two or three paragraphs, unless your instructor indicates otherwise.

Notice in the above example that **every factual statement**, such as, "Arsenic is widely distributed in the environment as a result of both natural processes and our use of arsenic-containing chemicals," **is supported by a reference** to one or more papers from the primary literature. These references enable readers to obtain additional information on particular aspects of the subject and to verify the accuracy of statements made in the proposal. Backing up statements with references also protects you, by documenting the source of information; if the author of your source is mistaken, why should you take the blame? Finally, it shows that you are well-read and knowledgeable.

## Background

In this section, you demonstrate your complete mastery of the relevant literature. Discuss this literature in detail, leading up to a specific objective of your proposed research. This section of your proposal follows the format of a good review paper or essay, as already described in Chapter 9. **In a proposal, however, the Background section will end with a brief summary statement of what is now known and what is not yet known about the topic as well as a clear, specific description of the research question(s) you propose to investigate**. In the following example, the writer has already described the importance of understanding the biogeochemical cycling of elements, the roles of arsenic and selenium in human health, the particular problems of arsenic-contaminated drinking water, the evidence that arsenic can detoxify selenium in animals, and the difficulties of measuring relevant arsenic and selenium compounds.

Ion-exchange and ion-pair, reversed-phase chromatographic methods have been widely used for separating arsenic and selenium compounds in biological materials including urine.[20–21] Arsenic species have been mostly separated by ion-exchange, while selenium species have been mostly separated by ion-pairing, reversed-phase procedures.[22] Eight arsenic compounds were separated on both anion- and cation-exchange columns.[23] Separation of anionic, cationic, and neutral selenium species was achieved on a reversed-phase column with sodium 1-butanesulfonate and tetrabutylammonium hydroxide as ion-pair reagents.[24] Only a limited number of the separation systems have been reported for the simultaneous speciation of arsenic and selenium. Orero Iserte et al. devised an anion-exchange separation on a Hamilton PRP-X100 column with a $NH_4H_2PO_4$ mobile phase[25] and applied the method to the analysis of sediment extracts. Do et al. separated ten arsenic and selenium species, mainly found in the environment and in mammals, on a reversed-phase column, with tetrabutylammonium phosphate as the counter-ion.[26] The retention time of chloride, a key interferent if ICP-MS detection were to be used, was not investigated. Le et al. achieved baseline separation of thirteen inorganic and organic arsenic and selenium species on a reversed-phase column.[27] For urine analysis the separation time was 37 min.

Thus only a limited number of procedures for the simultaneous determination of arsenic and selenium compounds have been developed, some of which are lengthy and require elevated temperatures. In the proposed study I will develop an ion-pair, reversed-phase, HPLC procedure with ICP-MS detection for the simultaneous determination of six arsenic species, AsC, AsB, DMA, MMA, AsIII, AsV, and six selenium species, TMSe, SeCys, Se(IV), SeUr, SeMet, and SeEt, in human urine. The procedure will have a target separation time of 10 min, which will include chromatographic separation of the chloride interference. The method will be used in a study of possible interactions between arsenic and selenium metabolism as evidenced by urinary temporal profiles of compounds containing these elements following ingestion of arsenic-containing seafood and/or a selenium supplement.

Notice that by the end of the second paragraph in this example, the author has already indicated what topics the proposal addresses and what work will be done. This section of your proposal has the potential to lead a double life: it can later serve as the basis for the Introduction and Discussion sections of a thesis or research article. In fact, **the Introduction section of any well-written, published research paper can serve as a model for what you are trying to accomplish in the Introduction section of your proposal. Only the verb tenses will differ.** This section of the published research paper will be written in the past tense, ending with a concise summary of what the researchers set out to accomplish and what they achieved, while your Introduction will end instead in the future tense, with a concise summary of what you *plan* to explore.

## Proposed Research

The proposed work portion has two interrelated parts:

1. What specific question(s) will you ask?
2. How will you address each of those questions?

Different instructors will put different amounts of stress on these two parts. For some of us, the formulation of a valid and logically developed question is the major purpose of the assignment, and a highly detailed description of the methods, experimental procedures, and techniques will not be required. For such an instructor, you may, for example, propose to extract and separate proteins without actually having to know in detail how this is accomplished. Other instructors may feel that your mastery of methodological detail is as important as the validity of the questions posed. Both approaches are defensible, depending largely on the nature of the field of inquiry, on the level of the course being taken, and on the amount of laboratory experience you have had. Be sure you understand what your instructor expects of you before preparing this section of your proposal.

Before you begin to write this section of your proposal, we recommend that you sketch a flowchart of your proposed study, as shown in Chapter 6 (p. 103) in the section on notebook entries. This will help organize your thinking and will also serve as a template for your writing. Often it is helpful to include such a flowchart in your proposal, making it easy both for the reader to grasp the complete experimental design and for you to write about it. Be mindful, however, of any length limitations.

As you describe each component of your proposed research, **indicate clearly what specific questions each experiment is designed to address,** as in the following two examples:

To examine the nature of the environment in the interior of the micelles, the fluorescence spectra of pyrene as the probe molecule will be obtained. The relative intensities of two peaks that are sensitive to the composition of the solvent will be compared with those obtained in solutions of known composition of pyrene in water.

The His-tagged mutant protein will be purified by affinity chromatography on a column in the nickel form. The retained protein will be eluted with a solution of Factor X cleavage buffer and isolated by anion-exchange chromatography.

**If the proposed research has several distinct components, it is helpful to separate** the components by **using subheadings**. For example, your first subheading might read "Formation of fibrils in the presence of copper," your second might read "Characterizing fibrils by size exclusion chromatography and mass spectrometry," and your third might read "Monitoring copper concentration in solution as a function of time."

Model your Proposed Research section on the relevant parts of the Experimental section of a well-written published research article. Only the verb tenses will differ. Consider these paragraphs from the Experimental section of a paper written by Rodriguez and Tyson.[3] Remember, however, that the research report is written with the benefit of hindsight, and only those experiments with a positive outcome will be reported. The full experimental section in this article contained the following subsections:

Experimental
    Reagents
    Instrumentation
    Method Development
        Column dimensions and type of resin
        Optimization
        Analytical performance
        Interference studies
        Analysis of water samples

Here is the optimization section of the method development in full:

## Optimization

The multicycle alternating variable search method[22,23] was used for the optimization of the following parameters: the borohydride concentration, the time the borohydride solution was passed through the column, the flow rate of the borohydride and carrier solution, the sample acidity and the stripping gas flow rate. The figure of merit was maximum net peak height sensitivity, though conditions that did not permit multiple injections without reloading the column were considered suboptimal. Parameters were optimized for a sample solution of 10 $\mu$g L$^{-1}$ of Sb(III) and a column size of 50 × 3.3 mm i.d. packed with Amberlite IRA-400 anion-exchange resin. The effect of the borohydride concentration and sample acidity were studied by varying these parameters within the ranges 0.1–2% m/v NaBH$_4$ in 0.05% m/v NaOH, and 0.05–4 mol L$^{-1}$ HCl. The length of time that the borohydride was passed through the column was varied from 30 to 120 s and the effect of three different concentrations of this reagent was studied. The borohydride and carrier flow rates were varied from 2.3 to 8.2 mL min$^{-1}$ and from 8.6 to 25 mL min$^{-1}$, respectively. The argon stripping gas flow rates were varied between 113 and 600 mL min$^{-1}$. Preliminary experiments with gas-liquid separators confirmed that the glass device containing beads performed satisfactorily.

[3]Rodriguez, Y.; Tyson J. F. Determination of antimony by atomic absorption spectrometry with flow injection hydride generation by a tetrahydroborate-form anion-exchanger. *J. Anal. At. Spectrom.* **2006**, *21*, 757–762.

You will see that there is much detail that would not be known until after the experiments had been conducted. You are not expected to be able to predict what these details would be. Here is the same material written as it would appear in a proposal. We have bold-faced the words that differ in tense in the two versions.

### Optimization

The multicycle alternating variable search method[22,23] **will be** used for the optimization of the following parameters: the borohydride concentration, the time the borohydride solution **passes** through the column, the flow rate of the borohydride and carrier solution, the sample acidity and the stripping gas flow rate. The figure of merit **will be** maximum net peak height sensitivity. Preliminary experiments with gas-liquid separators will identify the best device.

You'll note that the proposal version is much shorter, because, at this stage, you don't know what values of the various parameters might be realistic to investigate, nor do you know what the outcome of the preliminary experiments with the gas-liquid separators, column dimensions, or packing materials will be. In a short research proposal, you don't have the space to set out experiments in great detail, but you do need to include sufficient information to convince the reader—that is, a reviewer—that you have a plan.

You should also give some thought to the statistical evaluation of your results if this is relevant to your proposed work.

## Citing References and Preparing the References Section

Cite references directly in the text by one of the two number formats, as in the examples given earlier in this chapter. The References section of your proposal is prepared as described in Chapter 3, subject to any specific requirements of your instructor or the granting agency if you are writing a proposal that will be submitted to an external organization.

## Choosing a Title

One of your last tasks is to change the "working" title to the one that will greet the reviewer at his or her first glance at your proposal. It is worth giving some thought to this: you only get one chance to make a first impression, and it is worth making sure that this impression is as favorable as possible. It is not necessary to include the words *study of* or *investigation into* in your title; your reviewer knows that you are proposing to carry out an investigation based on experimental work. **You should refer to the big picture to which your research will contribute as well as to some feature of the specific topics you will be investigating**. One way of doing this is to break your title into two phrases separated by a colon. Look at the titles of the articles that you read in preparation for writing the Background section of your proposal and decide, as not all titles are constructed with the same care, whether you think the title is an informative, accurate representation of the article's contents. Not all journal article titles are good models for research proposal titles, because journal articles often contain descriptions of just a portion of the results from a bigger project. Here are two examples of titles: the unsuitable version is given first, followed by a more suitable revision.

 Study of the possibilities of determining cyanobacterial toxins.

 Measuring cyanobacterial toxins: determination of microcystins by matrix-assisted laser desorption ionization time of flight mass spectrometry following extraction into reverse micelles.

In the revised version, the big picture is presented first followed by a brief description of what the basis of the specific measurements will be.

 Investigations into the formation of volatile compounds of arsenic by soil bacteria acting on the arsenic leached from pressure-treated wood

 Tracking arsenic from pressure-treated wood: the role of soil bacteria in the formation of volatile arsenic compounds.

Again, notice that the big picture is presented first, followed by information about the particular feature of the big picture that will be addressed in the proposal.

Sometimes you can phrase your title as a question. For example:

 Can selenium supplements offset the toxic effects of arsenic in drinking water?

 Does copper catalyze the formation of $\beta$-2-microglobulin amyloid plaques?

## TIGHTENING THE LOGIC

Read your proposal aloud, slowly and thoughtfully, before deciding that the work is finished. If you listen while you read, you can often catch logical and typographical errors that you might otherwise miss. We think this is a good strategy with any piece of writing, since it forces you to articulate every word. Often when you read silently something you have written, you tend to skim through the text, and your brain registers what you think you wrote, not what you actually wrote.

Unlike a conversation you might have with someone about what you propose to do, a written text is not interactive. Once you have sent off the proposal or have submitted it to your instructor, there is no opportunity for additional dialogue, for the reviewer to ask whether you have thought of the role this variable might play, or how you intend to deal with this possible interference in your measurements. Therefore it is essential that you anticipate the needs of your reader, which in this case will be someone whose job it is to ask such questions about this proposed work.

In rereading your description of what you propose to do and how you propose to do it, imagine that the potential reader is skeptical, maybe even hostile; that is, **try to envision the specific objections that an interested, critical reviewer would raise**. Can you argue those objections away? Do so in your proposal if possible. If not, can you modify your approach or add additional components to the study that will address those specific objections? Perhaps you need to add additional experiments or to modify your experimental design. In some cases, you may need to modify the question that you are proposing to address.

It is part of the reviewer's job—and your instructor's—to act as a skeptical reader, to find flaws in your proposal, as well as to report on what is new and exciting about what you propose to do. Thus it is your job, as the writer, to be your own your harshest critic and anticipate and address as many shortcomings as you can before anyone else judges your work.

## A REAL RESEARCH PROPOSAL

All real research proposals contain the sections you have been asked to write (Introduction, Background and Proposed Experiments), together with additional sections relating to the results of preliminary work, details of how the money will be spent (the budget section), how students will be involved in the proposed work, what facilities are already available, and the prior accomplishments of the researchers involved. Quite often proposals are submitted by a team of researchers who are collaborating, in which case one of the researchers is designated to be the leader, known as the principal investigator or PI. The designation *PI* is also applied when only one person's name appears on the cover sheet of the proposal document.

Many granting agencies require that proposals be submitted electronically via a Web site, and PIs need to be knowledgeable about how the particular Web site functions. For example, if you create your proposal as a Microsoft Word document that contains lots of diagrams and special symbols, you need to ensure that when it is uploaded, the formatting has been retained. Granting agencies rigidly enforce deadlines. There is no flexibility or discretion; if you miss the deadline, your proposal is "dead" in the sense that you will have to resubmit it for the next deadline, which could be 6 or 12 months away. Even with electronic submission, the deadline for the PI may be several days prior to the granting agency's deadline, because the proposal may first have to be reviewed in-house for compliance with the college's or university's operating procedures. This detail of campus bureaucracy is clearly irrelevant when you are writing a proposal for a course, but beware: the world beyond college operates with deadlines and, if you are to contribute effectively, you need to develop time-management skills so that you meet them consistently.

## CHECKLIST FOR A RESEARCH PROPOSAL

(See also the checklists at the end of Chapters 4 and 5 dealing with revising and editing.)

- ❏ The title gives specific indication of the proposed work.
- ❏ The introductory statement leads to a clear statement of the specific goals and hypotheses.
- ❏ The questions posed follow logically from previous work in the area of interest.
- ❏ The logic behind all hypotheses presented is made clear.
- ❏ The final paragraphs of the Introduction and Background address the issues raised in the introductory paragraphs.
- ❏ Statements are supported by reference, data, or example.
- ❏ Proposed experiments will address the questions posed and are designed to distinguish among all alternative hypotheses.

❑   Each sentence follows from the preceding sentence and leads logically to the next.

❑   Rationales are provided for each step proposed.

❑   Plans for data analysis are clear.

❑   References are provided for every source cited.

❑   Each listing in the References includes the names of all authors, title of paper, year of publication, volume number, and page numbers, in the correct format.

❑   Work has been carefully proofread and revised according to guidelines presented in Chapters 4 and 5.

❑   Text is double-spaced.

❑   Pages are numbered.

# 12

# ANSWERING TIMED ESSAY QUESTIONS

## BASIC PRINCIPLES

Answering essay questions on examinations differs from other forms of scientific writing in only two respects: the essay examination must be completed within a short time, usually between 15 and 50 minutes, and you have little, if any, choice in the subject of the essay. In the case of the analytical writing component of the Graduate Record Exam (GRE), administered by the Educational Testing Service, you have 45 minutes for the "Issue Task" and you must choose between two specific topics. You have 30 minutes for the "Argument Task" on which you have no choice: you are presented with an argument that you are asked to critique. In both tasks, your goal is to demonstrate your ability to think critically and to develop, organize, and express your ideas clearly and concisely in Standard Written English.

Many of the guidelines given in Chapter 1 are applicable to a timed writing situation. A general guideline for getting high marks on any examination question is to **write in such a way that clearly reveals your train of thought to your instructor**. Your performance on essay questions can be strengthened by keeping in mind the principles discussed below.

**Principle 1: Answer the question asked.**  Read the question carefully before writing anything. **You must answer the question posed, not the question you would have preferred** to answer. In particular, note whether the question asks you to list, discuss, compare, or contrast. A list will not satisfy the requirements of a directive to discuss or compare. A request for a list tests to see whether you know all components of the topic; a request for discussion asks you to present arguments for and against a component, testing what you know about the subject relative to some other concept and asking for your opinions; a request to compare and contrast examines your understanding of the similarities and differences among these components. Note that *compare* means that you should write about the similarities and the differences; *contrast* means that you are only asked about the differences. *Compare and contrast* contains a redundancy.

Consider this list of the characteristics of zinc, cadmium, and mercury:

| Property | Zinc | Cadmium | Mercury |
|---|---|---|---|
| Abundance ppm | 132 | 0.16 | 0.08 |
| Relative abundance | 24th | 65th | 66th |
| Melting point ° C | 420 | 321 | −39 |
| Boiling point ° C | 907 | 765 | 357 |
| Density g $cm^{-3}$ | 7.14 | 8.65 | 13.53 |
| Ionic radius pm | 74 | 95 | 102 |
| Ionization energy kJ $mol^{-1}$ | 906 | 876 | 1007 |
| Electronic structure | $[Ar]3d^{10}4s^2$ | $[Kr]4d^{10}5s^2$ | $[Xe]4f^{14}5d^{10}6s^2$ |
| Oxidation states | +2 | +2 | +1, +2 |
| Reduction potential V $M^{2+} + 2e^- \rightarrow M$ | −0.76 | −0.40 | +0.85 |
| Toxicity | nontoxic, essential | toxic | very toxic |

Suppose you were asked to write an essay presenting the features of these three elements. This is a "list" question. Essentially you are being asked to turn the information in the table into Standard Written English. You are also being asked to demonstrate that you understand what some of the chemical properties mean. Your essay might start like this:

Zinc, at a concentration of 132 ppm, is the 24th most abundant element in the earth's crust. It melts at 420 °C and boils at 907 °C and has a density of 7.14 g $cm^{-3}$. The most common chemistry is that of the +2 ion, which has a radius of 74 pm, corresponding to the loss of both 4s electrons, the first of which requires 906 kJ $mol^{-1}$ to remove. Zinc will dissolve in a 1 M solution of hydrochloric acid. It is essential for human biological function.

You would then continue with similar paragraphs for cadmium and mercury. You will almost certainly be given a periodic table with your examination paper from which you can extract relevant information such as atomic number, atomic weight, and location in the periodic table.

**If you are asked to compare, or to compare and contrast the elements, your essay must be written differently.** All too often, when asked to compare and contrast A and B, students first write everything they know about A, then everything they know about B, and then conclude with something like, "And so you can see that A and B have many similarities and many differences." Once you have generated a list of similarities and differences, you are off to a good start, but you have not yet done what you were asked to do. Listing is not the same task as comparing and contrasting: listing is a much easier task and you should never expect to be rewarded for taking the easiest path available. When asked to consider two or more things, elements in this case, in the same frame of reference, be aware that your instructor is setting you up to demonstrate that you know or see something significant and that you have some understanding of the relationship between the characteristics listed in the table. If all you can conclude is that "they are similar in some ways, and different in others," you can assume you have missed something important and have not provided the sort of insight and analysis your instructor expecting. You have not answered the question asked.

Suppose you were asked to compare the properties of zinc, cadmium, and mercury. In this question, you are again being asked to convert the information in the table into Standard Written English and also to point out the similarities between the elements. Here is an example of how to do this.

Zinc, cadmium, and mercury are the metals forming group 2B of the periodic table and have similar electronic structures, with outer shells consisting of filled d and s orbitals. As a result, the elements have somewhat high first ionization potentials of 900–1000 kJ $mol^{-1}$. All the elements have a well-established chemistry of the +2 oxidation state and are naturally occurring at minor concentrations in the earth's crust with numerous uses, many of which are related to their electrochemical properties: all three elements are used in the manufacture of batteries of various sorts. The elements all have melting points below 500 °C and boiling points below 1000 °C, values that are the lowest of the all the elements in the d-block. In fact, the elements do not behave as typical transition metals; they have complete d shells whose electrons do not participate in bonding.

There is a limit to how many similarities one can find for chemical species since, by definition, all chemical species are different. It is probably not sensible to go on with statements such as the densities are all less than 14 g cm$^{-3}$, as the elements are more different in terms of this property than they are similar.

Usually, when you are asked to compare, the intended meaning is to examine both the similarities and the differences. To remove any ambiguity, often questions are worded as a request to "compare and contrast." In this case, you would continue your essay on the properties of zinc, cadmium, and mercury by pointing out the differences between the elements. For example,

> Both zinc and cadmium are electropositive metals (i.e., have a tendency to lose electrons forming positive ions) whereas mercury, with a positive reduction potential, is relatively inert. Mercury also has a well-defined chemistry of the +1 oxidation state, which is unknown for zinc and cadmium. This pattern of similarity between zinc and cadmium, but difference from mercury, is apparent in a number of characteristics, including density and melting point. Although the melting points of all the elements are below 500 °C, that of mercury is the lowest for any metal at −39 °C, meaning that mercury is a liquid at room temperature. This pattern of similarity and difference is in contrast to the behavior of other groups in the d-block, in which the greatest similarities are between the two heavier members rather than the two lighter members. Having said that, zinc is essential for biological function, whereas both cadmium and mercury are toxic.

Notice that the structure of the response to a compare and contrast question is to select a property or characteristic, describe how the three elements are similar or different with regard to this property, and then move on to the next property. In order to get full points for an answer to a question like this, you need to demonstrate that you can think "like a chemist." In this case, you must demonstrate that you understand something of how the chemical characteristics of elements are related to their position in the periodic table, which in turn means how they are related to the number of electrons and their arrangement in orbitals around the nucleus.

An important feature to note about the relationships among the data in the table is that all of the properties, except one, form sequences in which the values continue to decrease or increase as one moves from Zn to Cd to Hg (i.e., the sequences are monotonic increasing or decreasing). The "odd one out" is ("ah ha!") ionization energy. Therefore, your answer should show that you have noticed this. For example:

> With regard to ionization energy, there is an anomaly in the trend of values with increasing atomic mumber compared with all the other properties listed. The ionization energy for Cd is less than that for Zn, but the value for Hg is higher than that for Cd (and for Zn for that matter). This means that the shielding of the outer s electrons by the others is less effective in the case of Hg. Therefore, the attraction between an s-electron and the nuclear charge is such that it takes more energy to remove an outer electron from an atom of Hg than from atoms of Cd or Zn, but that is not the case when comparing Zn and Cd. It takes less energy to remove an electron from an atom of Cd than from an atom of Zn. Thus, the shielding of nuclear charge by the inner electrons is more effective for Cd than for Zn.

If you are asked for a comparison and respond with a list, you will probably not score full points. This is not because your instructor is being picky, but because you have failed to demonstrate your understanding of the relationship between the characteristics in question. **It is not the instructor's job to guess what you understand; it is your job to demonstrate to the instructor what you know.**

If you are asked for a list, give a list; this response requires less time than a discussion, giving you more time to complete the rest of the examination. When you are asked for a discussion, discuss: present the facts and illustrate them with specific examples. When you are asked for a comparison, you will generally discuss similarities and differences, but the word *compare* can also mean that you should consider only similarities. If you have any such doubts about what is required, ask your instructor during the examination.

**Principle 2: Present all relevant facts.**    Although there are many ways to answer an essay question correctly, your instructor will undoubtedly have in mind certain facts that he or she would like to see included as evidence that you grasp the concept in question. That is, the ideal answer to a particular question will contain a finite number of components; the way you deal with each component is up to you, but each of the components should be considered in your answer.

**Before you begin to write your essay, list all the components of the ideal answer**, drawing both from lecture material and from any readings you were assigned. For example, suppose you are asked the following question:

Discuss the factors that may affect the rate of a chemical reaction.

What components will the perfect answer contain? Begin by making a list of all relevant factors as they occur to you. Don't worry about the order in which you jot these factors down. Write the list in the answer book so that your instructor can see your thought processes.

 Temperature, pressure, concentration of reagents, activation energy, catalyst, open or closed system, equilibrium or not, solvent, nature of bonds to be broken, nature of bonds formed, $\Delta G$, $\Delta H$, $\Delta S$, number of steps, reaction mechanism, phases involved, rate changes as a function of time, forward and reverse reactions, steric effects, collisions, intermediates.

This list is *not* your answer to the question; it is an organizing vehicle intended for your use alone. Feel free to abbreviate, especially if pressed for time (T, P, [reagents], $\Delta E$), but be complete enough that you won't misunderstand your own notes while you are writing the essay. When writing this list, don't worry about including topics that may not be relevant. You will come back and edit the list later in the process.

In preparing to write your answer to the essay question, arrange the topics in some logical order, for example, from most to least important or by grouping related topics. This grouping and ordering is most quickly done by simply numbering the items in your list in the order in which you decide to write about them. You may decide that some of the topics on your list are not relevant: this is not a problem. Just cross them out neatly, but don't erase or obliterate them. A benefit of writing this list is that it has given you a chance to think about the question, and you may realize that the question is somewhat ambiguous (not all factors affect all chemical reactions). Write a note about this, so that your instructor can follow your train of thought. You also give yourself a chance to think about how you might start the essay, bearing in mind that the question asks you to discuss the factors and not just list them. Make some notes about this (e.g., reactions involve breaking bonds). You have now outlined your answer; the most difficult part is finished.

Incorporate into your essay each of the relevant ordered components of your list. Avoid spending all of your time discussing a few of these components to the exclusion of others. If you discuss only half of the relevant factors, your instructor will be forced to assume you don't realize that the other issues are also relevant. Show your instructor you know all the components of a complete answer to the question.

**Principle 3: Don't waste time by repeating the question.** Start with a strong topic sentence. Do not indulge in unnecessary throat clearing such as repeating the question or writing general introductory material. Just dive in with the answer.

**Principle 4: Provide evidence in the form of examples or facts.** An examination essay is not an exercise in creative writing, and it is not the place for you to express personal, unsubstantiated opinions. As with any other type of examination question, your instructor wishes to discover what you have learned and what you understand. Focus, therefore, on the facts and, as with all other forms of scientific writing, support all statements of fact or opinion with evidence or example. You may wish to suggest a hypothesis as part of your essay; if so, be sure to include the evidence or logic upon which your hypothesis is based.

**Principle 5: Keep the question in mind while you write.** Don't include superfluous information. If what you write is irrelevant to the question posed, you probably won't get additional credit for your answer, and you will most likely annoy your instructor. If what you write is not only irrelevant but also wrong, you will probably lose points. Certainly, you will waste time that might more profitably be applied elsewhere on the examination. When you wander off topic, you gain nothing and risk losing points, precious time, and goodwill of your instructor. Listing the components of your answer before you write your essay will help keep you on track.

**Principle 6: Leave some space for later revisions.** As a general strategy you might want to leave a few lines of empty space between the paragraphs of your response, so that you can add items that may occur to you as you continue to write or as you work on the other parts of the examination. It is also a good idea to write on alternate lines and, if permitted, to write in pencil, so that you will be able to make changes and insertions while still preserving a legible response.

**Principle 7: A picture is worth a thousand words.** This is a slight exaggeration, but the inclusion of a clearly annotated diagram or two can be an effective strategy for getting a good grade on an essay question in chemistry. Instructors are always impressed by students who can integrate diagrams into text, because it shows a greater command of the material—always assuming the diagram is relevant—than that which is displayed by writing just one or two paragraphs.

## APPLYING THE PRINCIPLES

To see how these principles are applied, let us continue the discussion of the question posed earlier about the factors that affect the rate of a chemical reaction. We have already applied principles 1 and 2 (answer the question asked and present all relevant facts), so we can continue with principle 3. You would not write

 In this essay, I will attempt to identify the factors that affect the rate of chemical reactions and explain the role of each.

Instead, you would start with

Chemical reactions involve the breaking and making of bonds between the atoms of the reactant and product species.

You would then continue with

Most reactions take place in a series of steps involving the formation of intermediate species from just two reactants. One of these steps is typically much slower than the others and is thus the rate-determining step. To evaluate the effects of reaction conditions, the effect of each on the rate-determining step must be considered. To form an intermediate, the reactants must collide with each other with sufficient energy to rearrange the electron distribution between the nuclei of the constituent atoms such that there is a reasonable probability that when the nuclei recoil, due to the repulsion of the positive charges, the atoms will rearrange to form the products rather than the original starting species.

Now you have got to the heart of the matter: reaction rates depend on the number of collisions in unit time between the reactants in the rate-determining step that result in the formation of products. You can now go on to take each of the relevant factors in turn and discuss how each affects the energy, the geometry, and the frequency of the collisions. You can also go back to your list and cross out (lightly) those factors that do not affect reaction rates, such as the various thermodynamic parameters (enthalpy and entropy).

In getting to this point, you have applied principle 4 (provide evidence) and have not included words such as "in my opinion." In finishing your answer you will adhere to principle 5 (keep the question in mind while you write). In the production of your text you will observe principle 6 (leave space for revisions) and seriously consider principle 7 (include a diagram or two). In this particular example, it could be very effective to include a sketch of the distribution of molecular speeds, indicating that (a) only molecules above a certain speed will collide with enough energy to pass through the transition state to the products and (b) increasing the temperature has a significant effect on the numbers of molecules above this threshold. You might also consider an eighth principle: provide some signposts for the reader in the form of subheadings.

Even if you run out of time before completing a thorough discussion of each issue, you will earn substantial credit by having indicated all of the specific topics of relevance. You can't help but do well on an essay exam, on any topic, if you follow these principles.

## THE ANALYTICAL WRITING SECTION OF THE GRADUATE RECORD EXAM

Many graduate programs in chemistry require that applicants submit scores on the GRE as part of their application. If you plan to continue your education in chemistry beyond college, you will probably need to take this exam. The test consists of a Verbal Reasoning section, a Quantitative Reasoning section, and, beginning in 2002, an Analytical Writing section designed to test an applicant's analytical and critical thinking and writing skills. This additional Analytical Writing section clearly confirms that these skills are regarded as essential for success at the graduate level.

Most of the principles outlined above are certainly relevant to the GRE Analytical Writing section, but, because the tests are designed to measure different capacities, not all the approaches suggested above apply. Whereas a typical timed essay test in a chemistry class seeks to measure understanding of a particular chemical concept, the questions on the GRE will never require factual information or be designed to test the writer's knowledge of a particular academic discipline. The tests are intended to be taken by applicants in a wide range of disciplines; therefore, they are carefully designed and field tested not to require special content knowledge.

Even though the Analytical Writing test does not test content knowledge, preparation for the test can improve your performance significantly. The GRE program has a Web site that offers a great deal of useful information for test takers including the entire pool of topics from which your test topics will be selected. You may find it useful to **visit** the Web site—**www.gre.org/issuetop.html—and view the published pool of topics**.

Your performance on the writing section can be strengthened by keeping in mind a few basic principles. Be sure you are answering the question asked. This is every bit as important in the GRE Analytical test as in any other timed testing situation, whether on the Issue Task or the Argument Task. Do not make the mistake of assuming that as long as your response presents a compelling argument on something *merely related* to the claim embedded in the prompt that you will earn a high score. Not responding to the claim itself will be judged as evidence that you did not understand the issue or the argument to which you were asked to respond. In the Issue Task question you are presented with a choice between two claims, but in the Argument Task question, you are given no choice. In both cases, **read the prompt carefully and fully—two, even three times**—to make sure that you understand it before you begin to formulate an answer.

**Before you begin to write, jot down some notes in which you identify key terms, concepts, or examples that you will use to illustrate and support your position**. As we said earlier in this chapter, in an essay that tests your knowledge of some content area, there are certain facts that need to be incorporated into your answer. In contrast to a test question that asks you to list "factors that affect the rate of chemical reactions," on the GRE there is no pool of privileged facts that you need to work into the essay because there are no correct or incorrect answers. A wide variety of arguments, for or against the proposition, can earn perfect scores as long as they offer clear evidence of superior critical and analytical thinking together with the appropriate writing ability. However, since your goal is to present a compelling case for whatever position you choose to argue, it is important, especially in the Issue Task, to provide support that includes specific reasons and concrete examples. Identifying the key terms you will use in building your argument and creating a skeletal outline of the sequence in which you will present them will provide structure and organization to your answer.

# CHECKLIST FOR ANSWERING TIMED ESSAY QUESTIONS

- ❑ Answer the question asked.
- ❑ Make notes before starting your essay.
- ❑ Present all the relevant facts.
- ❑ Don't waste time repeating the question.
- ❑ Provide evidence in the form of examples or facts.
- ❑ Keep the question in mind while you write.
- ❑ Leave some space for later revisions.
- ❑ Incorporate annotated diagrams into your answer when relevant and appropriate.
- ❑ Demonstrate that you can think like a chemist.

### Basic Principles for Approaching the GRE Analytical Section

- ❑ Visit this Web site at www.gre.org/issuetop.html to view the published pool of topics and familiarize yourself with the format of the exam.
- ❑ Answer the question asked.
- ❑ Read the prompt carefully and fully—two, even three times.
- ❑ Before beginning to write, jot down notes to identify key terms, concepts, or examples.
- ❑ Before beginning to write, create a skeletal outline to provide structure and organization to your answer.

# 13

# GIVING ORAL AND POSTER PRESENTATIONS

Most chemists go to at least one scientific meeting each year to share their research progress with others in related fields. The standard meeting involves oral presentations, exhibitions by equipment manufacturers and publishers, workshops, short courses, social events such as receptions and dinners, and poster sessions during which chemists communicate, through visual displays, text, and personal explanation, the work that they are doing.

To give students practice in developing oral-communication and poster-preparation skills, chemistry instructors often include talks and poster sessions as part of a course. You may also be asked (or even required) to present the results of an independent study research project or a summer research experience at a poster session. Many undergraduates present the results of their research at a regional or national meeting of the American Chemical Society or other professional organization.

## TALKING AND WRITING

Oral in-class presentations of published research papers are often assigned in conjunction with, or in place of, the written summaries discussed in previous chapters. As a member of a research group, you may be asked to lead the discussion when the group is in "journal club" mode.[1]

---

[1]Members of a journal club meet regularly to critically evaluate work published in the primary literature. There are several possible ways of doing this. Typically a club will meet once a week to scrutinize one recent article. Everyone reads the article prior to the meeting at which one member (or a small group) presents the contents in some detail together with some critical evaluative comments. Everyone then participates in discussion of the material.

Research projects, or even experiments and projects in a laboratory class, may also culminate with oral presentations. Although this book is about writing, we include this short chapter because oral and poster presentations are constructed in the same way as their full written counterparts and can, in fact, provide an ideal framework for later expansion into written papers of any size. **Indeed, in writing any paper—summary, critique, research report, research proposal, or literature review—it helps to think first in terms of giving a talk.**

Despite the major similarities, an oral or poster presentation differs from a written presentation in one important respect: a written page can be read slowly, pondered, and reread as often as necessary, until all points are understood; an oral presentation, however, gives the listener only one chance to grasp the material. For maximum impact, it must be very well organized, developed logically, stripped of details that divert the listener's attention from the essential points of the presentation, and delivered clearly, smoothly, and enthusiastically. With a poster presentation, your visual aids are accessible while you engage in a conversation with a small number of visitors.

One of the skills that employers of chemists value highly, whether at the BS, MS, or Ph.D. level, is oral communication. You should also bear in mind that to get a job, you will need to participate in a very high-stakes oral communication situation—an interview. Giving in-class presentations is one way of developing the needed oral communication skills.

We will discuss oral presentations first and then poster presentations.

## ORAL PRESENTATIONS

We will assume that you are going to give a talk about a research investigation to an audience of your peers and that you will be using PowerPoint (or similar software) to generate visual aids that will be projected, under your control, during the presentation. The goal of your presentation is virtually identical to that of a written assignment: you seek to capture the essence of the research project (whether it is yours or someone else's)—why it was undertaken, how it was undertaken, and what was learned—and to communicate that essence clearly, convincingly, and succinctly.

Before you give your first talk, make sure that you have attended several oral presentations given by other students and visitors to your department. Pay attention to the details of these presentations, such as the amount of information in the visual aids, the speed with which the information is presented, and what makes the speaker interesting (or

not). Not every oral presentation is a model that you might want to imi-
tate: even presentations given by professional scientists can be quite poor.

## Preparing the Talk

Start by writing an outline of your talk, which will assist you in making
decisions about the text you want to show and the pictures or diagrams
that you want to include. Here are some guidelines:

**1. Do not simply paraphrase.** If you wish to keep your audience awake,
do not simply regurgitate the information given in the Introduction,
Experimental, Results, and Discussion sections of the paper or papers that
you are presenting. To make an effective presentation, you must reorganize
the information. Begin your talk by providing background information, so
that the listener can appreciate why the study was undertaken. You can
draw this information from the Introduction and Discussion sections of the
paper and from outside sources if necessary. End your introductory comments with a concise statement of the specific question or questions
addressed in the paper under discussion. Let the audience know where you
are taking them and why you are taking them there.

**2. Focus your talk on the questions addressed and the results
achieved**. Time goes by quickly when you are talking in front of an
audience. You do not want to use it inappropriately by featuring material that is not strictly relevant to the objectives of the study and what was
found.

**3. Draw conclusions as you present each component of the study.** It
is important that you lead your audience, in a logical fashion, from one
part of the study to the next. Consequently, integrate the Experimental
and Results sections to form a continuous story. If you are discussing several experiments from a single paper, state the first specific question,
briefly describe how it was addressed, present the key results, lead into
the second specific question, describe how that question was addressed,
present the key results, lead into the next question, and so forth. For
example:

 Smith and Wesson first tried extracting the arsenic species with
Coca Cola, but found that only the organic species were dissolved.
However, they also found that the organic species were solubilized
with Liquid Plumber, and concluded that sequential extraction with
acidic and basic extractants was needed. They then tried extraction

with dilute phosphoric acid followed by extraction with sodium hydroxide solution.

Lead your audience by the nose from point to point.

**4. Be selective; delete extraneous details.** Much of what is appropriate in a research paper is not appropriate for a talk about that paper. Since the listener has only one chance to get the point, some of the details in the paper, particularly methodical details, must be pruned out in preparing the oral presentation. Streamline—include only the details needed to understand what comes later. If, for example, you will not discuss the influence of microwave energy or ultrasound on the results obtained, do not burden the listener with such details in your talk.

**5. Use visual aids appropriately.** Make sure you present new terms or names in writing, so that your audience is not distracted by trying to make sense of unfamiliar words. When numbers are being discussed, a simple summary table or two is helpful; numbers floating around in the air are difficult for listeners to follow. A diagram or flowchart of experimental protocol can help the listener follow the plan of a study. (An example of such a flowchart is shown on page 220 in the section on Poster Presentations.) Data can often be summarized in a few graphs, even when those data were presented in the original paper as complicated tables. Keep the graphs simple, and be sure to label both axes. You need not reproduce graphs exactly as given in the paper, and you need not display every entry from a particular table. Use large fonts for everything—legends, axes, labels, and text on graphs. Focus on showing the trends in the data, and omit anything that fails to help you make your point clearly. Do not present too much information in one image; build up complicated images in stages, or split them into two or more slides.

**6. Summarize the major findings at the end of your talk.** Drive the points home one by one. It is often helpful to include a summary visual of major results. You may wish to end your talk by suggesting what research questions should be asked next, but do not discredit the researchers. End on a positive note, reinforcing the points you want your audience to remember.

**7. Be prepared for questions about methods.** Listeners often ask about interpretations of data; to answer these questions, you must be thoroughly familiar with the way in which the study was conducted.

## Giving the Talk

You should give the talk in a room that allows you to see the screen of the computer as you stand and face the audience. You should have a pointer of some sort. Consider buying a laser pointer; otherwise use the computer's mouse or track pad to direct the audience's attention to the parts of the image where you wish them to focus. A remote slide changer, which will allow you to move about during your presentation, is also very useful (but quite expensive). Not every college classroom is designed so that the screen can be seen by everyone regardless of where the presenter is standing; bear in mind that wherever you stand you will probably be blocking someone's view.

**1. Know what you're going to say and how you're going to say it.** Hesitation, vagueness, and searching for words will all suggest a lack of understanding and will lose the attention of your audience. Write an outline of your talk and practice until you can talk smoothly while maintaining eye contact with your listeners. Note cards can be an effective aid; be sure to number them in case you drop them before or during your presentation. Avoid reading from a script; unless you are a talented actor, your presentation will sound dull and lifeless.

**2. Don't rush.** With PowerPoint, you can reveal the key aspects of a figure by building up the complete image in a series of stages as you talk about each one. Even when showing completed graphs or tables, **take the time to orient viewers to the axis labels or column headings before plunging into results.** You might say, "Here we see percentage conversion on the $y$-axis as a function of time on the $x$-axis." Remember, your audience has not seen these images before; if you don't first orient your listeners, you will be blithely talking about how interesting the results are while your audience members are still busy figuring out what it is that they are viewing. Be sure to point to exactly what your listeners should be seeing.

**3. Make the data work for you.** Draw the listeners' attention to specific aspects of the graphs and tables that represent the point you wish to make. Don't simply say, "This is clearly shown in the graph." Rather, say, for example, "Changing the pH did not affect the rate of reaction." Point to the graph or table as you speak.

**4. Write out unfamiliar terms and avoid acronyms whenever possible.** There is no justification for referring to APDC instead of ammonium pyrrolidine dithiocarbamate when the term is used only once or twice in the talk. Remember your goal is to communicate, not to impress or confuse. If you are unsure how to pronounce a word you have only read but never heard spoken, look it up in a dictionary or ask a suitably knowledgeable person. In a similar vein, make a real effort to pronounce correctly the names of the researchers whose work you are describing. Never, ever make any kind of comment about how difficult it is to pronounce the names of researchers or of the institutions or locations where the work was done.

**5. Use the laser pointer responsibly.** Don't turn the pointer on unless it is pointing at the screen. Point it first, turn it on, point out the relevant feature, and then turn it off. Any nervousness you are feeling could translate into a conspicuous tremor on the screen, so it is wise to minimize the time the pointer is on.

**6. Don't put large amounts of text on your slides.** You want the audience to be *listening* to you, not concentrating on reading. Your audience will be able to read short phrases while still listening to what you are saying.

**7. Speak clearly and loudly.** Don't mumble. Don't talk to the screen. Face your audience and make eye contact with them.

**8. Try to sound interested in what you are saying.** No matter how many times you have practiced your talk, be enthusiastic. If you seem bored by your own presentation, you will almost certainly bore your audience.

**9. Pay attention to pronouns.** Don't automatically refer to a researcher as *he*. Many papers are written by women, and many are written by two or more researchers. If you use *they* be sure that it is clear to whom you are referring.

**10. Don't end abruptly.** Warn your audience when you are nearing the end of your talk by saying something like, "I would like to make one final point," or "In summary. . ." We suggest that you have a summary and conclusions slide, perhaps including suggestions for further work.

**11. End your talk gracefully.** A self-conscious giggle or a "well, I guess that's it" isn't the best way to close an otherwise captivating presentation. We suggest that you first acknowledge any people who gave you advice, let you use their equipment and supplies, or helped in other ways, and then say something like, "Thank you for listening. I would be happy to answer any questions."

**12. Do not allow your presentation to exceed the time allotted.** You will lose considerable goodwill by rambling on beyond your time limit. Here again a few practice sessions come in handy.

**13. Paraphrase each question before answering it.** This serves the dual purpose of buying yourself a few precious seconds to think and also makes sure that your audience has heard and understands the question. For example, say "The question is 'does the technique used to isolate the DNA interfere with. . .?'" Then address your answer to the entire audience, not just the person asking the question.

**14. Do not feel compelled to answer questions that you don't understand.** Politely ask for clarification until you figure out what is being asked. If there is a moderator of the event, you can ask this person for help.

**15. Be willing to admit that you don't know the answer to a question.** You can easily work your neck into a noose by pretending you know more than you really do; nobody expects you to be the world authority on the topic you are presenting, and audiences usually appreciate honesty. Avoid appearing or sounding apologetic or defensive. Acknowledge the question in a positive way: "Good question," but then simply saying "I don't know the answer" is the safest way to go.

## Talking about Proposed Research

This is similar to presenting a research paper except that you have more literature to review. The preparation and delivery of your talk should follow all the points detailed earlier in this chapter. Highlight a few key papers that show particularly clearly why the question you wish to address is a worthwhile and logical one, and focus on the results of the studies you discuss. Then state the specific question you plan to address in your own work, being sure the question follows logically from the work you have just summarized. Finally, describe the approach you will take, focus on what you will do, and make clear what each step of the study is designed to accomplish. Conclude by briefly summarizing how the proposed work will address the question under consideration.

## The Listener's Responsibility

It can be disheartening to deliver a talk to an audience that appears indifferent. When you are a member of the audience, you bear a responsibility to listen closely and to show the listener that you listened closely. Try to formulate at least one question by the end of the talk: something you didn't understand, something you thought was particularly interesting ("I was surprised that the reaction rate was independent of temperature, do you have any explanations for this?"), or something unusual you saw in the data ("In that table you showed us, why were the arsenic concentrations so high in the control-animals' tissues?").

Even if the speaker can't answer your question, he or she will at least detect some interest in the talk and feel flattered that you cared enough about his or her development as a chemist and seminar speaker to have paid attention.

## Preparing Effective Visual Aids

A figure or table that works well in a published paper may not work nearly as well as a visual aid for a talk. When reading a journal article, readers can scrutinize your data as long as required—over several cups of coffee if necessary. For a talk, however, you want the audience to understand the slide quickly, so that you can concentrate on the results. If the slide is too complicated or too difficult to read, you may be finished talking about the results while your listeners are still trying to figure out what your axes are! **Make your visual aids simple and clear**. They should ease communication, not hinder it. Consider Figure 13, which was developed for publication: there is clearly too much material to be shown in one image.

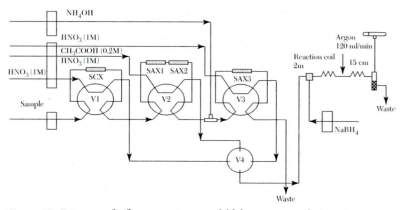

Figure 13. Diagram of a flow-injection manifold for separating four arsenic compounds by solid-phase extraction developed for publication in a journal. This picture contains too much detail for an oral presentation. There are too many lines and they are too close together.

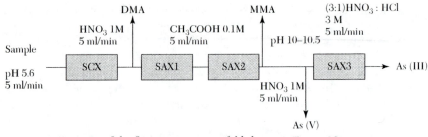

Figure 14. Diagram of the flow-injection manifold shown in Figure 13 developed for an oral presentation.

However, it can be considerably simplified as shown in Figure 14. Be careful about graphs that have been prepared for publication, as they too can contain more information than is suitable for a visual aid in support of a talk. Often the font sizes are too small to be read by those sitting toward the back of the room.

## The Pros and Cons of PowerPoint

PowerPoint makes it easy to show pictures of your instrumental setup and sample preparation: you can insert photographs taken with a digital camera, photographs or images obtained from Web sites (be sure to acknowledge your sources), and images scanned from books and magazines or copied from pdf files of journal articles (again, be sure to cite your sources). And it's easy to add labels and pointers to the slides and to highlight particular features as you talk.

PowerPoint is undeniably a tremendously useful tool, which can be used to brilliant effect to communicate your research. However, **you must not lose sight of your overriding goal: to communicate information**. It is easy to create backgrounds that are distracting, and some combinations of colors are unreadable: purple lettering on a blue background may look great to you on a computer screen, but for audience members sitting more than five feet from the screen, the words are illegible—or even invisible. Maximum clarity is achieved with maximum contrast, and the best contrast is achieved by putting black letters on a white background. Remember too, that some people are colorblind and will not be able to distinguish among several colors.

Resist the temptation to put your notes on the PowerPoint slides. If you give us the material to read, we'll be reading; we won't be listening to you. If you're saying what we're reading, then it doesn't really matter if we have tuned you out . . . but then again, doesn't that make you superfluous?

Talk to your audience. That's hard to do if you're facing the screen reading your notes—and it is very boring. Although you shouldn't use PowerPoint as a teleprompter, if you position the computer strategically between yourself and the audience, you can glance at the screen to remind yourself what the audience is seeing.

**Be sparing with animations.** This is a very useful feature of PowerPoint that allows you to bring in information to build up a complex picture in a controlled fashion, but you don't want it to be a distraction. Unless you have remote control over your presentation, you have to initiate every animation with a mouse click, and this can be difficult to manage while you are talking and making eye contact with your audience. It also requires a prodigious effort on your part to remember what material on each slide is animated. You spoil the effect if you have to press buttons to find out if anything else is going to appear.

Beware: **style is no substitute for substance**. It is fine to be high tech and colorful, but be sure you have something to say.

## CHECKLIST FOR JUDGING ORAL PRESENTATIONS

Many scientific societies give awards for the best student presentations at annual meetings. Knowing the criteria in advance can help you prepare a more effective presentation. We'll conclude this section by listing those things that judges and other listeners consider important. Your instructor will probably be looking at the same criteria when judging an in-class presentation.

- ❑ Was there a clear statement of the specific research question(s) addressed?

- ❑ Was all the background information relevant? Was it sufficient to understand why the question was posed? Did it lead logically to an understanding of why the question(s) was stated?

- ❑ Was the talk free of unnecessary and unexplained jargon?

- ❑ Did the speaker deal thoroughly with one issue at a time?

- ❑ Did the methods described follow logically from the questions posed?

- ❑ Were methods presented in the right amount of detail, including sample sizes, numbers of replicates, and use of controls? Too little detail? Too much detail? Was the design of the study easy to follow?

❑   Did the speaker lead listeners through the results to appropriate conclusions?

❑   Was the talk delivered clearly, at an appropriate pace, without reading word-for-word from notes, without distracting mannerisms, and with a graceful ending?

❑   Had the speaker clearly practiced the talk in advance?

❑   Did the speaker's talk fit in the allotted time?

❑   Did the speaker maintain eye contact with audience members?

❑   Did the speaker respond well to questions from the audience?

## POSTER PRESENTATIONS

In a poster session at a conference, displays containing text, figures, and pictures are lined up in rows, like billboards, for all to see. Each display, called a poster, represents the research of one person or a research team. Each group of posters is usually displayed for only an afternoon or evening, and 50 or more posters—sometimes several hundred—may be on display at any one time, each competing for the attention of conference attendees.

In contrast to the format for oral presentations in which one speaker has the attention of many listeners, in a poster session many scientists can be "talking" about their research simultaneously in a single room, and "listeners," as they stroll about the room browsing among the many posters, can have detailed conversations with the presenters of the posters they find especially interesting. The disadvantage of the poster presentation is that the "speaker" no longer has a captive audience: poster presentations are like flea markets, with all the noise and crowds. To be successful in selling your information, you must create a display that captures the attention of browsers and then leads them through an especially clear, logical, and interesting presentation of the research. Otherwise, much of your potential audience will simply pass you by, lured elsewhere by another's more compelling presentation.

How do you create a poster that will prompt people to stop and read, and from which even the casual reader will take away something of substance? Plan a two-pronged strategy:

1. **Limit the amount of information you present.**
2. **Arrange the information advantageously.**

We will assume that your poster is a presentation of your own experimental work. Although your poster will contain most of the elements of a research report (Title, Abstract, Introduction, Experimental, Results and Discussion, Conclusions, Acknowledgments, and References), simply creating an enlarged version of a report is not a good way to attract an audience. It is not reasonable to expect people to read through dozens of research papers during the hour or so they may spend at a particular poster session.

To be effective, your poster will contain just the essential findings of your work. It will **include fewer details than you would include in a formal publication or even in a talk**. Your poster should be designed to inform people both within and (largely) outside your immediate field about what you have done and what you have found, and it should provide a basis for discussion for those who wish to find out more. **It should highlight the major questions asked, the major results obtained, and the major conclusions drawn, and it should contain the least possible amount of text**. This means that you will not necessarily write in grammatically correct complete sentences, but rather in an abbreviated style in which nonessential words are omitted, much like the style employed for the titles of journal articles.

Bear in mind that a conference presentation, whether it is a poster or a talk, usually describes work in progress, that is, work that is not yet complete and ready to be written up for publication in a journal; consequently, it is all right to present results that are preliminary and say that you cannot yet account for some of your observations.

We strongly recommend that, before making your first poster, you scrutinize some examples of posters that others in your department have prepared. Quite often faculty will display recently presented posters outside their offices or labs. If a course is culminating in a poster session, try to attend; this might be especially useful if you plan to take this course in the future. Examine these examples critically to learn what works and what doesn't. One of the features you will discover is that if there isn't enough "white space" (space with no text) you will not find the poster visually appealing.

Before we discuss the content of a poster, we need to say something about the production process. Handwritten or hand-drawn material is not acceptable, and you should create your poster with the aid of suitable software, such as PowerPoint, and a printer. A basic design criterion is that the text should be readable from several feet away and thus the font size must be at least 24-point. After the material has been assembled electronically, you have two choices: if you have access to a poster printer (either on your campus or at a local print shop), you can create a poster the exact size for the board; or, if you do not have access to such a printer, you can print your material onto several regular letter-sized (8.5 × 11 inch) sheets of paper.

Determine the dimensions of the space you have been allocated. If you are going to a professional society meeting, you may have received an e-mail from the organizers giving you this information or directing you to the conference Web site. The American Chemical Society, for example, makes available boards that are 4 feet high and 6 feet wide. Next, decide whether you are going to use a poster printer or not. In making this decision, you might bear in mind (a) the lead time needed (if several students and faculty are all presenting at the same meeting and want to use the poster printer, you may be asked to submit your material a week in advance), and (b) the costs. It may cost $50 to print your poster; who is going to pay?

If you decide to use regular 8.5 × 11-inch paper, the need for "white space" means that, allowing for a strip at the top for a title, you will not be able to accommodate more than 15 pages if they are all in landscape format (i.e., with the longer dimension horizontal) or 18 pages if they are all in portrait format (i.e., with the longer dimension vertical). Although there are no "rules" about this, in our experience most chemistry poster presentations employ the landscape format, presumably because it accommodates the graphs and figures generated to support research in chemistry more readily that the portrait format.

You attract an audience with your title, which appears in large letters (2–3 inches high) across the top of your poster. The title needs to convey as much specific, substantive information as possible. For example:

Stability of selenized yeast dietary supplements: formation of selenomethionine $Se$-oxide and $S$-(methylseleno)cysteine

The poster should contain an introduction consisting of an explanation of the "big picture," an explanation of the "small picture," a brief description of previous work, and the goals of the work described in the poster. Here is an example of the "big picture" for the poster whose title is given above.

Selenium: essential micronutrient occurs in many foods, especially grains.

Deficiency: some countries have low soil concentrations leading to diets containing <55 µg day$^{-1}$, the US Recommended Dietary Allowance (RDA).

linked to heart disease, arthritis, cancer, AIDS, and arsenic toxicity.

Nutritional Prevention Trial (US 1996): extra 200 µg day$^{-1}$ as selenized yeast decreased lung, prostate, and colorectal cancer.

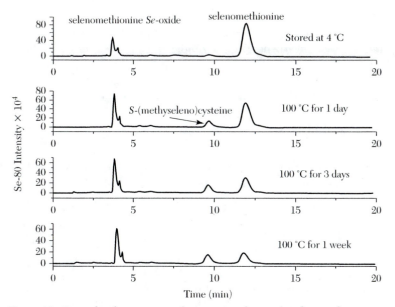

Figure 15. Example of a poster panel presenting the results of a set of experiments.

When this is blown up to 24-point font size, it fits comfortably on a letter-sized page in landscape orientation.

After you have created similar panels for the small picture and the goals, the rest of the poster should focus on the results. Only the most important results should be displayed, and you should, as a general rule, present figures, not tables. An example from the selenized yeast poster is given in Figure 15.

On a separate panel, give the information needed to understand the figure. This is a combination of the material that would appear in the figure caption, if this material were presented in a journal article or research report, and a brief extract from the results and discussion section. In this case, the material for this panel would be as follows:

Selenium-specific chromatograms (HPLC-ICP-MS) of the enzymatic hydrolysates of SelenoPrecise™ yeast after heating.

As time at 100 °C increased: selenomethionine decreased, oxide and S-(methylseleno)cysteine increased.

Experimental procedures should be described as briefly as possible in a flowchart mode. A convenient way to do this is to present the procedures as a set of instructions. For example:

Remove $TiO_2$ coating → crush tablets → take 0.2 g add 0.02 g protease XIV, 5 mL water → shake for 24 h → centrifuge 3000 g for 20 min → filter 0.45 µm → filter 10,000-Da cutoff filter → mix 900 µL with 100 µL HFBA → inject into chromatograph

You might consider changing the orientation, since chemists are used to seeing such flowcharts in the vertical direction, like this:

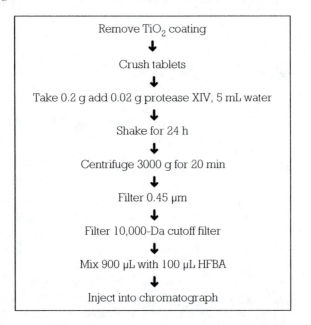

## Layout of the Poster

You should divide the poster into two or three sections, each highlighting one key issue and each separated from the others by substantial white space. You should start on the upper left-hand side with a panel that summarizes the major findings. This is the equivalent of the abstract in a research report, but it should be less detailed. For example,

Major differences found in Se speciation in currently available selenized yeast supplements and archived material from the Nutrition Prevention of Cancer trial.

When heated for several days, selenomethionine degraded. Selenomethionine *Se*-oxide and *S*-(methylseleno)cysteine formed.

Not all supplements currently on supermarket shelves are correctly labeled in terms of Se species content.

The general layout of the poster is shown in Figure 16 . Of course, this is only a suggested outline to get you started. The specific details of the work you wish to present may warrant some changes. You may also want to include some pictures. These may be an integral part of the scientific content, such as showing how a particular apparatus was assembled), or they may be part of your advertising to attract potential readers. If you are printing the poster on one large sheet, you should avoid the box outlines. These are used here to show you how the poster has been constructed.

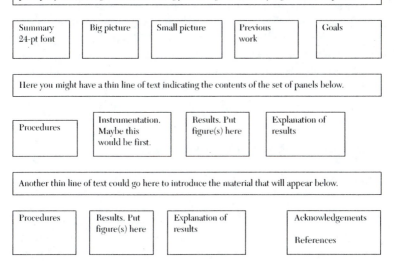

Figure 16.  Suggested layout of a poster.

## Making the Best Use of Color

Unless you are a particularly gifted graphic artist, you should be cautious about how much color you introduce into your poster. You want to aim for high contrast between the text or figures and the background, and the most effective combination is black text or lines on a white background. The occasional use of color to highlight a key word or two in each panel can be effective. Any pictures should be presented in color. If you create your poster as a series of regular letter-sized pages, you can enhance the impact by mounting each of them on a colored card so that a border of an inch or so of color shows. You can select the colors so that all the panels that are linked to a particular subtopic have the same border color. If you create a poster with colored text on a colored background, you will find that you can use quite a lot of ink, which could prove to be rather expensive.

## Other Design Features

With the possible exception of the title, do not write in capital letters. Text is more easily read if it is the usual combination of upper and lower case letters in some clear font. It can be helpful to present some of the key words or phrases in bold type, but you should use italics only where chemical nomenclature requires it, and you should not underline any text, with the possible exception of the name of the presenter. You can enhance the impact of your work if you create a miniature version of the poster as a handout. Make sure that relevant information, such as names, mailing addresses, and e-mail addresses, are clearly readable. If you have created a single sheet of paper with a poster printer, you will need a sturdy cardboard or plastic tube in which to store and transport your poster. Currently, most airlines appear to allow poster tubes as an additional carry-on item over and above the maximum of other personal items.

## CHECKLIST FOR MAKING POSTERS

### Check That

Poster includes all required information (such as institutional affiliation, names of all coauthors).

❑    All components will fit within the space provided for the display.

❑    Title is readable from a distance of 15 feet (letters 2 inches high).

❏ Text letters are readable from 5 feet [1 cm (3/8 inches) high; 24-point font].

❏ The amount of text in each area is the minimum required and not excessive.

❏ The flow of information on the poster is easy to follow.

❏ Methods are presented in flow chart form or as a simple listing.

❏ The introduction states the specific issue that is addressed.

❏ Each figure or table is self-sufficient.

❏ The significance of each result is stated explicitly, as a take-home message.

❏ There are no typographical errors.

❏ There is good contrast between text and background.

❏ The colors are not distracting.

❏ If supplementary handouts are provided, they include the poster's title, names of all authors, and the mail and e-mail addresses of the lead author.

# 14

# WRITING APPLICATIONS

## WRITING AND THE WORKPLACE

Major employers of trained chemists view an ability to write clearly and cogently as a threshold skill—that is, one that is necessary even to enter into the workplace. It is a mistake to assume that knowledge of software, experience with chemical instrumentation and techniques, or excellent laboratory skills will compensate for an inability to communicate well. The ability to write well has never been more important: talented, capable chemists must also be capable, efficient communicators.

According to the recent report from the National Commission on Writing (see Chapter 1), many blue-ribbon companies express strong disappointment with the preparation of college graduates to do the kind of writing necessary in the modern workplace. One respondent predicted that those "who cannot write and communicate clearly will not be hired and are unlikely to last long enough to be considered for promotion."

Poorly written application materials are regarded by interviewers as "the kiss of death." Those doing the hiring assume that an applicant who is careless with important personal documents may not be careful with corporate documents, technical reports, and professional communications. They also assume what research has repeatedly confirmed: **good writing reflects good thinking**. As one corporate recruiter noted, "We're almost always looking for writing skills when hiring. . .We're looking for professionalism in every respect."

Ads for positions almost always explicitly mention written- and oral-communication skills, and, as a general rule, the greater the responsibility and higher the status—and pay—for an advertised position, the stronger the requirement. The message is clear: it is not enough to be enthusiastic and knowledgeable about research and experienced in lab techniques; to be an employable and valuable participant in the scientific enterprise, whether in academia or in industry, you need to be able to write well. Therefore, when presenting *yourself* in writing—your skills, abilities, interests, and qualifications—it is essential that you do so in writing that is clear and correct and conveys a sense that you know how to communicate effectively. This is true whether it be for an entry-level position in industry or the opportunity to pursue further study in chemistry.

## THE APPLICATION PROCESS

To apply for a job, you will generally need to supply a résumé and an accompanying cover letter, both of which you write, and, if requested by a prospective employer, several letters of recommendation, which you generally never see. To apply for admission to a graduate or professional program, you will usually complete an on-line form including a personal statement (or statement of purpose) that addresses questions specifically asked in the application form. To apply to graduate or professional schools, and sometimes to apply for jobs, you will also include a transcript of your college course work and any special examination scores—for example, the Graduate Record Exam (GRE) scores. You have no control over your GRE scores and what your transcript contains; what is done is done. Nevertheless, you can still influence the message transmitted through your cover letter and résumé, or, in the case of an application to graduate school, your personal statement. That influence works both ways: it can strengthen an otherwise weak case or weaken an otherwise strong case.

There are many places you can get useful advice about résumé preparation. We list some in the Additional Resources section in the back of the book. Your university or college will have a careers office, and counselors are available to discuss your résumé and other materials related to job or graduate school applications. The American Chemical Society (ACS) offers an extensive careers service to its members, including on-line seminars and workshop materials. Some of this may be available to nonmembers, such as the booklet entitled *Tips on Résumé Preparation*; if you are not a member of the ACS, now is the time to join.

In this chapter, we will consider **the art of writing effective cover letters and writing personal statements for graduate school**. As you will see, all the various principles we have invoked throughout this book about writing well are also applicable to these writing tasks.

## BEFORE YOU START

As with every writing task, you need to think about your audience and anticipate the needs of your reader. Always try to put yourself in the position of the people who will be reading your application. What will they be looking for? In the case of a job, they will probably be considering your application with five main questions in mind:

1. Is the applicant qualified for this particular position?
2. Does the applicant truly understand what the position entails?
3. Is the applicant really interested in our program or company?
4. Will the applicant fit in here?
5. Can the applicant communicate clearly?

Your application must address all five issues.

When you prepare your application, you should also consider that the number of applications received by a potential employer usually exceeds the number of positions available, often by a considerable margin. For a large multinational company, the ratio of applications to offers may be 200:1 or higher. Many applicants will be qualified for the position, yet not every applicant can be interviewed or offered a position. Whoever first reads your application will necessarily be looking for any point of comparison upon which to disqualify you from the competition; your goal, then, must be to get the reader's interest at the start and hold it to the end.

Conveying genuine knowledge about the company to which you are applying is an effective way to attract and hold your reader's interest. According to one corporate recruiter, "We are greatly impressed when it is obvious that the candidate has researched us and can speak to what we do. Otherwise we are apt to keep looking for others." Taking some time to learn about an organization before you start to put together the actual application package will enable you to present yourself more effectively and will increase the chances that your application will not be overlooked. Given that nearly all companies have a Web site with substantial information about them, failing to learn about the company can place you at a considerable disadvantage.

## PREPARING THE COVER LETTER

The résumé summarizes your educational background, relevant work experience, relevant research experience, goals, and general interests in a condensed, accessible format. The accompanying cover letter identifies the position for which you are applying and draws the reader's attention to the aspects of the résumé that make you a particularly worthy candidate. The cover letter is usually the part of your application that a prospective employer reads first. Depending on how carefully it is crafted, it can either help counteract the impact of a mediocre academic record or do much to annihilate the good impression made by a strong academic performance. **Keep revising this letter until you know it works well on your behalf**. Have some friends, or perhaps an instructor, read and comment on your letter; then revise it again. Neatness counts, and a professional appearance also conveys seriousness of purpose. The time you put into polishing your cover letter is time well spent.

The cover letter for an entry-level position should be one printed page. Be sure you know how to format a formal business letter. An example is given later, but it helps to look at other examples. In the case of a cover letter, do not simply write,

Dear Mr. Faraday:

I am applying for the position advertised in the *Chemical and Engineering News*. My résumé is enclosed. Thank you for your consideration.

Sincerely,

*Aurora Orealis*

Aurora B. Orealis

Although the letter does not have any grammatical errors, its beginning is vague and its midsection does nothing to further the applicant's cause.

Here are some **basic goals** to set for yourself when writing the cover letter:

1. Identify the specific position for which you are applying. (Mr. Faraday may have several positions open. Ms. Orealis is applying for the position of research assistant, but how is Mr. Faraday to know?)
2. Draw the reader's attention to the elements of your résumé that you feel make you a particularly qualified candidate.
3. Indicate that you understand what the position entails and that you have the skills necessary to do a good job.
4. Convince the reader you are a mature, responsible person.

5. Convey a genuine sense of enthusiasm and motivation. Do not focus on what a wonderful opportunity the position will be for *you*. Many students assume that the employer they are writing to is primarily interested in helping them. Wrong! The employer is looking for someone who will help the company.

Before you begin to write the letter or statement, ask yourself some difficult questions, and jot down some carefully considered answers. For example:

- Why do I want this particular job?
- What skills would be most useful in such a job?
- Which of these skills do I have?

Once you have answered these questions for yourself, your next task is to convey them clearly and effectively to your reader.

It is wonderful if you have made the Dean's List every semester or have had research experience in three different labs, but if not, focus in your cover letter on the experiences that you *have* had. In lieu of having had much research experience, perhaps you have taken numerous laboratory courses. Perhaps acquiring certain skills in one or more of these laboratory courses has prepared you for the position for which you are applying. Or perhaps you can draw from experience outside chemistry to document reliability, desire, and willingness to learn new techniques quickly. We all have strengths: **decide what yours are and which ones to highlight in your application**.

Tailor each letter to the particular position for which it is being prepared. **Back up all statements with supporting details**. Avoid simply saying that you have considerable research experience. Instead, briefly explain what your research experience has been in a way that **shows** that experience and allows the readers to draw the conclusion for themselves that you have substantial, relevant research experience and skills. This can easily be achieved in your writing by following a simple order— context, actions, results—also known as CAR. When describing your experience, first put the effort or problem into **context**, then state the **actions** you took, and finally describe the **results**. Additional advantage can be gained by selecting words that convey leadership. To do this, limit the use of words like *worked, studied, completed, experienced, learned*, and *provided* and when possible incorporate words like *created, envisioned, championed, invented, conceived* and *led*. Do not state that you are a gifted leader; describe your leadership roles in a way that allows the reader to reach that conclusion. State the facts and let the reader draw the proper inferences. In other words, practice the time-honored prescription for good writing of all kinds: **show rather than simply tell** (see p. 234). Avoid making pat, unsupported statements, such as the following, and expecting the reader to take your word for it:

 My summer intern research experiences have improved my problem-solving ability.

Put this way, the statement offers the readers no evidence and no opportunity to draw conclusions for themselves. It is far more effective to describe what you actually did during those two summers in a way that allows readers to infer the value of that experience and much more readily accept the validity of the observation above.

> Starting last summer, I have been working closely with a graduate student to repair and optimize an electrospray time-of-flight photo fragment spectrometer and to utilize this spectrometer in exploring the nature of charged transition metal centers. During the previous summer, I assisted a graduate student in creating and debugging several modeling programs to better understand the statistics of instrumental limits of detection. Through these experiences I have improved my own problem-solving methodology in ways that apply not only to the sciences but also in formulating persuasive arguments and in solving the challenges of daily life.

**Sign the letter with your given name, not a nickname**; again don't run the risk of not being taken seriously.

Here is an example of a weak letter. Similar letters have, unfortunately, been submitted by people with very good grades, test scores, and letters of recommendation. The writer is applying for a position with an environmental-analysis lab. Remember that the laboratory manager reading these applications is looking for any reason to disqualify applicants; this letter gives ample reasons regardless of what the résumé contains.

Dear Laboratory Manager:

From the very first day of my high school chemistry class, I realized that chemistry was for me. The pursuit of academic research is amazing. I marvel at the advances that have been made, but at the same I am very concerned about the various environmental crises confronting the modern world. Therefore I would like to work for your company so that I can address these problems and provide solutions.

As my transcript shows, I have taken all the courses required for the chemistry major and three additional ones and have done well in most of them. Because of my concern with the environment, I am very interested in learning more about the global carbon cycle. I have been a member of a research group specializing in research chemistry. During my junior year, I participated in a project on detecting toxic biological molecules in natural waters and gained extensive skill using techniques that would be useful to your organization.

I would like to be considered for a position in a laboratory where I can work with other people as I have good interpersonal skills.

I look forward to hearing from you.


Sincerely,

*Skip*

Skip Toomalu


This letter conveys enthusiasm, but it is a very naïve enthusiasm. Avoid telling the professionals what they already know or what their discipline is about. Most professional chemists already know that their field is "amazing." It is unlikely that an entry-level position in an environmental company will provide an opportunity to address major environmental problems and provide solutions. The opening paragraph sounds more like the beginning of an application to graduate school and is inappropriate in a letter to a prospective employer, but the major problem is that although the writer mentions that he has some relevant experience, he fails to provide any convincing details of that experience. "Hire me, I'm great!" is not a convincing argument. The writer also seems unaware that all laboratory positions involve working with other people. In fact, nearly all jobs in chemistry involve working with other people.

Mr. Toomalu's letter also sounds somewhat generic: there is no indication that he knows anything about the company to which he is applying. The letter should be addressed to the individual who is the personnel recruitment manager (or the equivalent position in the organization). Sometimes, you will have to do some research to find this person's name. If necessary, call the company and ask for the information. Don't forget to ask if this person has a credential that might affect how you address him or her. If the personnel manager has a Ph.D. it never hurts to address him or her as *Dr*. If you know that the individual doesn't have a Ph.D., make sure you know whether the person is male or female. No one likes to be addressed as "Dear Sir or Madam," but these days no one will be offended by being addressed as Mr. or Ms.; we have moved on from the conventions of formal address that acknowledge a woman's marital status.

## A Sample Cover Letter

Here is an example of a much better letter.

321 Madderling Drive
Anytown, MA 01234
(413) 545-1234
rtoomalu@student.umass.edu

April 7, 2007
Dr. Joseph Blackstone
Corporate Recruitment
Farmatox Research Laboratories
Cambridge MA 01001

Dear Dr. Blackstone:

I am writing in response to the recent advertisement in *C&EN* (April 1, 2007) indicating that Farmatox is searching for a number of scientists in the analytical development area. I will soon graduate from the University of Massachusetts Amherst with a BS in chemistry. My goal is to pursue a career as an analytical chemist working in support of the biomedical applications of chemistry.

In addition to the required courses for the major, I have taken two graduate-level courses: bioanalytical chemistry and spectroscopic identification of organic compounds. I have always wanted to be involved in research, and following a fascinating introduction to some of the issues relating to the biologically mediated transformations of arsenic in the environment and the associated chemical measurement challenges with Professor Tyson's arsenic project in my freshman year, I have worked in several research groups. In Professor Vachet's group, I helped to study the effect of copper on the formation of fibrils of $\beta$-2-microglobulin, characterizing the various protein complexes involved in the initial stages of fibril formation by using size-exclusion chromatography with electrospray-ionization mass spectrometry. In Professor Gierasch's group, I learned how fluorescence resonance-energy transfer spectrometry was helpful in studying the folding of bacterial proteins SecA and Ffh. I spent the summer of 2006 working as an intern at Schering Plough, where I developed capillary zone-electrophoresis procedures for separating mixtures in high-ionic-strength solutions. For my senior thesis, I have been working in the Maroney group studying the redox-active Ni center of the hydrogenase isolated from the purple photosynthetic bacterium *Thiocapsa roseopersicina* by EPR. For this research, I expect to assist a graduate student in the analysis of the X-ray absorption data to elucidate the nature of S- and N- or O-donors that coordinate to the metal.

I would welcome an opportunity to interview for a position with Farmatox and will call you next week to confirm receipt of my résumé. Thank you for your time and consideration.

Sincerely,

*Richard Toomalu*

Richard Toomalu

Enclosure

This letter conveys enthusiasm that reflects knowledge, experience, maturity, and commitment. Notice that he did not **tell** Dr. Blackstone that his background made him a suitable candidate for a position. The applicant **shows** that he has considerable research experience and that he has worked with a number of techniques relevant to the work in progress at Farmatox. Moreover we see that Mr. Toomalu thinks clearly and writes well.

His letter conveys knowledge of the position, a sincere interest in chemistry, and a high level of ability and commitment. Your letter should do the same. Your research experience may not be as extensive as Mr. Toomalu's, but if you think about the experience you have had in relationship to the skills required for the position, you should be able to construct an effective letter. Take your letter through several drafts until you get it right (see Chapter 4, on revising).

## The Cover Letter: Some Suggestions

**Avoid passive voice in a letter when discussing your own accomplishments.** We discuss the merits of both active and passive voice in Chapter 5 (p. 81)

Rather than:

 A great deal of terminology was learned quickly.

Use the active voice and describe what you personally gleaned from the experience:

 I quickly learned a great deal about the. . .

Keep in mind that your cover letter (or personal statement) should summarize your own individual strengths and experiences, what *you* in particular did or learned, not what *anyone* in that position might have done or learned. According to a high-level recruiter at one of blue-ribbon companies we mentioned earlier, which are major employers of trained chemists, "We look for 'I did' in the cover letter, the résumé, and during the interview."

**Avoid offering vague, sweeping generalizations about the value of a particular course of study.**

 In order to expand undergraduate knowledge and experience, industrial experience is needed.

This is simply a variation on throat clearing and serves no useful purpose.

**Don't come across as presumptuous.** No matter how impressive your GPA or your credentials, a certain amount of humility is in order when you are the applicant. Tone is extremely important when presenting yourself. While you very much hope to be interviewed, don't presume that you automatically will be. Nor is it a good idea to advise the personnel manager about what he or she *should* be looking for in an applicant or how best to spend his or her time.

 I have the education, background, and professional experience for which you are undoubtedly searching.

 Since I have three years of experience, I would, of course, be an ideal addition to your company.

 I can assure you a meeting with me would be a good way to use your time.

It is more effective to present yourself as hopeful and eager, but not overly self-assured and cocky. So it would be much more appropriate to say something like,

 I would welcome an opportunity for an interview to discuss my qualifications further.

**Remember: show rather than tell.** Simply telling the reader that you are well qualified for a particular job and that you have very strong organizational and leadership skills does nothing to convince readers that you are indeed qualified and do actually have those skills. Instead, provide sufficient evidence for the reader to draw his or her own positive conclusions, as in this example:

> In addition to being certified in Massachusetts to teach math and chemistry, while in college I worked for three summers for American Computer Experience, a small company that offered computer-programming summer camps on college campuses to talented high school students. I started as a classroom teacher the first summer and designed my own course. By the second summer I was promoted to head teacher in charge of supervising the work of five other teachers and I designed the syllabi they all used. By the third summer, I was hired as the Academic Director of the summer program on the Amherst College campus, responsible for six different sessions and the academic program of over 120 high school students.

After reading such a description of a college student's summer job experience, readers can't help but nod their heads and conclude that, yes indeed, this is a young person with impressive organizational and leaderships skills. Remember that hiring managers are actively looking for those "I did," "I worked," and "I started" type sentences that offer specific information that serves as compelling evidence of your work ethic, initiative, skill set, or leadership ability—whatever the particular strengths that you, as an individual, have to offer at this stage in your career.

Even if the job advertisement asks you to respond to an e-mail address, do not interpret this as an invitation to submit anything other than a formal communication, with your contact information (mailing address, phone number, and e-mail address) at the top. Write your letter with word-processing software, and, when it is ready, copy and paste it into your e-mail software. Fix as many of the formatting issues that you can before sending it. Remember: you get only one chance to make a first impression.

## PREPARING THE GRADUATE SCHOOL PERSONAL STATEMENT

The procedures for applying to graduate school differ in detail among institutions and programs, so you will need to pay attention to the specific instructions given on the relevant Web sites. The process is similar to the one you went through when you applied for admission to your undergraduate institution, although there is no counterpart of the common application process. The admissions office in the graduate school at the institution to which you are applying will collect the materials relevant to your application and then pass them on to the appropriate department or program.

Unlike the situation for your undergraduate studies, you will be paid to be a graduate student in a doctoral program in a science discipline! The main criterion that will be used to evaluate your application is whether you have what it takes to successfully complete the program of study. A graduate program in chemistry consists of essentially two parts: formal course work and original research. Your job is to convince the admissions committee that you will do well in advanced courses and that you have the potential to contribute new knowledge to the discipline through your experimental work.

For many institutions, two sources of funds are available to support graduate students and, therefore, two types of jobs—teaching assistants (TAs) and research assistants (RAs)—are available. Most first-year graduate students become TAs. This means that, in addition to applying to be admitted to a program of study leading to a higher degree, you are applying for a position as a teaching assistant. You need not worry too much about the applications for the TA position, because most admission committees realize that you will not have had much, if any, direct experience of the kind of teaching you will be doing (working with students in laboratory classes and tutoring small groups or even one student), but you certainly don't want to be negative in your attitude toward teaching. The other source of funds that will support you as you progress in graduate school is the grant money allocated by faculty advisers to the RAs in their groups.

**Consider the audience for the personal statement: the admissions committee.** Most chemistry graduate programs will appoint a committee of research-active faculty (mostly associate or full professors) to look for the next cohort of students to work in their research groups and those of their research-active colleagues. They will be knowledgeable about current research in chemistry, about what is reasonable to expect an undergraduate to have accomplished in four years of study, and what sort of students have succeeded in their program in the past. They will also have zero tolerance for bad writing or writing that does not conform to the accepted conventions of Standard Written English. Do not sprinkle your personal statement with smiley faces or IM abbreviations if you want your readers to take your application seriously.

Here are extracts from two Web sites relating to the graduate school application process.

The University of Massachusetts, Amherst requires applicants to

... write a brief, but carefully written, Personal Statement detailing (1) the reasons why you want to do graduate work in this particular field, (2) your specific interests and experiences in this field, (3) any special skills or experiences that may relate to an assistantship, and (4) your career plans.

Tufts requests a

... Personal statement elaborating on your reasons for wanting to pursue graduate study at Tufts. The heading should read "Personal Statement of (your name)." Please give your reasons for deciding to do graduate work in the field you have chosen. We are particularly concerned that you cover these points: What previous experiences and commitments have brought you to consider applying for graduate training? What are your chief objectives in applying now? How do you think this Tufts program will help you in the pursuit of your objectives and vocation?

Tufts also requires a résumé.

You will deduce from these examples that you need to have a statement prepared in which you address issues related to your future research interests and plans, and you describe your past research experiences and accomplishments. Clearly, you need to invest some time and energy investigating the current research activities and interests of the faculty so that you can demonstrate how you will fit into the particular program to which you are applying. Check out the department Web site. Any résumé you submit for a graduate school application should be specifically tailored for that purpose and should be different from one you might submit for a specific job opening. Before giving you an example of a well-written personal statement, we will discuss some of the "don'ts."

## The Personal Statement: Some Suggestions

**Avoid the written equivalent of throat clearing.** While throat clearing (p. 73) is an understandable strategy when you are put on the spot when speaking, it does not result in a fluid, elegant delivery. It is just a way of getting started when caught off guard. The written equivalent serves much the same purpose; however, you have the invaluable opportunity to revise and eliminate the throat clearing before anyone reads your writing. You may well produce a lot of unnecessary verbiage when writing early drafts of a personal statement; most of us do. By all means, edit out these awkward bits and move as directly as possible into saying the sensible thing you are finally able to articulate. Here are some typical examples of written throat clearing that might appear in a personal statement:

 The next choice I have to make is to select a graduate school that suits me best.

I am interested in doing graduate work in organic chemistry because I found organic laboratory classes to be enjoyable and interesting.

I have a great interest in chemistry because of the great variety in the discipline. I hope to learn as much about chemistry as I can because I have enjoyed what I have learned thus far.

Each of these vague observations represents a bid to buy time before moving on to say something specific about what sort of graduate program the writer is looking for, what specifically he or she finds compelling about organic chemistry, or what in particular, amid the vast discipline of chemistry, interests this student most. While such mindless observations may help you to get the real ideas flowing, you should always edit out such instances of written throat clearing when you revise.

**Avoid diction that is too casual.** Each of us has a wide range of voices in which we can communicate, ranging from informal to formal, all of which still genuinely reflect who we are. When presenting yourself on paper in a personal statement, you should use the voice that reflects your best intellectual self, your thoughtful, formal self. Here are some examples from personal statements of diction that is simply too casual, followed by a slightly more formal and appropriate expression of the same idea:

 I would like to visit the campus to check out the facilities.

I would welcome an opportunity to visit the department and tour the facilities.

I am very solid in organic chemistry.

I have extensive course work and laboratory experience in organic chemistry.

I feel that I am a people person.

I have had ample opportunity to develop my skill communicating and negotiating with people from a wide range of backgrounds. For example, . . .

I kind of like the sound of Joe Shmoe, Ph.D.

 My ultimate goal is to earn a Ph.D. in hopes of becoming a professor or researcher in the area to which I can contribute the most.

**Put a positive spin on potentially negative aspects of your application.** Sometimes your performance has not been what you had hoped for, or you really don't yet have as much experience as you would like. Don't be dishonest, but present things in the most positive light possible.

I have had no experience in this field.

Although I have had little practical experience in this area, I do have experience with . . . [something related or similar]

Although thus far I have had no actual experience in this area, my plans for next summer include . . . [something that will provide relevant experience]

Because I have not yet narrowed my focus into a specific area of chemistry, I am particularly attracted by Dream University's strong overall program and the opportunity to rotate though different research groups to gain a clearer view of what each area involves.

**Avoid toadying to the experts.** Do not assume that members of the admission committee are eager to be flattered and that gushing about the fame or status of a particular institution will make you a more attractive candidate. Instead, **demonstrate that you have done your homework** and actually know something about the institution and its faculty and see it as a good match for your interests.

 The prestige and academic excellence of The University of My Dreams as well as its reputation for top-notch research make it an easy choice.

 Given my academic interests, the chance to participate in research such as that being done by Professor Nubbelpryse on the synthesis and study of surface-modified nanoparticles represents an exceptional opportunity.

**Be as specific as possible.** The more detailed and concrete you can be in describing your interests, the better.

 I would like to expand my knowledge.

At the moment, I am especially interested in the syntheses of functionalized dendrimers that have application for light harvesting and the evaluation of their potential in photovoltaic devices.

From my work this summer, I have developed an interest in the field of organic chemistry.

This past summer I worked in the protein engineering department at Genentech, Inc. in San Francisco. I was involved in the anti-VEGF project (vascular endothelial growth factor), which is aimed at finding an anticancer drug.

I am interested in Hevyhitta U because it is large and well known.

I consider Hevyhitta U, with its initiative in the study of the molecular basis of disease through its CBPM interdisciplinary research program, to be an ideal place for professional growth. I am particularly excited about Professor Drugge's work on HIV treatments.

**A *word of warning:* it can be a mistake to be so specific that you come across as inflexible.** If it turns out that it is not possible to pursue the topic of research about which you are so passionate at Hevyhitta U—for whatever reason, maybe because Professor Drugge has retired or moved on to another institution—then your application might be rejected. Make sure that, if you pick just one topic, there are several research groups in which you could work at the institution.

**Anticipate the reader's needs.** The effectiveness of any piece of writing depends on how well it succeeds in achieving its objectives. When it comes to presentation of self, much depends on how well you are able to anticipate and accommodate the needs of your audience. The more successfully you do so, the more effective your writing will be.

Ask yourself continually whether the reader will readily grasp the meaning or significance of the terms you use. Abbreviations that are familiar to you may be puzzling to readers who are not part of your university discourse community, (e.g., working as an R.A. or volunteering at the ABC House). Also, think about how you can usefully characterize such things as special awards, membership in honor societies, and work commitments in a way that allows readers to draw reasonable conclusions about what these activities and honors represent.

## A Sample Personal Statement

Let us assume that you are submitting an application to UMass Amherst. Here are the instructions: provide a brief, but carefully written Personal Statement detailing (1) the reasons why you want to do graduate work in this particular field, (2) your specific interests and experiences in this field, (3) any special skills or experiences that may relate to an assistant-ship, and (4) your career plans.

Ever since my first encounter with chemistry, via the charismatic 10th grade teaching of Ms. Molly Khul at Empire Falls HS, I have been fascinated with the impact that chemicals and chemistry have had on our quality of life. While I appreciate all of the major positive contributions of the pharmaceutical industry—the spectacular array of synthetic materials, fabrics, and colors that dazzle us and the stunning advances in electronics—the problematic impact of chemistry on our lives interests me most. I grew up in a town that seemed adversely impacted by chemistry: the houses contained lead (from the paint and the water piping), the soil was contaminated with arsenic, and the wells were contaminated with chlorinated solvents and gasoline. There were no fish in the river in the town center and, most summers, the local lake contained more algae than water.

I am interested in environmental chemistry and in particular the study of the fate of chemical species introduced, inadvertently or deliberately, through human activities. I am particularly interested in developing chemical measurement strategies that will provide reliable information about the transformations of chemical species, particularly those mediated by biological systems. My goal is to become proficient in the application of chemical measurement technologies for the determination of contaminant species in the environment and then to apply these techniques to a study of some of the problems we currently face, such as (a) why is perchlorate so widely distributed in the environment and (b) can contaminated aquifers be remedied in situ with zero valent iron?

I find the work currently in progress in the groups of Professors Max Pecktromtry and Mike Rorginism to be of particular interest. For my senior honors thesis work at Libra Larts College, I studied the transformation of inorganic arsenic, leached from CCA-treated wood to trimethylarsine oxide by various methylation processes in the soil. To follow these reactions, I developed an HPLC separation with plasma-source time-of-flight mass spectrometry detection and evaluated various schemes for the extraction of the relevant arsenic species from the soil. I concluded that two mechanisms were in operation: one involved soil bacteria, and the other involved naturally occurring but abiotic methylating agents. Although I have never lectured in the classroom, I did perform TA duties for the laboratory sections of Instrumental Analysis (Chem 513) and Bioanalytical Chemistry (Chem 545). I also served as a tutor in the college's Quantitative Skills Center in support of the general chemistry classes. I look forward to the opportunity to develop my teaching skills further. At this stage, I plan to pursue a career in which I can influence the way chemistry impacts our environment, although I am undecided whether this would most effectively be achieved by working for a large chemical corporation or for a government agency such as the EPA. However, I recognize that many things can change as a result of the graduate school experience, and I intend to approach the new ideas to which I am exposed with an open mind.

This statement is 499 words long. It also appears to be written by someone who has completed her studies, as the writer indicates that she has considerable research experience in a senior thesis project. A student applying to graduate school in the first semester of her senior year would probably not have achieved so much. So here is an important point: if you apply to graduate school no later than the end of the fall semester of your senior year (a) you may not be able to impress the admissions committee with all the fine research you are going to do in the second semester of your senior year, and (b) your transcript may only be 75% complete, if, when you ask for an authorized copy to be sent to the schools to which you are applying, the institution you attend does not list classes that are in progress. If this information is included, then the admissions committee members will still not know what courses you are planning to take in the final semester of your senior year. In either case, you should find a way of telling those who review your file what courses you are taking and will be taking before you graduate. There are several ways of doing this:

1. You can include the information somewhere in the personal statement.
2. You can use one of the other documents that you may be asked to submit, such as a résumé or an optional statement of purpose.

3. You can get one of your letter writers to include this information on your behalf.
4. You can write directly to the graduate program director or chair of the admissions committee.

We recommend the fourth option only if you have something in your record you particularly want to address. For example, suppose you have a rather indifferent academic record in the second semester of your sophomore year, which was the semester you experienced some legitimate extenuating circumstances such as contracting mono or coping with the serious illness of a close family member (but keep in mind that your cat Fluffy's appendicitis is not likely to rouse much sympathy). In this case, write to the chair of the admissions committee and explain what happened or include this in the application in some way. Make sure that at least one of the faculty who will write on your behalf addresses this issue in his or her letter.

Bear in mind that if you plan to go to graduate school in September after graduating the previous May, you need to have amassed enough experience to impress the admissions committee by the first semester of your senior year. So make sure that you get some experience in your junior year and the summer before your senior year. Better yet, start to build your list of research experiences in your sophomore year or earlier. If you participated in science fairs in middle school and high school, that's wonderful. Don't forget to include these activities in your list.

## CHECKLIST FOR APPLICATIONS

### The Cover Letter

❑ The cover letter is no longer than one printed page.
❑ The letter calls attention to relevant personal strengths in a modest, appropriate way.
❑ The letter is tailored to the particular position in question.
❑ The letter provides details to support and illustrate all statements.
❑ The letter is signed with your given name as opposed to a nickname
❑ The letter is written in the active voice (I learned) rather than passive voice (it was learned).

❑ The letter offers evidence that shows rather than tells that you are a viable candidate.

## The Personal Statement

❑ The statement is concise, precise, and direct, with no written throat clearing.

❑ The statement has been carefully proofread and corrected.

❑ The statement is written in an academic voice, avoiding diction that is too casual.

❑ The statement puts a positive spin on potentially negative aspects of the application.

❑ The statement avoids stating the obvious or informing the experts.

❑ The statement avoids toadying to the experts.

❑ The statement demonstrates knowledge of the particular institution, its faculty, and its programs.

❑ The statement conveys a balance between academic focus and flexibility and openness to new ideas.

# Appendix A

## Using Punctuation

A writer uses punctuation to ensure that a reader can readily grasp a sentence's intended meaning without having to back up and read the sentence again. In this sense, punctuation marks serve much the same purpose as road signs: they are signals posted by the writer to assist the readers in their journey through the text. Road signs announce steep hills and upcoming detours or caution drivers to reduce speed in the interest of safety. If drivers do not heed road signs, they are likely to make a wrong turn and lose their way and will need to back up and start again. If readers don't have punctuation to help them navigate a sentence, they too may get confused. Punctuation used correctly and effectively by the writer supports the flow of ideas and makes the reader's journey through the sentence or paragraph much easier. We offer here an overview of the way in which three punctuation marks—the comma, the semicolon, and the colon—can be used as tools to keep the reader moving forward.

### EFFECTIVE USE OF COMMAS

Read the following sentences silently to yourself, noting what happens in each instance.

1. As it dried the paper towel became wetter.
2. While the solution was boiling over ten more samples were pre-pared.
3. Write your name on the front cover and the first few pages should be left blank.
4. To prepare the students put on their safety glasses.
5. Faculty teach first-years and seniors tutor small groups.
6. As the hotplate was heating the filter funnels were prepared.
7. Fruit flies like a banana and time flies like an arrow.
8. To slowly evaporate the lab technician placed the solutions on top of the oven.
9. In addition to the measurement errors he made many miscalcu-lations in the lab report.

10. Two weeks before the recipients of the Nobel Prize in Chemistry were announced.

In all likelihood, you reached a certain point in each of the above sentences and realized that, because there was no punctuation to guide you, you had misunderstood the direction in which the sentence was headed. Think of a comma as a signal to the reader to pause. Unlike the semicolon, which is a linking device, the comma is a separating device. It has no linguistic epoxy, no glue to hold together independent clauses. It simply divides and, in most cases, cautions the reader to pause, ever so briefly, before proceeding, in order to grasp the writer's intended meaning. Here is a simplified summary of the main reasons to use commas:

1. **Do use a comma to separate introductory words, phrases, or clauses** from the main (independent) clause.

   If _____, main clause.

    If a mixture is homogeneous, the composition and physical properties are uniform throughout.

2. **Do place a comma before a coordinating conjunction** (for, and, nor, but, or, yet, so) that joins the independent clauses of a compound sentence.

   independent clause, and independent clause.

    An element is made up of only one kind of atom, and a compound is composed of two or more kinds of atoms.

   independent clause, but independent clause

   Extensive properties depend on the size of the sample, but intensive properties are independent of sample size.

   **TIP:** A good way to remember the coordinating conjunctions—there are only seven—is by the acronym FANBOYS (F for *for*, A for *and*, N for *nor*, B for *but*, o for *or*, Y for *yet*, s for *so*).

3. **Do NOT use a comma before a conjunctive adverb** such as *however* or *nevertheless* that joins the independent clauses of a compound sentence (see rules for semicolons, p. 247).

    Extensive properties depend on the size of the sample, however, intensive properties are independent of sample size.

4. **Do NOT use a comma to separate pairs of words, phrases, or dependent clauses joined by a coordinating conjunction (any of the FANBOYS words).**

> noun and noun                    infinitive or infinitive
> spectroscopy and spectrometry    to dissolve or to melt

5. **Do use a comma to separate a series of coordinate words, phrases, or clauses.** A comma should also be used before the conjunction that adds the final element in the series.

> noun, noun, and noun             phrase, phrase, or phrase
> gas, liquid, and solid           in a flask, in a tube, or in a jar

6. **Do set off a nonrestrictive adjective clause** (one that supplies information about the noun it modifies that is not crucial to identifying that particular person, place, or thing) **with a comma or commas**. Nonrestrictive clauses may be introduced by *who* or *which* but not by *that*.

> _____, nonrestrictive adjective clause, _____,

Another term for a nonrestrictive clause is a **nonessential clause**. While the information in the following sentence about where the results can be found is **useful,** it is **not essential** to the meaning of the sentence. The sentence is phrased and punctuated as an answer to the question "Are your results conclusive?"

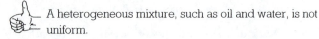 Our results, which are shown in Figure 1, are conclusive.

The meaning is "Our results are conclusive, and oh, by the way, if you would like to take a look at them, they are shown in Figure 1." In the following sentences, we are again given interesting, related information, but it is **not essential** to the meaning of the sentence; therefore, in each case the clause is separated from the rest of the sentence by commas.

A heterogeneous mixture, such as oil and water, is not uniform.

My advisor, who is very supportive, provided the funding.

7. **Do NOT set off a restrictive adjective clause** (one that supplies information about the noun it modifies that is essential to

the meaning of the sentence) **with commas.** Restrictive clauses may be introduced by *who* or *that* but not by *which*.

_____ restrictive adjective clause _____.

A restrictive clause can also be referred to as an essential clause because the information it provides is crucial to the meaning for the sentence. In the following sentence, the information about where the results can be found in the report is essential because the implication is that not all the results were conclusive; some results were conclusive and some were not.

 The results that are shown in Figure 1 are conclusive.

The conclusive results constitute a restricted group and have been placed in Figure 1. Removing the clause would change the meaning of the sentence in a fundamental way, so it is essential. The following sentences offer examples of clauses that are also essential to the meaning of the sentence and are therefore not set off by commas.

 A mixture that is heterogeneous is not uniform.

The person who provided the most support was my advisor.

### Reminders:

- If the added information is essential or restrictive, it can be introduced by *who* or *that* but is not set off by commas. *that* = restrictive = no commas
- If the added information is nonessential or nonrestrictive, it can be introduced by *who* or *which* and is set off by commas. *which* = nonrestrictive = commas

## EFFECTIVE USE OF SEMICOLONS

In contrast to the comma, think of the semicolon as having some glue to it—the power to hold together two independent clauses. In contrast to the colon, which directs the reader's attention forward to what follows the punctuation, the semicolon encourages

the reader to consider the two independent clauses as equal in importance with respect to one another. Think of the semicolon as an old-fashioned pair of scales, balancing the equal weights on either side.

1. **A semicolon can be used to join two independent clauses that are not joined by a coordinating conjunction.**

   Independent clause; independent clause.

   An element is made up of only one kind of atom; a compound is composed of two or more kinds of atoms.

2. **When two independent clauses are joined by a conjunctive adverb, a word such as *however, therefore,* or *consequently,* or by a transitional phrase such as *for example* or *as a result,* the joining word should be preceded by a semicolon and followed by a comma. Remember that two independent clauses joined by any of the FANBOYS words (*for, and, nor, but, or, yet, so*) require only a comma before the joining word.**

   Independent clause; therefore, independent clause.

   Butanol is not very reactive; therefore, the technique of refluxing was used.

   **Using *however* intensifies the suggestion, implicit in the choice of the semicolon to join these two clauses, that the two ideas should be considered in reference to one another.**

   Independent clause; however, independent clause.

   Perhaps the most complicated natural substance ever synthesized in the laboratory was Vitamin B12; however, the first natural substance ever synthesized, urea, was much simpler.

3. **When a series ordinarily using commas has commas within the items, the semicolon can be used as a less confusing, additional separator between the items in the series.**

   _____, _____; _____, _____; and _____,

   We wish to thank Bill Vining, State University College of Oneonta, for moral support; Kevin Shea, Smith College, for editorial support; and Ed Voigtman, University of Massachusetts, for technical support.

# EFFECTIVE USE OF COLONS

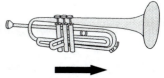

Think of the colon as signal to the reader that something important is just ahead, much as a road sign might caution a driver of something important ahead on the high-way—a steep hill or children at play—or a trumpet or an arrow that heralds something more important about to be revealed. It is a way of saying "pay attention!" The most important thing to remember about using the colon is that **what precedes a colon must be an independent clause**, that is, a clause that could function independently as a sentence on its own. The colon is the punctuation equivalent of "dah-da-da-da-dah."

1. **Use the colon after an independent clause to introduce, supplement, explain, or add something to what has already been said.**

   ———, ———; ———, ———; ———.

   Independent clause: a list.

    Matter occurs in three states or phases: solid, liquid, or gas.

   ———: ———

   Independent clause: another independent clause.

    A mixture has no unique set of properties: it possesses the properties of the substances of which it is composed.

   ———: ———

   Independent clause: a single word or two

    The term *mass* is often incorrectly used in place of another word: *weight.*

2. **Use a colon to introduce a quotation *only* when the clause that introduces the quotation is independent, that is, capable of standing on its own as a sentence.**

    Pasteur was right about luck and hard work: "Chance favors only the prepared mind."

   **If the words that introduce the quotation are not an independent clause, do not use a colon.**

    Louis Pasteur said: "Chance favors only the prepared mind."

   Louis Pasteur said, "Chance favors only the prepared mind."

# Appendix B

|   | Content | Form |
|---|---------|------|
| A | • Excellent content<br>• Deftly synthesizes primary sources into a thorough, insightful narrative<br>• Adroitly anticipates the inevitable "so what?"<br>• Unassailable conclusions and logic | • Organization unerringly clear and strategic<br>• Transitions between sentences, paragraphs, topics effective, precise<br>• Target length precise<br>• Headings and subheadings used to sparkling effect<br>• Figures form an integral part of the narrative, enhance meaning |
| B | • Solid, ambitious content<br>• Aptly synthesizes primary sources into a coherent narrative<br>• Adequately anticipates the inevitable "so what?"<br>• Reasonable conclusions and logic | • Organization effective<br>• Transitions between sentences, paragraphs, and topics consistently clear and helpful<br>• Target length achieved<br>• Headings, subheadings, and figures present and helpful |
| C | • Problematic content<br>• Synthesis of primary sources questionable, sense of narrative minimal<br>• Insufficient effort to anticipate the inevitable "so what?"<br>• Questionable conclusions and logic | • Organization discernible, but problematic<br>• Transitions present, but mechanical, not always helpful<br>• Target length inaccurate<br>• Headings, subheadings, and figures missing or confusing |
| D | • Seriously deficient content<br>• No sense of synthesis of primary sources<br>• Fails to anticipate the inevitable "so what?"<br>• Logic? What's that? | • Organizational pattern difficult to discern<br>• Transitions confusing, inadequate, or missing<br>• Target length ignored<br>• Headings, subheadings, and figures missing |

# Suggested Rubric For Evaluating Science Writing

|   | Expression | Mechanics |
|---|---|---|
| A | • Word choice consistently idiomatic and precise<br>• Prose unerringly concise, pithy, and polished<br>• Control of active and passive voice is dexterous | • Mechanically perfect<br>• Meticulous observance of the conventions of chemistry and SWE*<br>• No irregularities that impede clarity or distract attention<br>• Punctuation used to artful effect to enhance meaning and invigorate prose |
|   | • Word choice clear, idiomatic, and appropriate<br>• Prose consistently concise and polished<br>• Control of active and passive voice is competent | • No spelling errors<br>• Infrequent minor mechanical errors regarding the conventions of chemistry and SWE*<br>• Few irregularities that impede clarity or distract attention |
|   | • Word choice occasionally inappropriate, vague, unidiomatic, wordy<br>• Prose lacks sufficient concision and polish<br>• Control of active and passive voice is problematic | • Isolated serious errors or frequent minor errors regarding the conventions of chemistry and SWE*<br>• Frequency of mechanical and punctuation errors sufficient to impede clarity or distract attention |
|   | • Word choice impedes clarity<br>• Prose wordy, vague, occasionally garbled<br>• Control of active and passive voice not evident | • Consistent and frequent errors regarding the conventions of chemistry and SWE*<br>• Mechanical and punctuation errors seriously impede clarity and distract attention |

* Standard Written English

# Additional Electronic and Print Resources

## Suggested References for Further Reading

### BOOKS AND ARTICLES ABOUT SCIENTIFIC WRITING

Coghill, A.M., Garson, L.R. Eds., *The ACS Style Guide: Effective Communication of Scientific Information*, 3rd ed.; Oxford University Press: New York, 2006.

Davis, M. *Scientific Papers and Presentations*, 2nd ed.; Academic Press: New York, 2005.

Day, R.A. *How to Write and Publish a Scientific paper*, 5th ed; Oryx Press: Phoenix, 1998.

Day, R.A. *Scientific English: A Guide for Scientists and Other Professionals*; Oryx Press: Phoenix, 1992.

Kanare, H. *Writing the Laboratory Notebook*; American Chemical Society: Washington, DC, 1985.

King, L.S. *Why Not Say It Clearly? A Guide to Scientific Writing*; Little, Brown: Boston, 1978.

Kovac, J. *The Ethical Chemist: Professionalism and Ethics in Science*; Pearson Education, Inc.: Upper Saddle River, NJ, 2004.

Kovac, J., Sherwood, D. *Writing Across the Chemistry Curriculum: An Instructor's Handbook*; Prentice Hall: Upper Saddle River, NJ, 2001.

O'Connor, M. *Writing Successfully in Science*; Chapman & Hall: New York, 1991.

Penrose, A.M., Katz, S.B. *Writing in the Sciences: Exploring Conventions of Scientific Discourse*; St. Martin's Press: New York, 2003.

Wilkinson, A.M. *The Scientist's Handbook for Writing Papers and Dissertations*; Prentice Hall: Englewood Cliffs, NJ, 1991.

# BOOKS ABOUT ACADEMIC WRITING

Faigley, L. *The Brief Penguin Handbook*, 3rd ed.; Pearson Longman: New York, 2009.

Zinsser, W. *On Writing Well: An Informal Guide to Writing Nonfiction*, 4th ed.; Harper Collins: New York, 1995.

# BOOK ABOUT STATISTICS

Miller, J.N, Miller, J.C. *Statistics and Chemometrics for Analytical Chemistry*, 5th ed.; Pearson/Prentice Hall: New York, 2005.

# USEFUL WEB SITES

## Writing Conventions in Chemistry

**http://portal.acs.org/portal/acs/corg/content**
This is the home page of the American Chemical Society. Search the site for tips on résumé preparation, writing research reports, and lab notebooks, as well as for information about what is happening in chemistry. Look for ACS Careers and you'll find information on ethics, plagiarism, and professional conduct.

## Advice on Grammar and Punctuation

**http://owl.english.purdue.edu/handouts/** (Select "Grammar, punctuation, spelling")
http://writing-program.uchicago.edu/resources/grammar.htm

## Evaluating Web Sites

**http://lib.nmsu.edu/instruction/evalcrit.html** provides not only good criteria for evaluating a web source but also a helpful explanation for why careful scrutiny is so important.
**http://www.ithaca.edu/library/training/think.html** offers useful quizzes on evaluating web sources.
**http://www.lib.berkeley.edu/TeachingLib/Guides/Internet/Evaluate.html** offers some practical techniques to apply and questions to ask for evaluating web sites.

## Giving Effective PowerPoint and Other Oral Presentations

http://www.swarthmore.edu/NatSci/cpurrin1/powerpointadvice.
htm (Courtesy of Professor Colin Purrington)
http://www.kumc.edu/SAH/OTEd/jradel/effective.html
(Courtesy of Professor Jeff Radel)

## Preparing Effective Poster Presentations

http://www.swarthmore.edu/NatSci/cpurrin1/posteradvice.
htm (Courtesy of Professor Colin Purrington)
http://www.kumc.edu/SAH/OTEd/jradel/effective.html
(Courtesy of Professor Jeff Radel)

## Useful Advice on Résumé Preparation

Just enter "resume preparation" into Google and take your pick
from the many useful sites that appear.

# Answer Key

## Key to "Plagiarism Challenge" from Chapter 9

1. **YES.** This is a particular kind of plagiarism called "patchwriting." Such shifts in voice and style are often more obvious than students realize, and when you fail to place these phrases or sentences in quotation marks you are claiming to the reader that you are their author, which, in such a case, is clearly dishonest.

2. **YES.** This is plagiarism. An eminent scholar has sufficient knowledge to make this sort of statement; a novice does not. You can, however, incorporate this assertion into your paper and harness the authority of the speaker by citing the source. You should give the name of the speaker, his or her affiliation, the title, the date, and the location of the talk. The simple fact that you heard it rather than read it does not absolve you of the obligation to credit the source of such a specific original observation that is not your own.

3. **YES.** This is what is called self-plagiarism. It is an act of fraud because each class is intended to represent acquisition of additional knowledge, and submitting the same paper twice suggests that you have done more work and acquired more knowledge than you actually have.

4. **YES.** This is plagiarism. Forming study groups as a means of preparing for exams is a common and generally approved practice throughout academia, but it raises the question of "what are the boundaries?" Clearly, the actual writing on an exam must be produced individually by the person who puts his or her name on it.

5. **YES.** This is plagiarism. Just because you didn't find the ideas already written down, it does not mean that you need not acknowledge their source. Since informal discussions occur quite often, chemists and other scientists have a formal way of dealing with this situation known as a "personal communication." You should put a reference

number in the text and cite your uncle by his surname and initials, followed by his affiliation, city, state, "personal communication," and the year. It is considered ethical to ask the person concerned if he or she can be cited in this way. Material received by e-mail should also be cited as a "personal communication."

6. **YES.** This is plagiarism. This is dishonest because you have not disclosed that the idea of using household chemical formulations is not your original idea and, furthermore, that the Coca Cola article presents results that are the principal evidence that your suggestions have merit.

7. **NO.** This is not plagiarism, but as a student you must be very careful to publicize your credentials or personal experience as the source of any special knowledge you may have that is clearly not common knowledge, so as to avoid appearing to have plagiarized. You must establish your own authority to the extent that any other scholar who reads your work would cite you as the knowledgeable source. This scenario is based on an actual recent event at a major university. The student was ultimately vindicated, but it went all the way to the honor board.

8. **YES.** This is plagiarism. Whenever you use more than three words from a text in the sequence in which they occurred originally, you are plagiarizing. You must use some judgment here since "copying" phrases such as "high-performance liquid chromatography" is not plagiarism.

9. **NO.** This is not plagiarism, but it is still an act of academic dishonesty to fabricate data. You must never, ever make up data and pass it off as though it came from an authoritative source. You will get into very serious trouble if you do.

10. **NOT NECESSARILY.** If you take the technical words and phrases (such as capillary electrophoresis with atomic fluorescence detection) and write your own narrative that describes the work done by several research groups, this is not plagiarism. If, however, you simply link together the abstracts of several papers, this would be considered plagiarism, because you are presenting the words of other writers (whoever wrote the abstracts) as though they were your own.

# Key to "The Citing Sources Challenge" from Chapter 9

1. **YES.** It is acceptable not to incorporate this information without citing it because it falls within the category of common knowledge and is readily available.

2. **NO.** This is profoundly dishonest. It suggests that you have done what the professor hoped and expected you would do: read, analyze, and synthesize a number of differing points of view into a coherent, thoughtful response to the assignment, when you clearly have not.

3. **NO.** This is not acceptable for a student. Journalists are, by law, exempt from revealing their sources of information; however, scholars at all levels are obliged to identify their sources.

4. **YES, This is Acceptable, but. . .** If it is an undisputed statement of fact (e.g., the legitimacy of the rating system itself is not a subject of controversy), you would not be compelled to cite the source; however, it would be an act of scholarly courtesy to cite the source to enable other scholars pursuing similar lines of inquiry to benefit from your efforts. "Having light we pass it on to others."

5. **NO.** This is not acceptable. Writing on the Web is protected by copyright, and it must be cited, even if no author is listed.

6. **NO.** This is not acceptable—or wise. It is always risky to make statements of this sort without any evidence unless you are the acknowledged world's expert in the field, and even then it is risky. As it happens, not all arsenic compounds are toxic, and there is evidence that arsenic may be beneficial, even necessary, for some organisms.

7. **YES.** This is acceptable. If the authors of articles in professional journals do not cite a source, this indicates that, even though this is not the sort of term that pops up in dinner conversation or even in a high school chemistry text, among the community of chemists it is considered common knowledge.

8. **NO.** This is not acceptable. The question is whether this is common knowledge among chemists. We suggest the following guideline: if it appears undocumented in five or more sources, treat it as disciplinary common knowledge. Pay close attention to what the authors

you are reading are doing and follow suit. If they cite a source, you should too.

9. **NO.** It is never acceptable to fabricate evidence of research productivity. First, you need to have direct evidence (from the probable senior author—the faculty member for whom you worked) that a manuscript is, indeed, being written. You should also find out what the title is, and then you should list this in your résumé as "in preparation."

10. **NO.** This is not acceptable practice. A Ph.D. dissertation represents original work by the writer, and it is just as much a publication as a journal article or a book. Most universities require that doctoral dissertations and masters theses be deposited in the library, from where they can be borrowed by anyone with appropriate access, not just students on the home campus. If you pass off the writing of a doctoral student as your own, you are committing plagiarism.

# Index